TELEPHON
WIEN 5045

TELEPHON
K.EBERSDF. 6817

KAISER EBERSDORFER

DAMPF-UND KUNSTMÜHLE

VON

MAX MALLOWAN

COMPTOIR: WIEN, III. Dampfschiffstr. 12

Wien, 30 April. 1896.

Mallowan's Memoirs

by the same author

NIMRUD AND ITS REMAINS (2 vols)

Mallowan's Memoirs

Max Mallowan

COLLINS
St James's Place, London
1977

William Collins Sons and Co Ltd
London · Glasgow · Sydney · Auckland
Toronto · Johannesburg

First published in 1977
© Max Mallowan 1977
ISBN 0 00 216506 6
Set in Monotype Bembo
Made and Printed in Great Britain by
William Collins Sons and Co Ltd Glasgow

To Rosalind
with love

Contents

Illustrations

Acknowledgments

The two drawings of the seated mother figure on p. 124 were made by Mrs Pat Clarke.

The photograph of Gertrude Bell with Lionel Smith at Eridu between pages 136–137 is reproduced by kind permission of The University of Newcastle-upon-Tyne.

The photograph of No. 4 Paternoster Row, Ur between pages 280–281 is reproduced by kind permission of The Trustees of the British Museum.

CHAPTER I

In the Beginning

I was born in London, on 6 May 1904 at Albert Mansions, in a flat which overlooked Battersea Park. My earliest recollections are of being taken out by our daily help to somewhere in the slums and being seated in front of a hob grate and roaring kitchen fire, in rough company where the men were in their shirt sleeves. The good and kindly woman who had transplanted me went by the Dickensian name of Mrs Pettigrew and enjoined on me never to mention to my mother where I had been. Alas, it appears that I was incapable of maintaining silence, and some account of my delectable visit eventually came out. Mrs Pettigrew was summarily dismissed for her irresponsible conduct – to my sorrow – such was the snobbery of the times.

My father Frederick, who was born in 1874 and died in London at the age of 85, was Austrian; his home had been in Styria, and my grandfather, of Slav origin, also named like me, Max Mallowan, had owned a steam-powered flour mill which took many prizes including a gold medal struck by the Emperor Franz Josef. After the First World War the mill was burned to the ground and as it was uninsured the family was in dire straits. My father, who was an officer in the Horse Artillery, left the army to seek his fortune abroad.

Frederick Mallowan was a born soldier; an artilleryman, competent in the care of men, and of horses, which he groomed with loving attention. He was free with his tongue and in the fashion of the day fought a duel with a brother officer. When I was small he showed me with pride the scar from a sabre cut on his skull and was unable to explain how he had survived the blow. The only other episode in his army career which came to my knowledge reflected his character which was inclined to disregard any order that he considered unreasonable. On manoeuvres in what was then known as Bosnia-Herzegovina, at the height of midsummer he was ordered to lead his squadron a twelve-hour ride back to base in the heat of the day. Alone among his brother officers he defied the order and led his troop through the comparative cool of the night. A stickler for appearance, he brought his troop home in immaculate condition and presented a striking contrast to the other battalions which arrived in a state of exhaustion and decimated by heat stroke. For this successful defiance of authority he was awarded a decoration and nothing could have pleased him more.

My father was not sorry to leave the army in which he saw no future, and he was not ill-equipped, for he had been through the hard grind of Continental education and was a competent, though not an outstanding all-round scholar. The hardships of youthful schooling in Austria would have seemed unbearable to the young nowadays, for he had an hour's walk from home, which he left at 6 a.m. and in the winter tramped through snow and ice to begin lessons at seven. At night he was plied with home-work, but no one shirked it for fear of failing in the final examinations. Failure meant conscription in the army as a common soldier for a term of five years and disbarment from entering the officers' corps, or the University. Frederick was successful, although like some members of our family he was a late developer, he had stamina and guts as well as intelligence. But to the end of his days he suffered recurrent nightmares from the ordeals he had experienced at High School.

Apt in chemistry, he soon prospered in London where he set up in business and traded in copra, fats and oils. Later he became chief quality-arbitrator to the firm of Unilever and came to be regarded in the City as the authority on the subject; he built up an international practice. On one occasion when involved in a law case because of alleged food poisoning he offered to swallow some suspected margarine in court. This kind of dramatic demonstration delighted him, especially in his youth, when he was inclined to be cantankerous and quarrelsome, qualities which did not make for an easy life when it came to marriage. None the less he had the gift of reconciliation, like my great-great-grandfather, who in the Austro-Hungarian war of 1866 served as a distinguished surgeon and was deputed by the emperor to minister to both sides.

My mother's maiden name was Duvivier; she was born in 1876, died at the age of 74 and remained a Parisienne all her life, although more than fifty years of it were spent in England. Her father had been an engineer and, I believe, a not very successful inventor; her mother Marthe was an opera singer of renown, well known in Brussels in the 1880s and sang under the name of Duvivier as Salome in the first performance of Massenet's *l'Herodiade*, an opera which took the house by storm. Her career was short for she had been trained by de Reszke whose exacting voice production overstrained many. She won the premier *Prix de Consérvatoire* in 1870 and went on to sing with Chaliapin who, she said, was possessed of all the gifts, magnificent in person and as an actor – I saw him sing in *Prince Igor* and *Boris Godunov*, an unforgettable experience. He was a stevedore from the Volga, singing the 'Boat Song' and the 'Song of the Flea' with inimitable gusto. I remember him sitting in the auditorium on an off night at Covent Garden, clapping enthusiastically with his vast hands as Thomas Beecham took the applause. My grandmother also sang in the opera house at New Orleans with the famous Patti and half a century later I saw the stage of the theatre where she had once performed, and stayed at the charming little hotel in the French quarter, named the Hotel de Ville, which she must have known in her time.

Marthe Duvivier in early youth eloped with a French aristocrat named de Verteuil whom she secretly married, without the consent of his parents, who in consequence brought an action against her and won a decree of nullity. Under French law at the time a marriage could in these circumstances be declared null and void if the man was under twenty-one. Grandmother earned much money, entertained lavishly and spent all she had. She was warm-hearted and possessed of a rollicking sense of fun. From this side of her family my mother inherited her artistic temperament and lack of business sense. My mother, generous to a fault, full of affection, a lively conversationalist and companion, loved the social round of entertainment and was only truly happy in town. Going to the country was an excuse for painting. Surprisingly, she was a brilliant copyist, and copied El Greco's 'Agony in the Garden' three times, to natural size.

Mother devoured romantic novels and all the classics and wrote poetry of a lyrical kind some of which had, I believe, merit and was published in high-brow reviews, for example, *La Revue des Indépendants*. She lectured on the arts with verve and style and had the love of

13

language that comes naturally to the Latin temperament.

A devoted mother who fretted over her children, her views about what should be done for them were diagonally opposed to my father's. This did not make for domestic peace since my father was by nature inclined to be a tyrant, though in practice he was the kindest of men. Both parents were egocentric and neither understood compromise. My father therefore sought peace outside the home where he was both irregular and unpunctual.

Our youth was thus enlivened by stormy scenes and the most violent quarrels which sometimes made us feel gloomy. But contrary to general opinion, quarrelsome parents can breed in their children a determination to make a success of marriage when their time comes. In this way I am indebted to both father and mother for inclining my temperament towards peaceful companionship and a proper feeling of regret when I have been bellicose. I believe that the same effect was induced on my brother, Cecil; my younger brother, Philip, remained celibate and by nature was not quarrelsome.

How difficult it is to speak fairly of one's parents and to judge them impartially – is it perhaps a matter of love-hate as they call it nowadays? I think of my mother with a mingling of love, of joy and of exasperation. In her youth she must have been radiantly beautiful – a petite Mediterranean brunette with brown eyes and immaculate complexion, much courted by men also for her vivacity and spontaneous conversation. She was restless and without a trace of self-consciousness. 'Ah, you boys,' she used to say, 'you have no go,' when all we wanted was to be left in peace. *Requiescat in pace.*

When I was four years old, in about 1908, we moved to No. 52 Bedford Gardens, off Church Street, Kensington. There was a small garden with a brick wall at the end of it and here I made my earliest excavations and still have a picture of the Victorian china sherds recovered deep from a jet black soil. The garden boasted a large pear tree and we ate the wooden sweet Williams freely and not without pain. My other memories are of being encouraged by my father to lean out of the windows and summon with a police whistle the hansom cabs which stood in a line at the end of the road together with a number of bath-chairs. Every Friday night there was the joy of awaiting through the open window the sounds of a German brass band and the glorious deep tone of the trombone. This now reminds me of the story of the great pianist Paderewski who was in his early days told by his music master, 'My boy, you are a born trombonist, you will never be any good at the piano.' Had he listened he might have ended up in a German band.

From Church Street we used to saunter down to Kensington Gardens for the morning walk with a nurse, and I was once in serious trouble for biting the succulent arm of my brother Cecil as it hung down from the pram. In Kensington Gardens we sauntered through the beautiful Orangery, flanking the Palace where Queen Victoria was woken up in the middle of the night to be told that she was now Queen. We drank at a small kiosk delicious bottles of Batey's stone ginger beer. We also derived some excitement as well as terror from watching the dog-fights in which our Chow, Choumi, was involved. All Chows are at a great advantage because of their thick manes which do not easily give their opponents a chance of coming to grips.

Later, in 1912, we moved to Mostyn Road, Wimbledon, where we lived in a half-timber sham-Tudor house named Bolingbroke, large enough for a family of at least six. It had a garden big enough to hold a grass tennis lawn. The house was rented for the sum of £52 a year. My father, who loved the game, taught us lawn tennis, and best of all took me regularly to the old Wimbledon, then a tiny club, where we saw at the closest quarters the great players of the day. Norman Brookes, A. F. Wilding, Mrs Lambert Chambers, and Max Décugis who used to cry freely when things went wrong.

At Wimbledon I went to a Preparatory School named Rokeby in a road called The Downs. The school had been founded by a Mr Olive who was a good Latinist and must have been singularly lacking in humour, for he named it originally St Olives, and took as its motto: *oliva semper viret*, 'the olive is always green'. He was succeeded by his son and a partner, G. R. Batterbury, who told me that he had only once come across the name in fiction, in a novel by Wilkie Collins where he figured as a common thief. At the age of eight I was assigned to the bottom class, where I was immediately taught the rudiments of Greek by a lady named Miss Vines who wore a large straw hat decorated with grapes. She imparted to me an early love for the language from which I have had nothing but enjoyment, in contrast to Latin which I found something of a grind by comparison, but I am happy now that I submitted to its austerities. At Rokeby I must have spent three or four years and ran the gamut from the bottom to the top of the school. I do not think that I received a better education anywhere and spent at least two years marking time at my Public School thereafter. The chief character at Rokeby was a mathematical master, an excellent teacher named J. P. Ferrier, a Manxman, who thrilled us by relating how the Bank on the Isle of Man had failed, and rendered his family penniless. This he said was what had caused him to take to teaching as a profession. He had a violent temper and was forbidden to handle the cane, freely used in those days, because he said that this instrument was only effective when it caused a boy to groan. Ordinary cries counted for nothing. But he was an effective teacher and delighted in exaggerating his natural ferocity. I was no good at algebra and remained at the bottom of his class until one day I was coached by my cousin John Duvivier. Under his clear guidance I rapidly saw the light and from being bottom, went to the top. I never forgot this lesson in after life, and when I came to teach, realized that if I was not getting across to my pupils, I was the stupid one.

Rokeby imparted to me also the love of cricket, and the joy of watching this uniquely English game on a fine summer afternoon, is for ever associated with that school. The game is a philosophy, and happy are those who can indulge in it and pass through the range of quiet and dreamy absorption which can suddenly and unexpectedly be galvanized into a lightning flash of excitement. Such experiences remain as a mellow background to life. I have only met one other Rokeby boy in later life, and that was Robert Graves, on whom J. P. Ferrier made the same strong impression. Robert Graves was of course the famous novelist, destined also to be a fine poet, one of the most distinguished boys that Rokeby has produced.

Next in order of my education came my Public School, Lancing, a rude awakening after my Preparatory School. I shall not forget the harsh impression of my first arrival at school on a cold midwinter afternoon, in January of 1917. This was my first sight of the grey granite prison walls, framed by the dark cloisters and the gaunt length of the tall Victorian chapel thrusting itself like a long spear against the bleak base of the Sussex Downs, and looking out on its other side towards the rushing waters of the river Adur.

This desolate scene remained in my mind for more than fifty years until I returned to behold in the summer a landscape unspoiled, which unfolded itself to me in its incomparable setting, untarnished by any modern building, pristine in its beauty and bounded by the sea, against the river Adur which was now transformed into a sweetly flowing silver ribbon. It was a discerning Housemaster, E. B. Gordon, who prophesied that one day the beauty of the scene would possess me and it is true that when at last I went back to Lancing, I felt like the soldiers in Xenophon's mercenary army when they caught their first sight of the Black Sea, after their long march from Mesopotamia, and set up the cry, *Thalassa, Thalassa.*

Gordon, or Gordo as we called him, wrote home to my parents before I left: 'I think he will be a great man some day.' At least I have had greatness thrust upon me by a kindly master. Posterity may judge if I have earned any right to such a title, whatever it may mean.

At Lancing I was placed in the Headmaster's House, that of the Reverend H. T. Bowlby, a strong Victorian character, whom I admired for his total lack of compromise. Lancing was one of the Woodard Schools, intended for the sons of clergymen, and the level of scholarship tended to be low. For this reason I had little difficulty in rising to the top of every class with the exception of the Sixth Form, in which I only remained for one year and left prematurely, just after my seventeenth birthday. There was a fanatical insistence on attendance in chapel and we were expected to worship twice on weekdays and sometimes as much as five times on a Sunday. For most boys these attendances sufficed for a lifetime and were calculated to knock conventional religion out for good. When the time came for Confirmation I refused, and this deviation from the norm was inexplicable to the closed mind of my Headmaster. He warned me that if I persisted in this attitude I could expect no promotion and no authority in the school. I therefore set about persuading my father, who incidentally was an agnostic, that as far as scholarship was concerned I was wasting my time and would do better to go to the University immediately, without divulging to him the real reason for my wish to leave. I had little difficulty in persuading him, for he had small faith in the virtues of the English Public School teaching after the brutal all-round education that he himself had received on the Continent and I was therefore released from school after four years, in 1921.

The years at Lancing, 1917–1921 were exceptional in the history of the school, for two of them coincided with the First World War: only towards the end were the younger able-bodied men released from war service and able to resume their teaching career. None the less even in the early years we had some good men in charge of us, but I suspect not enough of them. One man of high ability was a Fellow of the Royal Society, a Mr Tomlinson who was press-ganged to teach us mathematics. He was both ancient and far above our heads, unable to keep order and we made life a misery for him. But I owe a debt of undying gratitude to my Housemaster, E. B. Gordon, whom I have already mentioned, because he understood my loneliness and difficulties in conforming. Such kindness makes a lasting impression throughout life and anyone who has given it will not go unrewarded. He was a devotee of St Thomas Aquinas and had his own hand-printing press.

One effect of the war was to be expected; we had to devote many hours to the Officers Training Corps and this after peace was declared in 1918 was much resented except by the few who were militarily minded. Some rebellion eventually occurred and an Irish boy, named Flynn, who happened to be watching the parade from an upper window, threw out a cake of soap, a miraculous shot which landed from on high on the commanding officer's boot, much to the amusement of everyone not in authority. For this and other minor offences he received in the Headmaster's report, the comment, 'a type of boy fortunately rare'. Nevertheless, so far as I know, he did well in life and became a law abiding citizen. His father was a clergyman and burnt the report in solemn conclave. I remember that his father's photograph stood in a frame at the side of the son's bed and exhibited a bald head which his bedmates used to polish continually with beeswax. Such annoyances, often amounting to brutalities, were part of the schoolboys' make-up of the time, and for anyone below the norm, life was made unbearable. I felt particularly sorry for a boy named Bradshaw, otherwise known as the Biwi, or the Missing Link, who was mercilessly ragged. One or two boys could not stand the strain and had to leave, a reflection on magisterial lack of vigilance. Fear of exposure to this kind of treatment was I think psychologically damaging; it induced concealment of one's thoughts and feelings and left a permanent scar from which, until very late in life, I never wholly recovered, and it resulted in an inner dread of society which manifested itself finally in a bellicose outlook. The fact is that we were, as it seems to me, a brutal and a cruel generation and spent many years in eradicating this outlook. We had been brought up at an impressionable age to war, and to hearing our elders talk about it. I had an uncle in the front line in France, and on his leave he used to demonstrate the whistling of the *Obus* and wait for the dreaded explosion – Crump. I was then eleven years old, and could hardly bear to wait for the day when I should take part in similar experiences and have the thrill of fighting for king and country. We were brought up in an atmosphere that tended to make the young callous and cruel. No thought of pacifism or the morality of war then occurred to us.

At Lancing however, there was a change of attitude. Although we were not concerned with the brutality of war, as soon as it was over military training and parades begat a spirit of anti-militarism which made things difficult for those in charge of the Officers Training Corps. My House, Heads, was notoriously slipshod and slovenly on parade and on occasions we deliberately turned up with one boot unpolished and only half of our buttons burnished. We were regularly bottom of the OTC House competition.

The leading spirit in this rebellious activity was another member of my House, no less a person than Evelyn Waugh. On one occasion a plot was hatched to surprise the authorities by winning the OTC cup and we trained desperately in all the military exercises for a whole term. The effort was not wholly in vain for in the competition we came third out of six Houses and failed to win by only a few points. If we had won, the plan was to turn the normal triumphant race round the cloisters brandishing the trophy in triumph, into a funeral march to the accompaniment of a dummy coffin. Had we succeeded, Evelyn Waugh and one or two others were to have been expelled.

Evelyn Waugh was popular among the boys for he was amusing and always ready to lead us into mischief, but he had a way of getting others into trouble and himself invariably escaping. He was courageous, witty and clever but was also an exhibitionist with a cruel nature that cared nothing about humiliating his companions as long as he could expose them to ridicule. Deeply religious, it seemed to me that had he been self-effacing he could have dedicated himself to a monastic life and spent it in illuminating manuscripts, for he had the requisite gifts and was trained in script writing by a renegade Cowley father, a brilliant herbalist named Francis Crease who lived in solitude in a lonely cottage on the Sussex Downs.

I do not wish to give the impression that Lancing was at the time a bad school. Far from it. The level of teaching and learning at the beginning of the war was low, but the precocious revolutionary spirit on which I have touched was, as I believe, extraordinarily stimulating and made for original work in later life. Among my contemporaries in a relatively small school of three hundred boys we may count besides Evelyn Waugh; Roger Fulford, later famous for his work on the four Georges; Hugh Molson, later Lord Molson, a pillar of public life, and Humphrey Trevelyan, later Lord Trevelyan, diplomat who has also enjoyed distinguished careers in many other fields. Finally Q. T. P. M. Riley, an original character, lost his life at an early age in the course of polar exploration. It cannot be mere coincidence that four out of the five who made a name later in life came from the same House – Heads.

Another of Lancing's endowments for which we must be grateful was the chapel, perhaps the most beautiful example of modern Gothic in all England, and a reflection of the austere religious spirit in which it was built. As a boy I found it chilling but awe-inspiring and the music which emanated from it was never to be forgotten. We had a superb organist named Brent Smith who on the great organ notes played out Blake's 'New Jerusalem', and brought down a great pane of the vast chapel windows in doing so – thick tiles of sea green that nearly killed our French Master in falling. Blake's memorable hymn was played to the accompaniment of a bugle and came to a crescendo as three hundred boys sang out the New Jerusalem and the downfall of England's dark Satanic Mills. In recollection I still experience the strange incomprehensible thrill of an emotion about a visionary England that remains as an echo in my Utopian dreams.

One Master, the late J. F. Roxburgh, who joined us after the war and was in charge of the Sixth Form, made an indelible impression. He was indeed a prince among schoolmasters, an exhibitionist, who understood the fanciful effect that a histrionic talent can exercise on growing boys. He appeared to have a different suit for every day of the year and wore a variety of academic robes as he strode magisterially down the nave of the chapel. Partly educated in France, he spoke and wrote the language to perfection and every week devoted three-quarters of an hour to expounding the beauties of French lyric poetry. Several boys have told me that this gave them a taste in life that they have never forgotten. I firmly believe that these extra-curricular activities were the most valuable part of one's education, and it is my opinion that the rigid ties of cramming for examinations so detrimental to this kind of activity are pernicious.

Roxburgh who also loved English literature and good writing made us think about language, and his marginal comments on our essays were always thought-provoking. Frequent abbreviations would appear in the margin such as CCC which meant *cliché, cant or commonplace*, and OO – *'orrible oxymoron*. He was constantly pushing and probing to extract a spark of originality; he had a profound feeling for the classics and the beauty of metaphor in Aeschylus: there was never a dull moment when he taught. He loved poetry which he was constantly quoting and reading for our benefit. The crisp clear tones of his voice ring out in my ears after 60 years, a music matched by no other man except Gilbert Murray whose mellifluous voice was unique.

Thus I speak with mixed feelings of Lancing, a mingling of melancholy, not unmixed with the misery which was partly due to homesickness: gratitude I owe the school for inculcating a sense of fortitude, rays of enjoyment, and a capacity for bearing and surviving the harsh realities of life with a minimum of fuss. For me there was one valuable lesson, namely that in life every man has to learn that a modicum of injustice is inevitable and that from time to time it is better to bear it without complaint than to moan and seek difficult or impossible redress. I believe that in this country today we suffer from this ailment and it acts to our disadvantage, and to the detriment of an already undisciplined society which would be improved if its members were prepared from time to time to sacrifice their rights for the better ordering of the whole. This form of sacrifice, ill understood, was fundamental to primitive society which accepted the scapegoat as an act of atonement for its sins: we neglect it at our peril.

My happiest time at school was during my last year when I earned the privilege of enjoying a 'pit', the name for a private study room, where one was allowed to read in peace and to eat hot crumpets and doughnuts on a Sunday. The bliss of solitude in a tiny cubicle was a reward for suffering years of public pandemonium in the House common room.

My years at Preparatory and Public School were punctuated in the holidays by blissful visits to dear friends of my mother at Bossington House which enjoyed the advantage of one of the finest stretches of trout-fishing on the Test. Through the french windows of the dining-room we gazed out at the sundial on the green lawns and the meadows, to the white bridge with single handrail across the river and beyond that to the Horsebridge road with its innumerable hump-backs as it crossed the narrow tributaries of the river all the way from the little railway station to the mill that was the entry to Bossington. As boys we enjoyed wonderful breakfasts as we looked out at this superb rusticity: fresh home-made scones, butter from Jersey cows, the table groaning with luxuries – scrambled eggs and cold partridge, kedgeree and other delicacies that met us as the chiming clocks struck nine in near unison. At the round table in the dining-room there presided Judge Deverell, a severe but kindly Victorian character who at the end of our stay invariably presented me with a golden guinea and my younger brother Cecil with a golden ten shilling piece. His daughter Molly Mansel-Jones was the châtelaine of Bossington, another Victorian of the utmost probity and rectitude, beloved by the village, by her domestics, by all her friends, and by my brother as well as myself. She represented all that was best in the Victorian era and impersonated its virtues of faith, hope and charity. There was no compromise for her. No border line between right and wrong. The codes of conduct were strictly laid down by conventional standards. She was well-read in English, French and German. Her tragedy was that she was married to an alcoholic who was also the kindliest of men, and eventually drank himself to death, but not before running her into debt. His worst bouts of drink were suffered when he was supposed to be seeing his doctor in London and undergoing the Turvey treatment. He dissuaded me from entering the Chinese Civil Customs because, he said, of the pain that this separation would cause my mother who had been desperately lonely and depended much on me. This man of talent was despised by his family who treated him as a bounder. But his wife Molly had a touching faith in him till the end. Never have I forgotten the lovely meadows and the marshes of Bossington, one of them appropriately named Rushums, the pools that teemed with grayling and the cunning old trout basking under the bridge in his sixteenth year. The savour of the Hampshire meadows will remain with me till the end.

The transition from Lancing to Oxford University where I spent four years, 1921–1925, was a step from purgatory to paradise. At Oxford I achieved little, for I was not yet prepared: like all my family I was a late developer and did not shine in the Schools. But these were necessary years for lying fallow and had I not gone up too early the opportunity of doing archaeology might never have come my way: a better degree which I could have achieved by going up two years later would not have compensated for the loss of my proper vocation: destiny knew what it was doing.

I remember the delight of taking a first meal in the New College pavilion and being offered food at table by an unknown neighbour. We had rough manners at school where such a gesture was unknown: at last, I said to myself, I am being treated as a gentleman and found the life delectable.

For my first year, my rooms – sitting-room and bedroom we enjoyed in those days – were situated at the top of the Robinson Tower which commanded a magnificent view over Oxford. I thought nothing of climbing up and down the 300 stairs three or four times a day, or of walking a couple of hundred yards across the College for a bath. What is more my 'Scout' or college servant made no complaint about carrying two scuttles of coal a day to feed my fire: his name was Saxton, a right good fellow he was and cared for us as we cared for him. Not so long before my time an undergraduate had shared his rooms with a bear and I was delighted to recall this fact when many years later some row occurred over the keeping of dogs by Kathleen Kenyon in the University of London and I was able to add that in my opinion the society of animals was preferable to that of human beings.

Aesthetic appreciation of Oxford, its buildings, its history, the society of congenial friends and congenial books, weighed more with me than any curriculum which it had to offer. I took to heart the wise words which our Dean, Percy Matheson, addressed to us as freshmen in our venerable and beautiful hall. 'Get to know these stones,' he said, and I was truly rewarded by following his advice. He taught me ancient history and in his presence I felt as if I was entering a gold mine, though I was ill-equipped to extract the nuggets which needed a penetration beyond my capacity. For his love of New College, he deserved the Wardenship, but this office went instead to that great and pompous man H. A. L. Fisher.

Most stimulating of tutors to me was H. W. B. Joseph, anathema to Maurice Bowra, but he taught me how to set about thinking and had the art of making one feel ashamed when one had done ill-considered or slipshod work. How often I left his room, after a gruelling hour's talk, tail between my legs, but the beaten dog was devoted to his master who I think was in the end not ill pleased with the results. I am reminded of a remark made by the great Aristotelian Ross, when he said farewell to his pupil Kenneth Wheare after instructing him in metaphysics. It will not be long, he said, before you have forgotten all the philosophy you have learned in the exercise, but at least from now on you will always recognize nonsense when you encounter it. This was indeed the reward for doing Classical Greats and when I read the works of some of the renowned sociologists of our time, Marcuse or the like, I can but wish that they had read their compositions to my philosophical tutors and received the castigation that is their due. It is not now admitted that Joseph's philosophical work left any permanent impact. But the power of his mind is undeniable and he had the one talent which should be indispensable to any teacher – the gift of provoking thought.

Youngest and most amusing of my tutors was Stanley Casson the Greek archaeologist and historian. He was a man of ideas but not a profound scholar and consequently most stimulating to an aspiring archaeologist. He knew Greek ground well; he was killed in an air crash in the Second World War. He was ready to try his hand at any subject including the detective story. I owe him a debt of gratitude for recommending me to Leonard Woolley. 'I have written you a testimonial,' he said, 'and have not damned you with faint praise.' Of him the story is told that the famous Warden Spooner met him in the Quad one morning and said, 'I want you to come to tea this afternoon to meet our new young tutor Mr Casson.' 'But Mr Warden, I am Mr Casson.' 'Never mind, come to tea just the same.'

Of the lectures I attended, I remember most vividly that given on the Greek tragedies by the great Gilbert Murray. Himself a poet, he was imbued through and through with the spirit of both lyric and epic; with his incomparable memory he would recite at random long passages from the classics in a voice unmatched elsewhere that uttered a half-suppressed emotion in communication with a world that for him and for us had not vanished. The only difficulty was that the same dramatic tones were used for the recital of the stark movement of tragedy as well as for the ordinary conversational greeting of hail fellow well met, or good morning. But this was a difficulty which the Greek tragedians themselves were unable to overcome. Great man as he was, he addressed the humblest of us with deference as if he were earnestly soliciting our opinion on a subject in which he was deeply versed. His books still carry the record of a crystal clear and sometimes heretical mind. At the League of Nations the French called him *ce doux rêveur*.

A lesser but none the less unforgettable Oxford figure was an elderly grey-haired little don named S. G. Owen. He looked like an impish faun from the innermost depth of some forest. He was impregnated with the effusions of the cynical Latin poet Juvenal which he expounded to us with gusto. Every satire was a juicy fruit to be sucked dry and though he admired Juvenal for the wrong reasons and wrote an adulatory sonnet about him, he inspired us with his enthusiasm. I loved Juvenal's delicious epigrams such as *Nemo repente fuit turpissimus*, which may be best rendered, 'nobody suddenly becomes a thorough scoundrel', and other no less profound saws. But what we awaited week after week with a delicious sense of anticipation was Owen's venomous invective against the Latinist poet A. E. Housman whose views on Juvenal were regularly torn to shreds. Only later we discovered that this was his way of replying to the slating that he regularly received in the *Classical Quarterly* for his misguided views and I suspect that Housman was usually in the right.

One more notable figure that I must recall is that of Percy Gardner, Wykeham Professor of Greek Art and Archaeology, who lectured to us on Greek sculpture. For this subject I had some understanding, as this was for me a prelude to archaeology. Percy Gardner, a tall upstanding figure, lectured in a frock coat and winged collar of a type which must have gone back to the 1860s. He gave us of his incomparable store of learning with a permanently bored expression, in a monotone that somehow contrived to rivet our attention. I remember how he commended to us the learning of the guide lecturers in the British Museum – two men named Skeat and Hallett. Hallett's bored manner and monotone was a replica of the Master's; when he invited questions at the end of each tour, the reply frequently was: 'If I knew the answer to that one I should not be working here but in the offices of the Encyclopaedia Britannica.' Nevertheless these tours of the British Museum provided an incentive for taking up an archaeological career, and when I heard Percy Gardner lecture on the Hermes of Praxiteles I reflected on how wonderful it would have been to be present at the time of its discovery in the Temple at Olympia and thereafter thought of all sculpture in its original setting. At Oxford the only work that I did as an undergraduate with any claim to merit was a study of Greek sculpture in which occasionally I produced an essay that earned an alpha mark.

To Oxford I am mainly indebted not for any academic achievement but to an initiation into the significance of true learning and the companionship of books and buildings. Greatest of all however was the gift of congenial friends of one's own age. Never again did one have the opportunity of making friends with whom one lived at irresponsible ease in conditions where the means of entertainment was both easy and cheap. We went to the theatre at least once a week and enormously enjoyed the Repertory where sometimes the scenery fell on the actors' heads. I remember the continuous laughter of Gilbert Murray on seeing *Heartbreak House* and Bernard Shaw's speech to the effect that only in a provincial town such as Oxford could his play be greeted with laughter instead of an intellectual silence.

Three of my friends died at an early age, in their twenties, and have many times caused me to reflect on the unfairness of life now that I have reached the age of three score years and ten and the truth of the ancient Greek saying that he whom the Gods love dies young. Most gifted of all was Esme Howard, eldest son of Lord Howard of Penrith, successively HBM's Ambassador in Madrid and Washington where I had the privilege of staying with the family. Esme was endowed with his father's high talents; warm-hearted and generous, a lover of the arts with a sparkling wit and humour, the memory of his companionship still carries with it a warm glow. Without doubt he would have made a distinguished mark on life and his persuasion was such that I made a brief excursion into Roman Catholicism. He was carried off at the age of about twenty-five by Hodgkins disease; when I last saw him at Berne and Portofino, in the Dowager Lady Caernarvon's villa, Alta Chiara, he was pitifully wasted away. He accepted his suffering with a calm faith in God and a resignation that were the marks of the true saint – never to be forgotten in one's prayers.

Rupert Fremlin, a friend from my Lancing days, a delightful companion full of gentle mockery, died of Black Water fever in Nigeria, as did Richard Warner who lived with me in the Robinson Tower. Those were the days in which this dread disease claimed many victims in Africa. With Rupert I have the memory of a warm summer evening in May, after a game of tennis, drinking mulled claret to the accompaniment of strawberries and cream, a strange and inappropriate association which in our innocence we found delicious. Longer lived was another New College man, Ronald Boase, endowed with a truly Scottish caustic wit; on hearing a friend exclaim that the only thing he had ever learned at Eton was that honesty is never the best policy, he replied that honesty is never a policy.

Fortunately one old friend and companion remains with me – Rodney Kannreuther who many a time shared entertainment with me at the top of the Robinson Tower, in my delightful rooms in 'Pandy'; and in digs at No. 6 Ship Street, where our landlady kept in the cellar an inexhaustible supply of china vases which on enforced repayment she substituted for those that we had carelessly smashed in the living-room. At Oxford I had one stroke of good fortune that may well be unique in that I backed the winner of the Derby three years in succession and collected about ten pounds on each occasion. This sufficed to give a generous dinner party to about a dozen friends and most of us I fear were the worse for drink in the end; but such parties taught us our exact capacity for alcohol and were a necessary introduction to sobriety. I still remember my disgust when my scout,

'Daddy Hughes', roused me on the morning after the night before and asked if I would wish for a glass of brandy to revive me. Incidentally Daddy Hughes had accompanied one Dr Mayo to Fiji and there learned the language. When, as a result of this visit a Fijian prince came to Balliol, Daddy Hughes alone in Oxford spoke Fijian, and was regularly invited to tea by the prince.

Our entertainment at Oxford was usually on a more modest scale than at my Derby Winner parties. Rodney and I used to dine regularly at the 'George Grill' on a Saturday night. Our fare consisted of: soup, rump steak, sweet and cheese, washed down with a tankard of beer, all for the sum of five shillings a head, perfected for us by the addition of a sixpenny 'bouquet' cigar. That was indeed a Lucullan banquet. Such was my preparation for the next stage of my life which was to be set at Ur of the Chaldees.

As so often happens at a turning point in a man's career, my immediate entry into archaeology appeared to be the result of a happy accident. After finishing my examinations or 'Schools' as they are called in Oxford, I rose late on a fine summer morning and sauntered across the quadrangle in an agreeable and leisurely mood in search of breakfast. Thus by chance I ran into the Dean, the friendly chaplain of the College, known as 'holy Lightfoot', a distinguished theologian. 'Mallowan,' he said, 'what plans have you for the future?' 'I fear,' I replied, 'that I may be condemned either to enter the Indian Civil Service or to pursue the Law, for my father does not want me in the City – no business career for me.' 'And what do you really want to do?' 'Just one thing,' I said – 'Archaeology, to which I have been attracted by hearing Percy Gardner talk about the discoveries at Olympia. I want to go to the East and look for things there.' 'Go and see the Warden,' he said, 'he may help you.' This I did immediately and was courteously received by that affable, renowned public figure, H. A. L. Fisher, successor to Spooner who had urged Woolley to take up archaeology. Warden Fisher kindly gave me a letter of introduction to the well-known Orientalist D. G. Hogarth, then Keeper of the Ashmolean Museum, who that very morning had received and indeed had spread on his desk a letter from Woolley asking for an assistant to help him at Ur of the Chaldees – that was in 1925. Woolley, always in a hurry, practically engaged me on sight, in spite of my total lack of experience; partly because I was not bumptious and partly because my tutor Stanley Casson had sent him a kindly letter. But whatever he had said I survived the acid test which was meeting Katharine Keeling, soon to become Lady Woolley. Woolley was surprised to discover that on visiting the British Museum I had purchased and read his first report on Ur concerning the discovery of the Temple of the Moon God. I did not tell him that one of the attractions of seeing this report on the counter, was that its author went by the name of Woolley, then my hero, the famous Kent cricketer.

Such was the series of happy accidents which led me to Ur; but I have long come to the conclusion that provided one is born under a favourable star, opportunity comes to those who are ready for it. Everyone must be prepared to grasp his luck with both hands. By these apparently devious routes I was directed to Babylonia, that is to the southern end of the Euphrates Valley; I might just as well have gone to Egypt or to China and would have been ready to do so – but no one called.

PART I

Before the War
1926 - 1938

CHAPTER 2

Ur: An Introduction to Archaeology

I arrived at Ur on a dark night in October 1925, filled with great expectations. My companions were Leonard Woolley, and A. S. Whitburn, an architect who like myself was joining the expedition for the first time. We had travelled from Baghdad, a twelve-hour journey across desert and steppe, on a broad gauge Indian-type railway in the comfortable Pullman carriages made for pleasurable, unhurried travel even though the compartments were sometimes infested with hornets. At Ur Junction, two miles west of the ruins we were met by our motor car, an original 'T'-type Ford, picked up in a ditch some time after the First World War and set in motion for the sum of not more than ten pounds.

After all these years I still have a vivid memory of entering the house which was to be my home for the next five months. Surrounded by barbed-wire fences, as a protection against marauders, the approach was through a walled open courtyard flanked by the Antiquities Room and the Architect's office; the entrance was shielded by a veranda. The bright light of the hissing pressure lamps held up by our two lean Arab servants revealed a welcoming house, compacted with ancient burnt bricks gathered from the surface of the mound. The youngest brick was twenty-five centuries old, but of such quality that after we had finished the dig at Ur the house was picked up piecemeal and moved bodily to Eridu, twelve miles away.

Our expedition house consisted at the time of one main living-room, in which we dined and relaxed, seven bedrooms and a bathroom. Later it was slightly enlarged to accommodate Katharine Woolley. The bedrooms were small cubicles; the roof was of mud, the walls were mud-plastered and the living-room was apricot, the only colour available. The floor was of burnt bricks, some of them inscribed, and was partly covered with rush matting. Doors and windows were of the simplest deal. The effect was pleasing and austere, and I recall that until

Katherine arrived there was not a single easy chair in the place. The shelves in the living-room carried a small working library, but as at the time we were making history, few reference books were required. All this was revealed in a flash as the lamps were held aloft and we caught sight of our worthy but drunken Indian cook who had emerged from the kitchen to greet us. From outside the court came our two guards, both armed with rifles, and equipped with bandoliers rich in cartridges. We were soon to learn that the mud roof overhead was far from water-proof.

Not long after sunrise on the following morning we caught our first sight of the great mound of Ur. The *Tell*, as the Arabs called it, rose to a height of more than sixty feet above the plain, and consisted of a mixture of sand, mud and grit; we could see at a glance that this great monster was teeming with antiquities, and swollen with subterranean buildings of which a number had been exposed in the three seasons which preceded my arrival.

The attractions for Woolley of a return to Ur were at that time very powerful because it was a venerable, ancient city closely associated with the Old Testament. There was still a wide Bible-reading public. Woolley himself had been trained as a theologian and at one time destined to enter the Church. He thought that by going to Ur he would bring to life the Old Testament, a task in which he brilliantly succeeded. He had in mind the record in Genesis 11:27 that Abraham's grand-father died in the land of his birth, in Ur of the Chaldees, and sub-sequently in 11:31 that Abraham's father Terah migrated with his family from that city to go into the land of Canaan, and sojourned on the way at Harran (in S.E. Asia Minor). Excavations made this journey comprehensible for Harran, like Ur, has proved to be a centre of Moon worship. It was always Woolley's hope to discover some reference to Abraham and although this name never appeared in the cuneiform record he succeeded in reconstructing the background of that Old Testament prophet's original home before he migrated from Sumer (later named Babylonia) to Palestine.

Another memory from Genesis 10:10 was also prominent in Woolley's mind before setting to work at Ur. It was the legendary passage which described how Cush became the father of Nimrod, a mighty hunter before the Lord, and thus an echo of the ancient power of Assyria. The tenth verse more precisely stated: 'The beginning of his kingdom was Babel, Erech, and Accad, all of them in the land of *Shinar*' – that is to say Sumer, and this line of thinking made Woolley feel that the true object of his commission was to reconstitute the vanished picture of Sumerian civilization. This was his greatest achievement and will evermore stand as a memorial to his name, for his discoveries demonstrated that Sumerian Ur was indeed one of the cradles of civilization, no less important than Egypt. Here in the southern valley of the Euphrates the ancient scribes had, between 3500–3200 BC, devised a system of writing in the wedge-shaped, triangular cuneiform script which was one of the world's primary inventions and led eventually to the first alphabet brought into being for the convenience of traders by the Phoenicians shortly after 1400 BC.

Ur, which lies about half-way between Baghdad and the head of the Persian Gulf, was evidently one of the most important cities in the network of urban civilization which was ingeniously developed by the Sumerians, who established their lines of trade and the imprint of their culture by a complicated system of canals and waterways linking urban settlements in the vicinity of the Euphrates all the way from what later became Babylonia to the Persian Gulf.

Woolley's work at Ur demonstrated that here at the southern end of the river valley distinctive developments occurred which were in sharp contrast to those that were taking place in the northern confines of prehistoric Assyria above the narrow bottleneck where the Tigris and Euphrates rivers converge and are not more than thirty miles apart in the region well known through the city of Baghdad.

During the excavations, Woolley, always amiable, studiously polite and usually genial, was something of a tyrant as all successful heads of expeditions have to be, but he was always just and never expected more than he gave himself. Sometimes if one asked for something of which he disapproved, he would say, 'The Trustees would never allow that' or 'I cannot imagine what the Trustees would say to such a request'. Though young, I had the wit not to reply that the Trustees would not give a damn, and now that I am old and to my surprise have come to serve as a Trustee of the British Museum myself, I know that my response, if uttered, would have been correct. Nevertheless, I cannot but applaud my silence.

His assistants were never more than two or three in number but he transmitted his energy, and I doubt if any man could have extracted more from us. We rarely went to bed before midnight; Woolley himself sat up in his little office till two or three o'clock in the morning and we were expected to be on the dig not later than half an hour after sunrise. Once I ventured on a game of cards with the epigraphist and was told that if I did not possess the energy to work I would do better to go to bed.

His wife, Katharine Woolley, who always accompanied him, was a dominating and powerful personality of whom even at this time it is difficult to speak fairly. Her first marriage had been a disaster, for not long after the honeymoon her husband shot himself at the foot of the Great Pyramid and it was only with reluctance that she brought herself to marry Woolley – she needed a man to look after her, but was not intended for the physical side of matrimony. Katharine was a gifted woman, of great charm when she liked to apply it, but feline and described by Gertrude Bell, not inaptly, as a dangerous woman. She had the power of entrancing those associated with her when she was in the mood, or on the contrary of creating a charged poisonous atmosphere; to live with her was to walk on a tightrope. Many a man led on by her bewitching spells suddenly found himself cast aside with disdain, but she could inspire affection and was good company – well-read and never dull. Opinionated, Teutonic in overriding contrary opinion, ultra-sensitive and ready to take offence: there was no room for any other woman on the expedition. The Woolleys wisely saw to it that there never was one. Even the workmen on the dig were afraid of her and I remember an occasion when the male members of the expedition were vainly attempting to separate a tribal quarrel in the course of which the combatants were cracking each other's heads with maces: the sudden appearance of Katharine on the scene was enough to bring about an instantaneous end to the battle.

After such episodes there were heads and wounds to be bound up and as junior member of the expedition it fell to my lot to act as medical officer, even to indulge in some faith healing when required. My most remarkable case was a man who had fallen off our rubbish wagon and sprained his right hand which was swollen to the size of a football. I rubbed on some embrocation and perhaps blasphemously said to him,

' "thy faith shall make thee whole". Come back on the morrow.' He did so and displayed a perfectly normal hand. I was also expected to act as chief masseur to Katharine Woolley, who suffered from recurrent headaches, and I acquired no small skill as an operator, for I happened to be possessed of sensitive hands. It sometimes fell to me to apply leeches to her forehead – a visiting doctor had pronounced that some blood-letting would be beneficial. I had no great relish for this rather tricky task. Katharine, a bad sleeper, sometimes needed attention from Leonard Woolley in the small hours, but as he was always whacked, no amount of calling could rouse him although he slept in an adjacent bedroom. To overcome this difficulty, a string was tied round Leonard's toe and violently tugged when his services were required in the night. Fortunately, this method of rousing him was only applied in emergencies; but as the nearest doctor was in Nasiriyah, many miles away, and there was no telephone, we had to contrive to survive without him.

Katharine was an artist endowed with no mean talent and executed a bronze head of our foreman Hamoudi ibn Sheikh Ibrahim which was an impressive and powerful portrait of the man.* She also achieved a series of beautiful line drawings of the metal tools and weapons from Ur, but in spite of an authoritative manner lacked confidence in her own natural abilities and could execute little without minute consultation. Although her health was an anxiety to Woolley, and her exactions made constant demands on his time, marriage made him more human and with advantage often diverted a single-mindedness which otherwise would have left no time whatever for anything but work. Both the Woolleys were snobs and were unashamed to bend any potential helpers to their aid and likewise to cast them off when they were no longer useful, a short-sighted policy which made enemies. Both Woolley and Ur owed Katharine much for mobilizing private and public interest on behalf of the dig; her personal magnetism induced more than one Maecenas to provide generous financial support for the expedition.

Katharine died aged about fifty having struggled with bad health all her life. One night before going to bed she said to Leonard, 'Len, I am going to die this night. You will find me dead in the morning: you

* Now in the Horniman Museum, Dulwich.

must carry on exactly as you would if I were alive.' He received this statement with disbelief, for there had been many alarms, but the next morning she was indeed dead, and so ended the life of a remarkable woman who had exasperated many, but charmed more.

Woolley's epigraphist, at the time of my arrival, Father Legrain, had been sent out by the Museum of the University of Pennsylvania which partnered the British Museum in funding the excavations. Legrain, a tall, handsome man with grey hair, was an amusing character, cynical in outlook; although ordained he was sometimes mistaken for an agnostic; he had been induced to enter the priesthood by his mother, but a better vocation for him would have been the fathering of a family. After a promising start he failed to get on with the Woolleys and at the end of his second season refused to serve again. The more was the pity, for he was a brilliant copyist of formal inscriptions. To some of us he was a source of continuous merriment as he sang his way on a Sunday over the bumpy ten-mile track into Nasiriyah shouting jokes and ogling the hooded Bedouin women – a pursuit not without risk; he sometimes met with a good-natured mincing response to his innocuous approaches. He humoured us all but enraged the priggish side of Woolley by addressing one of our servants as 'the father of farts', which indeed he was.

Legrain found a ready friend in A. S. Whitburn, a young veteran of the First World War, who stumped about the ruins addressing his tape-boy in a strange brand of Arabic which was a language of its own. At the end of one season, when the expedition finances had sunk to a low ebb, there was very little money to spend for our journey, and Whitburn was my companion on a hard voyage from Alexandria to Athens in the course of which we travelled steerage, at a cost of £1 a head. I regret to say that we sustained ourselves by purloining onions and tomatoes from open crates on the deck, apparently a serious maritime offence: we ate them alternately, to acquire warmth and then to cool down. Our fellow passengers were kindness itself, and I slept next to an impecunious merchant from the island of Tenos who insisted on giving me frequent pulls at his wine bottle. We ate a vast breakfast on arrival at Athens and having finished it, started all over again on another one. At Ur Whitburn entertained us with a fund of cockney stories which kept us continually amused.

Two colleagues who shared the work of excavation deserve a special mention. The first was John Rose, a Scot with a quiet sense of humour, who became a life-long friend; a beautiful draughtsman, he made an invaluable contribution by disentangling the complex strands of brick-work in the ziggurat, a building which had experienced the most intricate alterations over a long period of time. John Rose was a man of exceptional modesty, and after leaving us went out to the West Indies and designed a new plan for Castries, but he was so far self-effacing that he never made the mark on the world that he should have achieved as an architect.

While we were together we helped to make a balanced team and became practised in holding our tongues, but after I left, a less sub-ordinate group joined the expedition, and Rose told me that one night four of them joined together after midnight and engrossed their grievances on sheets of foolscap paper, which after two hours they solemnly burnt in conclave. A good form of catharsis and psycho-logical relief.

The other delightful colleague was Father S. J. Burrows, a Jesuit priest from Campion Hall who served as epigraphist in succession to Father Legrain. This unworldly man, an endearing character, and per-haps something of a mystic, was so far removed from the small realities of life that he was little comfort to a young man such as myself who occasionally needed solace. Versed in ancient Oriental languages, Sumerian, Babylonian, Phoenician, Aramaic and Hebrew, he was un-able to bend his mind to the vernacular and had the greatest difficulty in asking for a jug of hot water in Arabic. When showing visitors round the dig his method of exposition was diametrically opposite to that of Woolley who was certain about everything. Burrows's hesita-tions, even at translating the simplest brick inscriptions, were not calculated to inspire confidence and only the expert would have sus-pected him of possessing profound academic learning. Whenever I was conducting a vistor around Ur, Burrows, wearing his little black hat, was invariably seen to be squatting in our unroofed open-air lavatory, clearly visible to visitors from the top of the ziggurat, and it was em-barrassing to explain to the enquirer that this was our epigraphist per-forming his morning office.

At that time I was a practising Roman Catholic and as this conscientious priest agreed to say Mass to the small Indian Christian community at Ur Junction Station on Christmas morning, I volunteered to be his server. This was something of a hardship, because it was a rare rest day and we had to rise at about 6.30 a.m. and make ourselves unpopular by starting up the old noisy 'T' Ford engine in order to cover the two-mile journey to the station, awaking our fellows who were enjoying a well-deserved rest in bed. When we reached the Rest House where Mass was to be said, the only man ready and in attendance was the Mohammedan watchman who had everything in immaculate order for us. The Christian Indians who had been carousing deeply on the night before were dead drunk to a man, and none of them turned up. We celebrated three Masses in succession and, having ended them, half a dozen dejected men, looking much the worse for wear, put in an appearance and asked us to begin again. This Burrows quite rightly refused to do, but he gave them a brief address, expatiating on the wisdom of the Church in ordaining a fast before a feast, incidentally a precept also inculcated by the Babylonian magicians. For my part I was unable to resist rubbing it in on Burrows that the only man who had kept faith with our tryst was a Muslim. He replied by enjoining me not to divulge to any of our fellows what had happened and to this request I was sympathetic. I trust that Burrows' shade will forgive me for revealing this secret after a lapse of fifty years.

I myself had left London to take up my duties as the junior member of Woolley's staff, on the understanding that I would serve as general field assistant and would be taught the job by Woolley as I went along, for I had had no initial training whatsoever. In addition, I was expected to learn Arabic and become reasonably proficient at the spoken language. I was never a good linguist, but by dint of keeping Van Ess's grammar in my pocket for several years on end I became tolerably competent in the speaking and understanding of it and at eliciting sense by a dialectic method of question and answer, which stood me in good stead during the war when better Arabists than I were often unable to put their Arabic across. Another of my duties was to help make up the pay-book which was no light task, considering the large number of men that we employed and also the fact that we paid in rupees and annas which were extremely difficult to add up. At the end of the day I acted as medical officer and attended to the men.

As the youngest member of the expedition I was frequently delegated to show visitors round the dig when necessary, especially those
en route for India. The guest we enjoyed entertaining most was the
celebrated missionary, Van Ess, author of my invaluable dictionary. He
had run a Dutch Mission in Basrah for over forty years and had long
memories of the country. He had paid his first visit to Ur as early as
1904 and related that when the Turkish Governor was sitting in his tent
the tribesmen used to practise shooting at him after sunset.

Another distinguished visitor of whom I must also speak was
Gertrude Bell, whose name and fame in the Arab world stood in her
time as high as that of T. E. Lawrence. When we were at Ur, she was
discredited politically, for she had swept aside the warnings of the High
Commissioner, Sir Arnold Wilson, that there would be serious trouble
in Iraq, and serious trouble there was, involving the loss of many lives,
particularly in the district of Diwaniyah, near to which a hospital train
was cut down. We had a suspicion that some of our workmen were
among the butchers. Thereafter, Gertrude Bell turned her attention to
the foundation of a museum and to establishing an Antiquities Service
in Iraq on a sound basis. For this Iraq owes her a debt beyond repayment, and one hopes that one day the Iraqis will make generous recognition of it. During my first two seasons at Ur, Gertrude herself acted
as the Director of Antiquities and would spend several days battling
with Woolley over the share of the finds. The division was supposed
to be on a fifty-fifty basis, but no tigress could have safeguarded Iraq's
rights better. Then aged 57, she was still a woman of extraordinary
energy and I well remember a tour of Eridu with her on a hot day,
when none of the men dared to be the first to suggest that she stop
tramping around in the dust and make a break for luncheon.

Whitburn and I called on her in Baghdad in her little house, on our
way home in 1926, in order to present our respects. She was glad to see
us, for she was lonely and mortified that she was no longer a power in
the land. Three months after this visit she died through an overdose of a
sleeping draught which was thought to have been taken deliberately.
We felt privileged to have met this remarkable woman, a brilliant
Arabic speaker and learned historian, an intrepid traveller whose two
principal books, *The Desert and the Sown* and *Amurath to Amurath* are
still classics. Remarkable also are her letters which she wrote stylishly

and with effortless ease, after the longest day's journey. The memory of her will endure, both in this country and abroad: I still remember the day when the Iraq Museum consisted of one shelf, half full of antiquities. Thereafter Gertrude Bell acquired a brick building near the Tigris which was to serve for some twenty years as Iraq's first Museum of Antiquities. This has now been succeeded by a great building equipped in the most modern fashion and houses one of the richest collections of Sumerian and Mesopotamian antiquities in existence. This achievement stands ultimately to the credit of Gertrude Bell who, incidentally, left a legacy for the foundation of the British School of Archaeology in Iraq.

But perhaps the most arduous task of all was at the beginning of the season. I used to go down with the foremen as advance party and such was the nature of the dust storms at Ur that one wing of the house, after the summer, was buried up to the roof under the sand, which usually took three days to shovel away. It was quite a heavy job to make the expedition house presentable, but in spite of the severity of the summer and the extraordinary dryness we were also liable to terrible rainstorms in the late autumn, they were the tail end of the monsoon from India.

During the excavations we employed 200–250 men, sometimes less, sometimes more. They worked for us from sunrise to sunset with an interval of half an hour for breakfast and an hour for luncheon. It was a strenuous day's work for which they were paid at the rate of one rupee, the equivalent of about eighteen pence. In addition, *bakshish*, that is tips, were awarded for all small finds as an encouragement to them to keep their eyes open. The gangs consisted of a pickman, a spademan and four, five or six basketmen according to the distance which the soil had to be carried. In addition there was a small gang of about eight men who worked our two trucks on the light railway.

These Arab tribesmen were desperately poor and lived next door to starvation. They could therefore hardly be expected to be possessed of any surplus energy and had to be driven along by exhortation and encouragement, and occasionally, I fear, by the sack. But the work was much coveted and was a tremendous boon.

The work necessarily had to move slowly, but over the twelve years these men shifted hundreds of thousands of tons and they were the backbone of the indispensable team which extracted history from the soil. They were controlled by our foreman, an elderly father, Hamoudi ibn Sheikh Ibrahim from Jerablus in North Syria who had worked for Woolley for many years at Carchemish before coming to Ur, and brought with him three sons. I can still see the old man, Hamoudi, perched like a great eagle on the side of a cliff, exhorting and encouraging the men, prevailing over them by a mixture of threats, invective and sarcasm.

In the course of four or five years an *esprit de corps* had developed, as it always will, if men are well led, bound by a common purpose and made to feel a sense of pride in their work. None the less we did experience one lapse of conscience. We found one grave which, we were certain from previous discoveries, must have contained a golden frontlet on the forehead of the deceased. When we came to clear the earth, it was not there – one of the men had abstracted it at an unwatched moment. On casting over in our minds who might have been the thief out of our 170 men we agreed that whilst it might have been any one out of 169 that had done the deed, only one workman whom we had named 'Honest John Thomas', must be innocent. On the next pay day therefore, Woolley asked the men if, one by one as they came up to the pay-table for their money, they would agree to swear their innocence on the Koran, and in chorus they assented to do so, under the eyes of the Chief of Police from Nasiriyah. About 150 men in succession swore that they were innocent, but when the guilty one was about to touch the book all of them rose as one man and pointed the finger of condemnation rather than witness the awful act of perjury which was about to be perpetrated: the guilty one was Honest John Thomas, who, like Iago, had over the years deliberately built up a reputation for honesty. Had we been wiser we would have remembered our Shakespeare.

After an initial training I became, at the end of each season, chief packer of the antiquities which were dispatched as a rule in no less than forty or fifty crates, and large crates at that, supplied by the RAF. The task of packing was a delicate and difficult one, as well as extremely dusty. I had to accompany the cases by rail all the way to Basrah and used to sit in the last open wagon, at the back of the train, a position which I enjoyed. At Basrah I accompanied the valuable cargo to the docks and finally saw it on to the steamer for the long journey home.

The year 1930, my fifth and penultimate season at Ur, was of crucial importance in my life, for it was the year of my marriage.

Agatha, or Agatha Christie, as she then was, had paid a visit to Baghdad in the spring when I happened to be ill with appendicitis and away; the Woolleys became friendly with her and asked her to stay in the autumn and travel home with them at least part way at the end of the season. They had read several of her novels and were admirers. When Agatha came down to stay in March of that year Katharine Woolley in her imperious way ordered me to take her on a round trip to Baghdad and see something of the desert and places of interest on the journey. Agatha was rather nervous at this request and afraid that it might cause me displeasure when I might be looking forward to journeying home on my own. However I found her immediately a most agreeable person and the prospect pleasing.

We set off together and inspected the ruins at Nippur, greatly impressed by their starkness, the gaunt ziggurat and the eerie nature of the site, which was one of the oldest in Sumer. We spent a strange night at Diwaniyah with the political officer, Ditchburn, who was extremely rude about all archaeologists and obviously displeased at having us to stay. Thereafter we made a trip to Nejeif, a wonderful old walled town, one of the Holy Pilgrim cities of the Shiahs. There we were not allowed to go into the mosque, but we saw one of the very last of the horse-drawn trams: I have only seen two others, the first as a boy at Kew and the second in San Francisco. From Nejeif we motored on to Kerbela where we were to spend the night, visiting on the way the lovely Ummayad* castle of Ukhaidir, so well described by Gertrude Bell in *Amurath to Amurath*. Walking round the parapets of those high battlements was a terrifying experience if you had no head for heights, but I led Agatha round them all, by hand, and she confided herself to me without too much trepidation.

After visiting the castle, as it was a boiling hot day, we decided to have a bathe in a salt lake near by, but in doing so the car became inextricably stuck in the sand and looked as if it would never get out.

* Expert opinion is now inclined to believe that it was founded early in the Abbasid period. Her book on the subject is one of her most important legacies, and includes a detailed survey of the site.

Fortunately we had with us a Bedouin guard supplied by the police at Nejeif to see us on the way to Kerbela and after praying to Allah he set off to make the forty-mile journey on foot in order to get help while we resigned ourselves patiently to a very long wait. I remember being amazed that Agatha did not reproach me for my incompetence in leading the driver to get stuck in the sand, for had I been accompanied by Katharine Woolley that is what would have happened, and I then decided that she must be a remarkable woman.

Our guide had hardly gone for five minutes, incidentally a very handsome Bedouin guide in the uniform of the desert police with a long flowing kefiyah, than there passed by on this lonely track an old-fashioned 'T' Ford filled to the brim with passengers. They stopped and all fourteen of them got out and lifted our car up bodily out of the sand; a minor miracle. Praising God we drove to Kerbela where we spent the night in the police station and were each allotted one cell, one for Agatha and one for myself. My last duty for the night was to escort her by the light of a police lantern to the lavatory. We had breakfast in the prison where I remember that one of the policemen recited to us 'Twinkle, Twinkle Little Star' in Arabic. The mosque at Kerbela was of singular beauty and the tiles a wonderful sky-blue that one does not easily forget. We reached Baghdad in good heart and arrived at the Maude Hotel where we had a very pleasant stay in that primitive inn. After being stuck in the sand on the way to Kerbela we never looked back and I don't think I guessed that the short journey to Baghdad would lead to a longer union which was destined to last for the best part of fifty years. We travelled home together part way on the Simplon Orient Express after accompanying the Woolleys as far as Aleppo where we parted company from them. Our journey on the Taurus Express at the end of March was wholly enjoyable and gave me the firm intention of seeking Agatha's hand when we reached home. We were married on 11 September 1930.

CHAPTER 3

Ur: The Excavations

The earliest remains of human habitation which Woolley revealed at Ur were found at the bottom of a great excavated shaft, 50 feet below the surface.

Deep down in the bowels of the earth he passed through many levels of stratified occupation which ran from the end of the Early Dynastic period about 2500 BC, through a large number of earlier sequences including Uruk and Jamdat Nasr, the periods at which writing was invented and first developed. Below these he observed a deep band of sandy alluvial clay interspersed as might be expected with grains of aeolian, windblown sand. Woolley, who had previously found similar but shallower deposits near by and had heard from Watelin of flood levels at Kish, soon came to the conclusion that here he was in the presence of something significant.

When he related his observations and read out his field notes to his wife, Katherine Woolley, and asked her what he had found, her quick intelligence immediately gave him the desired response – 'the Flood'.

The 'Great Flood', according to the eleventh tablet of the Gilgamesh Epic, had overwhelmed and destroyed mankind. Only one family, that of Ut-napishtim, the Sumerian Noah, had been saved, prompted by a merciful God to escape together with the males and females of an appropriate assortment of livestock. This was the Flood remembered in the Book of Genesis and recorded in the story of Noah. Many of the details, in particular the sending out of birds from the Ark were sufficiently close to the early cuneiform record to prove that this ancient Mesopotamian tradition had survived, doubtless through Canaanite records, into the Hebrew scriptures of the Old Testament. Here was a discovery after Woolley's heart; a plausible authentification of the Old Testament record, for the excitement of the Bible-reading public, and Woolley, a brilliant journalist, made the best of it.

As we descended into the great pit and looked up at Nebuchadrezzar's boundary wall, Woolley used to say, 'Here we leave history behind us. You may not realize that a greater period of time separated Nebuchadrezzar from the flood than separates us from Nebuchadrezzar.' In this alluvial bank Woolley found prehistoric graves of the late Ubaid period which he surmised contained the remains of persons drowned by the flood. Several feet below we reached virgin soil, whereon Woolley detected the beginnings of Ur and the reed huts built by its first inhabitants when the settlement was but an island in the marsh.

But Woolley's flood was in fact a deposit laid down at the end of the prehistoric period which goes by the name of Ubaid, in about 4000 BC, and therefore much too early to be related to the records of the Mesopotamian Flood, which are specifically associated with a king of Suruppak (Ut-napishtim) who flourished at the beginning of the Early Dynastic period in about 2900 BC. Traces of that same flood have been discovered at the site of Suruppak (Farah) itself and were identified not only in plano-convex houses much higher up in the Flood Pit at Ur, but also at Kish where these deposits were much less bulky.

Woolley thus, not for the first time, made a brilliant identification which missed the true mark. In spite of disbelief, there can be no question that he did indeed find the remains of a great flood, one of many which have ravaged Babylonia from time immemorial. Nothing would be more interesting than to return to these same levels and probe them again scientifically. A task inviting future exploration.

Woolley's most important discovery at Ur – and the second in antiquity – was the Royal Cemetery which brought forth a wealth of Sumerian treasure, the like of which had never been seen before and is never likely to be seen again. Woolley excavated and recorded more than two thousand graves, for the most part of the Early Dynastic period about 2750–2450 BC, and there were others which provided brilliant evidence of Sargonid art in the twenty-fourth century BC, followed by a series of great corbel-vaulted brick tombs of the Third Dynasty of Ur.

This marvellous excavation revealed in the most striking way

Woolley's strengths and weaknesses. No other man alive, and no one today, could have coped with this gigantic task as the finds poured in. The Antiquities Room was filled to the brim; there was gold scattered under our beds, and it says much for the security of Iraq under the British Mandate and for the vigilance of our good Sheikh Munshid of the Ghazi, that we were never raided or attacked, for rumour soon spread that among other things we had found a solid golden sphinx.

The masterly direction of this complicated operation is a tribute to Woolley's capacity for organization: no grave out of the two thousand or so went unplotted. This was achieved both with the tape and the prismatic compass as a check and it was no mean feat to take a reading in a high wind or a sandstorm when the needle waggled and spun to and fro like a ballet dancer. Woolley's choice of a boundary for the dig at a point where the stratification of the soil was most clearly legible was judicious. Here at a glance the observer could see the complete sequence of deposits through the mound on waste ground that had been used as a cemetery for a period of about three hundred and fifty years. Woolley appreciated the fact that over the whole cemetery area there ran a sealed stratum which gave a terminal date for its end. In other words, that everything underlying that stratum could not be later than the latest objects contained within it, and these consisted of seal impressions in a style familiar to Mesopotamian archaeologists.

Unfortunately, Woolley tended to have preconceived ideas and was determined to prove that his finds were older than anything of the kind hitherto discovered. In particular, he was bent on proving that the beginnings of civilization in Mesopotamia were older than the beginnings in Egypt, a misconception which led him and some of his colleagues astray. He preferred to play a lone hand and was reluctant to consult authority, particularly when he had built up a chronological framework which he considered to be satisfactory. Therefore he concluded that the terminal stratum above the Royal Cemetery contained nothing later than impressions of the First Dynasty of Ur which he dated to about 3100 BC. In this he was wrong, for some of the sealings were Sargonid, to be dated after 2400 BC; and likewise he dated the stratum below the bottom of the Royal Cemetery earlier than the evidence warranted. Moreover, the seal impressions underlying, and therefore earlier than the Cemetery, are apparently not older than the period known as Early Dynastic I. The royal graves can comfortably be accommodated between Early Dynastic II and Early Dynastic III, and most of them within the latter period. The bulk of the royal tombs is now generally accepted as falling between about 2750 BC and 2500 BC, and many of the commoners' graves are two centuries later still.

Egypt was his bugbear and distracted him from the truth. We can no longer agree with the assessment made in *Ur of the Chaldees* (p. 88): 'When Egypt does make a start, the beginnings of a new age are marked by the introduction of models and ideas which derived from an older civilization which, as we know now, had long been developing and flourishing in the Euphrates Valley, and to the Sumerians we can trace much that is at the root of ... Egyptian art and thought.'

For Woolley's not inconsiderable error there was a fair excuse at the time, for the dating of early seals was then in its infancy, and he in fact was producing the evidence that enabled the chronology to be established on a scientific basis. To his eternal credit is the written and graphic record which has put Babylonian chronology of the third millennium BC on soundly based lines. The fact is that both civilizations, Egyptian and Sumerian, developed more or less *pari passu*, in step, and that is what Woolley's own excavations have demonstrated.

The sight of the Royal Cemetery when we were in full cry was amazing – and I recall that one of the royal tombs, which contained no less than 74 bodies buried alive at the bottom of the deep royal shaft, appeared, when exposed, to be a golden carpet ornamented with the beech leaf head-dresses of the ladies of the court, and overlaid by gold and silver harps and lyres which had played the funeral dirge to the end.

The task of selecting the most striking and important of the multifarious objects discovered in the Royal Cemetery would be an invidious one. But I think one must give a place of high honour to the first of the treasures to be found, in 1926: the famous gold dagger, intact in its lattice-work sheath, the elegant lapis lazuli handle embellished with golden studs. At that time there was nothing comparable and a well-known archaeologist, de Mecquenem, mistakenly pronounced that it could not be Sumerian but must have been made under the Italian Renaissance. The quantity of lapis lazuli found in the tombs was remarkable and indicated a trade with the distant mines of Badakshan, in what is now Afghanistan. It is probable that the Sumerian demand for this stone exhausted the best veins of these mines, for never again has lapis lazuli been attested in such large quantities. Many of the golden vessels, thought by some critics to be barbaric, were sensitive works of art, as delicate in feeling and in controlled strength as the finest Queen Anne silver – for example, a little fluted trough-shaped silver lamp still in a pristine condition, a masterpiece.

No less striking were the musical instruments with bulls' and stags' heads; the lapis lazuli and shell mosaic box labelled as a 'Royal Standard' by Woolley was, in my opinion, the sounding box of a lyre. Most remarkable was Queen Shubad's (Pu-abi's) wig overlaid with golden ribbons, and the hundreds of superb lapis and carnelian beads discovered in her tomb. Perhaps pride of place should be given to the sumptuous electrum, hammered and chased wig of Prince Mes-kalam-dug, with its side flaps pierced to carry leather protectors and its perforated ears. Nor should we forget the lovely little golden onager or wild ass, which decorated the yoke pole found on one of the chariots in the shaft grave. But the catalogue continues endlessly. The variety and quantity of the objects found is significant of a lively trade connection with Anatolia and Iran, especially Susiana and Elam. Recently it has become apparent that some of the stone vessels were probably imported from as far afield as the Kerman district of south central Iran. The freedom of movement and widespread ramifications of trade in this period, Early Dynastic III, were remarkable and gradually developed over the centuries.

The Royal Cemetery had also witnessed significant architectural developments, as is attested by the corbel-vaulted masonry and the domed tomb of a princess, wherein the dome was carried, perhaps for the first time, on rudimentary pendentives. Woolley has contributed more than any other man to the history and archaeology of the Early Dynastic period.

With the discovery of the Royal Cemetery the world learnt for the first time of the extraordinary Sumerian practice of human sacrifice: the slaughter of many persons of the court, to accompany the dead ruler; the nearest equivalent of Indian Suttee. This expensive and wasteful practice, which for ever immobilized much treasure beneath the earth, was soon abandoned, doubtless because it was an uneconomical one both in human life, especially in women who were the chief victims, and in portable wealth. In Babylonia there was a literary remembrance of this ancient practice long after this type of burial had become extinct, for we possess a fragment of a funerary lament on the death of Gilgamesh, a legendary king who, according to a cuneiform text, was accompanied to the underworld by his retainers – described as 'all those that lie with him'.

Dominating the plain surrounding Ur, as it had done since it was built in 2100 BC, stood the ziggurat or staged temple-tower. Originally over seventy feet high, there is no ziggurat in all Mesopotamia to compare with it, both because of the rich red colour and unmatched composition of the brickwork and because of the magnificently contrived arrangement of the entire structure with its triple staircase of a hundred stairs apiece. At the time of excavation it was a thing of beauty because of its massive majestic presence and the subtle curvature of its façades; there is not a straight line in the building. But alas it has now suffered some deterioration and its reconstruction has not been happily executed.

Each of the burnt bricks with which this mighty monument was built was stamped with the name of Ur-Nammu, founder of the Third Dynasty of Ur, who, in restoring Ur and making it the capital city of Sumer, transformed the ancient city built of mud-brick to one of burnt-brick, as Augustus had transformed Rome from brick to marble.

The tower, which rose in three stages, was once crowned at the top with a small shrine, the scene of mysterious ceremonies. Even as late as Herodotus in the fifth century BC, tradition recorded that the top of the ziggurat of Babylon contained within it the god's shrine and couch on which the king impersonating the god cohabited with the goddess, and thus we may presume fertilized the land. This was also the practice at the time of the Third Dynasty of Ur when we have evidence of the sacred marriage ceremony. The king after a solemn ceremonial followed by a banquet enjoyed relations with a substitute for the goddess known as the *en* priestess, who was sometimes the king's daughter, sometimes his sister: hymns of the crudest imagery exalting the vulva were sung on these occasions.

Ur-Nammu, who reigned for eighteen years, ascended the throne in 2150 BC and consolidated the Sumerian empire within the bounds of the lower Euphrates and Tigris rivers. In order to defend the city he put up a huge rampart seventy feet thick enclosing a space which measured three-quarters of a mile long by half a mile wide.

But his permanent achievement was the establishment of an administration on sound lines and, above all, the construction of a network of canals which irrigated his own and other cities that came under his control. The effect of this irrigation was doubtless to improve the quality of the crops including the flax which sustained the royal house and its dependants.

The record of twelve years' excavations at Ur has nowhere been excelled as a contribution to archaeological and architectural knowledge of one of the great cities of Sumer and Babylonia, and has been enhanced by a wealth of historical documents which make the ancient monuments speak out loud and clear and turn prosaic discoveries into a poem.

Thus we know that the son of the builder of the ziggurat, Shulgi, who reigned for 48 years and embellished his father's tower, was a musician, who played eight instruments including a 30-stringed lyre with the onomatopoeic name of Ur-Zababa. For the first 28 years of his reign there is no record of this musician-king doing anything at all, but he commanded a highly competent administration and eventually it seems, having cut down on the time devoted to music, became a most effective ruler, whose authority extended far beyond Ur into Iran. He is perhaps comparable to the musician Paderewski who, having begun life as a great pianist, became Prime Minister of his country.

Shulgi established the royal weights and measures, as we know from a magnificent inscribed diorite duck-weight, weighing about four pounds, found near the precincts of the ziggurat. He also embellished the temples in his own and other cities and, as we learn from one inscription, 'Cared greatly for Eridu which is on the shore of the sea'. Since Eridu was a near neighbour this tells us, as we can also deduce from geophysical observations, that Ur was then not only near the river, but on the margin of a series of lagoons which linked it directly with the Persian Gulf about one hundred and fifty miles away, a situation that enabled Ur-Nammu to re-establish an ancient maritime trade with the south.

Third in succession within the same dynasty was a monarch named Bur-Sin, who in the course of only nine years' reign embellished and improved the city. He acquired prestige by building a temple named the *Apsu* at neighbouring Eridu and died from the 'bite of a shoe'. I have always supposed that he contracted a septic foot when tramping the blown sand which has long infested that site, for no doubt he personally supervised the building of his new temple.

The holy city of Eridu, according to the Sumerians, the first to be built before the Flood, was of immemorial sanctity and from Ur was an unforgettable sight seen at dawn or shortly after sunrise, shimmering in the mirage twelve miles away. Its ziggurat, a ruined pile, then suddenly appeared to assume its ancient form as a staged tower and mysteriously stood up in the soft light of dawn, its architecture dramatically reanimated and transformed through a fine film of gossamer.

After Bur-Sin had restored Eridu he was succeeded by two more monarchs who began to discover that the conquests of their predecessors were too much for them to contain, and proof that Ur had run into difficulties was revealed by the fact that neither of them was able to contribute any significant additions to the architecture of the city.

The history and monuments of Ur has no more colourful and dramatic span in its long life than that covered by the rise and fall of the Third Dynasty – and some of the outstanding monuments and sculpture of the period were dedicated to its divinities, the Moon god Nanna and his wife Nin-Gal known as the Great Lady. They were the principal divinities of Ur and appropriately so, for in those climes the moon shines with extraordinary clarity. Here we found the most extensive traces of burning and in the ashes the burnt fragments of statuary smashed by the brutal Elamites: the tragic end of a dynasty was never more vividly displayed.

I recall the dramatic discovery, in the debris at the foot on one of the high brick podia, of a statue of the goddess Bau, seated on a throne flanked by geese. She was, I suppose, a patron saint of the farm-

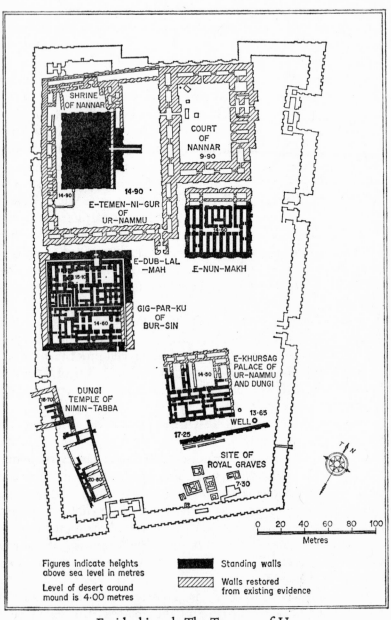

SHRINE OF NANNAR

COURT OF NANNAR
9·90

14·90

14·90

E-TEMEN-NI-GUR OF UR-NAMMU

E-DUB-LAL —MAH

15·10

14·60

GIG-PAR-KU OF BUR-SIN

.E-NUN-MAKH

14·50

14·50

E-KHURSAG PALACE OF UR-NAMMU AND DUNGI

13·65
WELL

DUNGI TEMPLE OF NIMIN-TABBA

18·70

20·80

17·25

SITE OF ROYAL GRAVES

7·30

N

0 20 40 60 80 100
Metres

Figures indicate heights above sea level in metres

Level of desert around mound is 4·00 metres

Standing walls

Walls restored from existing evidence

E-gish-shir-gal: The Temenos of Ur.
Third dynasty period c.2100 BC.

ing community whose fortunes had now reached their very depths, their protector lying on her face in a side chapel in the temple where the weavers' pit, the scribal offices, the hriests, apartments and the spacious kitchens were now deserted and forlorn.

From the excavated remains at Ur, the day-to-day activities of its citizens were most vividly revealed in the private houses for which a well-selected quarter of the city was set aside. The best preserved were built in the course of the centuries which succeeded the Third Dynasty of Ur, that is between about 2000–1400 BC or a little later. The strength of tradition and the extraordinary tenacity of land and property holders was constantly revealed. Indeed because of the claims of landowners which were never swept aside until the neo-Babylonian period after 600 BC, little town planning was possible, and the houses were approached through a maze of winding streets.

I remember looking at one house-site where we had preserved the stratification over a depth of about twenty feet, and seeing in the corner, suspended on a column of earth, a small altar which had retained its identical position in the same room over a period of six centuries. No one had dared to change the position of the brick offering-table dedicated to the god. In addition there was a public chapel which stood at the cross-roads, dedicated to wayfarers. In it we found a rustic statue of a goddess standing on its brick base and a little box containing copper statuettes. The wickerwork gate still stood ajar at the entrance, the impression of it still imprinted on the mud enabled us to record the details of its construction.

This house quarter, as Woolley delighted in saying, was the one in which the patriarch Abraham must have lived when he migrated from the moon city of Ur to the moon city of Harran, far to the north, on the borders of Asia Minor and Syria. Of Abraham himself, a sheikh of substance, who among the inhabitants of Ur must have been a prosperous but not a particularly important figure, we found not a trace. In this age when the Bible is a neglected book of literature it is hard to conceive how important the revelation of the scriptures was to the public mind, and indeed that the excavation of Ur was partly induced by this consideration. Woolley himself was the son of a parson and had been brought up on the scriptures; he had a remarkable memory both for the Old and New Testaments. At one time our epigraphist thought (mistakenly) that he had identified the name of Abraham on an inscribed clay tablet. Rashly I wrote home to an old friend and mentioned the discovery: on revealing that I had done so I was severely reprimanded by Woolley and made to send a telegram enjoining the recipient to silence until such time as the news was made public, but indeed it never was!

The standard type of house at Ur 2000–1400 BC was substantially built. Every balcony was supported by columns and in each courtyard there were four columns doubtless originally of wood, sometimes resting on a low brick step or pedestal. The front door which opened directly on to the street was flanked by a porter's lodge, near to which were the stairs, partly of brick, partly of wood. The arrangement by which admission to the house led immediately to the open, square courtyard was directly related to the economy of the ancient Sumerian city and its Babylonian successor. All merchandise had to be carried in on the backs of draft animals, namely asses or onagers, mules or even oxen. The unloaded bales were then stacked in the yard ready for distribution elsewhere, or else dispersed within the house. In so far as Abraham lived a city life, this was the way in which it was organized. Fifty years ago, when I worked at Ur, most of the houses in Baghdad were built on a similar plan which thus had an ancestry of more than 4000 years and was only discarded with the advent of the motor car which rendered the pack animal virtually obsolete.

Woolley was an incomparable showman, a man of knowledge endowed with a vivid imagination which sometimes got the better of him, but as a rule he did not deviate too far from probability. He was at his best when guiding the visitors to Ur through the houses. You walked through the narrow streets, knocked at the front door, and often, thanks to the tablets, knew the name of the occupant, a merchant, a dealer in cloth, a jeweller or a schoolmaster; you knew whether he had failed or prospered in business, for sometimes he had encroached on a neighbouring property, sometimes his own had been engulfed by another's.

Woolley's observations missed nothing and his imagination grasped everything. 'This is the Headmaster's house, take care of the bottom step, it is much too high to be practicable. There was once a wooden step in front of it, but this has long ago perished. You see, the owner

Right: Max, Philip and Cecil Mallowan at Engelberg, Switzerland, 1921.

Below: The sixth form at Lancing, 1921. *Back row, left to right:* no 2 T. E. N. Driberg, Evelyn Waugh, A. H. Molson, now Lord Molson, no 7 John Trevelyan, Q. T. P. M. Riley, C. F. H. Whittall, M. E. L. Mallowan; *front row, left to right:* no 3 F. E. Ford, now the Venerable Ford, J. F. Roxburgh, later headmaster at Stowe.

Left: Max in 1930, aged 26, then directing excavations at Arpachiyah

Below: Max in the porch of the expedition house at Ur, 1926.

Above: Burnt brick ziggurat at Ur, showing the northeast face with triple staircase. Built by Ur-nammu about 2100 BC.

No 4 Paternoster Row, Ur; northwest end of chapel.

The staff at Ur in 1926: *Back row, left to right:* Max, Hamoudi, Leonard Woolley, Katharine Woolley and Father Burrows (epigraphist).

Max, Agatha and Leonard Woolley at Al Mina

Katharine Woolley, Hamoudi and Max in the porch of the expedition house at Ur, 1926.

had to have the maximum possible rise before the turn of the stairs which ran over the lavatory behind you; in that way he was able to avoid bumping his head.' 'Now take a look at the roof,' he would say, as we stared up at the empty sky. 'I know you cannot see it, but we know everything about it that matters. The evidence is mostly on the floor in front of you.' He would point to the brick base of a vanished wooden column, one of four, which could only have been used to support a balcony three feet wide which allowed the rain to drip into an impluvium in the middle of the court; he would then point to the only possible place for the gutters and explain how a raised coping must have run along the gentle slopes between them. So it went on as we passed through the bazaar, past the big bread ovens in 'Bakers Square', past the house of the dealer in cloth, the chapel at the cross-roads and the three-storeyed inn.

This was an exhilarating tour and if sometimes we were taken by the hand and led gently up the garden path, what a wonderful path it was. If his solutions were not always correct, Woolley did an immense service to the advancement of science by provoking us to re-examine the evidence. Many a pedestrian archaeologist could do with a dose of such medicine.

At the time of excavation, however, Woolley little realized that a flood of historical and economic evidence was emerging from his discoveries in these houses, for it took years to decipher and digest the contents of the clay tablets found within them. Much of this was first revealed by A. L. Oppenheim in a fascinating paper entitled, 'The Sea-Faring Merchants of Ur', and in particular related to one merchant, named Ea-Nasir, who in about 1900 BC was trading and exchanging garments, silver, wool, perfumed oil and leather against large quantities of copper, ivory, beads, semi-precious stones and onions. Etched carnelian beads, perhaps Indian in origin, have often turned up at Ur and elsewhere in Babylonia. In addition there was a much-coveted ornament in the form of a bird, called the Meluhha bird, which may well have been a representation of the peacock, possibly from what is now eastern Baluchistan. We now know much about this trade both in earlier and later periods, and Woolley's discoveries have been one of the most important contributions to our knowledge of it. The countries which were concerned in the trade with Sumer from the twenty-sixth century BC and for another six centuries or so were known as Magan and Meluhha and between them the two place-names covered a wide range of southern Iran. In the end the trade through Meluhha extended to the very confines of India as is also suggested by the discovery of Indianesque seals at Ur and in the Persian Gulf.

Stimulated by Woolley's finds a French expedition is now working in the neighbouring city of Larsa, where one day another archive, the counterpart of the one at Ur, should come to light. It should also be recalled that the documentation found by him at Ur, literary, epic, religious, historical, was enriched by thousands of business texts many of which related to activities much earlier than the trade which we have described and were discovered in several buildings including the temple of the Moon goddess, Nin-Gal.

The sequences of discoveries in the houses correspond to the vicissitudes of Ur's fortunes from about 2150 BC through a thousand years. Here we witness the last of the Sumerian dynasties; the advent of the Semitic political régime under the cities of Isin and Larsa, followed by an uneasy acceptance of Hamurabi's dynasty in Babylon. The southerners, descended from the Sumerians, were natural enemies of the Babylonians and shortly after the new northern domination, one of Hamurabi's successors, Samsuiluna, was obliged to pull down the city walls which had been erected under Ur-Nammu, c.2110 BC. The once proud capital of Ur was now eclipsed for some centuries and came under the political régime of the Kassites, a dynasty of Iranian origin.

The revival of Ur was brought about by a monarch named Kurigalzu, 1407–1389 BC, whose extensive building operations were manifest throughout the city, and notably in a building named the High Platform which was arched and most probably domed. At one time the free-standing arch, an impressive sight, was proclaimed the oldest in the world. That record has, however, long been made obsolete. Kurigalzu, whose capital at the Aqar Quf near Baghdad is a landmark for all visitors because of its ziggurat, doubtless embellished Ur for political and religious reasons which had nothing to do with economic advantage. Ur still stood, although largely dismantled, as the relic of a once great Sumerian religious capital and through its renovation the Kassite king could not fail to acquire prestige because he was appeasing its ancient gods and priesthood. In no case did he claim to have initiated a building – the common formula was 'that which from of old had been in ruins he renewed, its foundations he restored': this was political piety.

The efforts of this monarch were instantly visible wherever he built. His bricks were often of a poor sandy composition, greenish in colour through under-firing. But we should not underestimate his efforts, for he pulled a decrepit society together: the stagnation is evident from the paucity of business texts.

These rude Kassites are indeed an interesting people who adopted a new stance in Babylonia. Assertive of all territorial rights, they carved formidable boundary stones with new symbols for the gods and adorned their buildings with brickwork in relief, both with simple geometric designs and, in the neighbouring city of Warka, with a unique frieze illustrating their dependence on the gods who supplied the city with water.

They introduced a form of mask-like sculpture with powerful features, to which realism was only secondary, both in stone and in faience, and a new type of cylinder seal fully inscribed and beautifully engraved. As smiths, particularly goldsmiths and jewellers, they were skilled, and they were competent glaziers. To their work at Ur Woolley has devoted an entire volume.

After the collapse of their régime, Babylonia entered a dark age: they had kept the fires of civilization burning, albeit dimly, for over four centuries. Three comparatively obscure Babylonian monarchs left records of their building activities when Ur was at a low ebb in the twelfth and eleventh centuries BC. Thereafter the revival of Ur coincided with the advent of two remarkable kings of Babylon which, however low its economic plight, never altogether lost its religious prestige.

One great figure, Nebuchadrezzar II, 605–561 BC who changed the course of Babylonian history left a significant mark in Ur. Throughout Babylonia he manufactured thousands of burnt bricks, elaborately stamped with his name and titles. In his passion for propaganda he was the Beaverbrook of his time who understood supremely well the art of publicity. His achievement was that he reaped the reward of the tremendous victory won by his father Nabopolassar who, in 612 BC, in alliance with the Iranian Medes, had extinguished Nineveh and all the great Assyrian capitals, Nimrud-Calah included. Nebuchadrezzar now turned his attention to the Egyptians, another foreign power which had to be eliminated outside its own country, and this he achieved at the battle of Carchemish on the upper Euphrates in 605 BC. It is yet further to the credit of Woolley that he dug at the site of Carchemish itself and in a house area traced decisive evidence of that great Babylonian victory. Nebuchadrezzar then proceeded to make himself master of Phoenicia and Syria: Babylon then dominated the west. So far as possible he saw to it that these conquests were made known throughout Babylonia, and Woolley found the most extensive traces of his work at Ur.

Besides reconstructing the ziggurat, Nebuchadrezzar built anew the sacred wall or *temenos* in the centre of the city, an area enclosed by heavy mud-brick walls with inter-mural chambers over a space measuring 400 × 200 yards and intersected by powerful gates. This was a showman's legacy with a proper feeling for a venerable foundation.

Nebuchadrezzar also instituted an innovation at Ur by remodelling an ancient temple named E-nun-mah. Originally the high altar was set apart and hidden in an innermost shrine. Now an altar or statue-base was erected in full view of the public and a cult once esoteric was thus transformed. Woolley with his knowledge of the Old Testament was quick to take the point and to reconcile this new form of worship with the account in the Book of Daniel wherein it was recorded that the Jews like all other inhabitants of Babylon were ordered to bow down and worship the 'golden image': it was a choice between idolatry and death. This discovery at Ur thus verified the record in the Bible as authenticating the new religious practice in Babylon.

After the death of Nebuchadrezzar three more neo-Babylonian monarchs of comparatively little importance spanned only six years between them.

Thereafter one of the most remarkable kings and the last to reign at Babylon was Nabonidus, 555–538 BC. It was he, not his predecessor, who according to the Old Testament appears to have been mentally unbalanced and for a time went out to grass! His profound concern for Ur and the care he bestowed on it was made manifest from the excavations and came as no surprise, for his mother was high priestess in the northern moon city Harran, a venerable old lady, buried with love and pompous offerings at the age of 104. Nor is it surprising in view of his ancestry that Nabonidus installed his daughter as high priestess of Ur in a nunnery near the ziggurat named E-gig-par. A Phoenician-style ivory box depicting a row of maidens holding hands was probably her property and must have emanated from Tyre or Sidon.

But the most remarkable discovery in this lady's official residence was a room containing flat discs of clay which were schoolboys' exercises endorsed as the property of the boys' class. In a second room adjacent to this one there was a collection of antiquities some fourteen hundred years older than the time of Nabonidus's daughter, ancient texts and a diorite statue of Shulgi, the second king of the Third Dynasty of Ur. Furthermore, on a drum-shaped clay object inscribed partly in Sumerian, then long an extinct language, and partly in the living Babylonian, was a museum label which stated that bricks of another king, Bur-Sin, were copied from bricks found in the ruins of Ur, the work of his governor discovered while searching for the ground plan of the temple 'which I saw and wrote out for the marvel of the beholders'. The copies were full of blunders but were the record of a deliberate antiquarianism and of excavations conducted at Ur about 2500 years before Woolley's. This veneration of antiquity in the time of the last king of Babylon was indirect evidence, as Woolley has stressed, of a very ancient pursuit of archaeology, but it was also I think steeped in magic which both respected and feared the past. There was danger in disturbing ancient monuments, especially in erasing them, and the activities of Nabonidus and his daughter, by no means unprecedented, expressed an awareness that it was both wise and historically important to reverence the legacies of ancient times. Ur was a city infested with ghosts of the past and it was prudent to appease them.

Nabonidus however, left his principal mark and record in the ziggurat which was evidently badly in need of repair and maintenance when he came to control Ur. Its three main stages were coloured black, red and blue, for in neo-Babylonian times the top was crowned by a sky-blue glazed brick shrine, probably surmounted by a dome which Woolley liked to think of as golden, like that on the mosque at

Kerbela. There was doubtless a magical significance in these colours which perhaps represented the underworld, the earth and the sky or firmament in accordance with well-established Sumerian concepts. Woolley also liked to associate the triple staircases of 100 stairs apiece with Jacob's dream, the ladder in Genesis, whereon he saw angels, ascending and descending from heaven. There was in one face of the ziggurat an interesting legacy of the superficial work conducted at Ur long before Woolley reached it. We could see the scars of a great tunnel which Taylor the British Consul in Basrah had in 1854 driven through it in the mistaken belief that this great monument like the pyramids of Egypt was a king's tomb.

Two more important buildings associated with the name of Nabonidus also excavated by Woolley deserve mention – one, the 'Harbour temple', probably abutting on a canal, was a perfect example of neo-Babylonian architecture, deeply founded because of the damp and preserved in its entirety to a height of some twelve feet: Woolley put a roof on it and the visitor to Ur was able to enter its dark satanic chambers and find himself in the presence of the Moon god.

The excavation of a vast palace adjacent to the temple was delegated to me by Woolley in my second season and I take pride in the plan which bears my name together with that of my old friend and colleague, the architect A. S. Whitburn, who aided me in a task which was difficult for a novice. At the time I proposed that this vast building was the residence of the high priestess, the king's daughter, and Woolley generously did not contradict me although the suggestion seems less plausible to me now because she had her own convent in the E-gig-par, already mentioned, not far from the ziggurat. It is however possible that one wing was reserved for her because there are within it three complete and self-contained units including one well adapted to a harem. The architecture has features peculiar to the neo-Babylonian period, notably walls nearly one hundred feet long in mud-brick relieved by no less than 98 shallow buttresses which happily broke the monotony of the façade and cast long shadows at the appropriate time of day.

The extravagant use of ground space at the time was encouraged by the long break in the city's history whereby many buildings had fallen into desuetude. Space was thus readily available for new building schemes and at this period we find private houses larger in scale than any that the city had hitherto witnessed. These vast buildings must have been very rapidly erected and remind us of the extensive palaces in stucco no less rapidly executed at Samarra in about AD 1000 when one of the Abbasid Califs decided to move his capital from Baghdad to a place of greater security.

The city of Ur is thus associated with the imprint of great monarchs who left personal memorials which mark some new and striking phase in the city's life. The last of them whom we have space to mention is Cyrus.

Cyrus the Great (558–529 BC), by his capture of Babylon, brought to an end the career of Nabonidus, the last of the neo-Babylonian monarchs.

Cyrus repaired the sacred *temenos* wall, restored one of its gates and inscribed his name on a diorite door socket. He also repaired and restored the venerable temple of E-nun-mah, thus associating the new Persian régime with a reputation for religious tolerance, and on a cylinder found at Babylon, the famous Cyrus cylinder, reviled the heresy of his predecessor who had introduced the worship of the moon in eclipse. There is enough evidence to show that Cyrus was careful to re-establish, as far as he could, continuity of administration, to provide for the security of the city and its guards, even to promote the welfare of the goldsmiths. But this was the last of Ur's many swan songs and thereafter apart from some traces of Hellenistic occupation the city rapidly declined. The real reason for a total economic decline was the decay of its waterworks and the new channel taken by the Euphrates which had once washed the walls of the city and had now receded to a new course.

Today the river flows some ten miles to the east of Ur. As Woolley has put it, 'the once populous city became a heap, its very name was forgotten; in the holes of the ziggurat owls made their nests and jackals found a hiding place'.

Of course the work connected with our discoveries at Ur was not confined to the site itself. Each year, during the months which we spent back in England, we continued the task of recording and cataloguing our finds. I was especially hard worked through the summer of 1930, for Woolley was determined to get as much as possible out of me before I ceased to be celibate. In addition to working in the British Museum Research Laboratories on the treasure that we had brought home from Ur, I was engaged in helping Woolley with the register of small finds that he was preparing for his great volume on the Royal Cemetery of Ur.

After completing the duties which had been assigned to me I was ready to set out on my honeymoon. Before leaving, however, Woolley read me a homily. He told me that I must arrive in Baghdad not later than 15 October and that no excuse whatsoever would be accepted if I were late. He said that I would be required to build a new wing on to the expedition house – a study and a bathroom for Katharine Woolley, and that when I arrived in Baghdad he would give me precise instructions about the plan and how I was to set about the work. I assured him that I would not be late and we parted with mutual expressions of esteem.

Agatha and I enjoyed a honeymoon first in Venice and thence in Athens after travelling down the Adriatic coast in a little steamer called the *SRBN* which we had entirely to ourselves; the food was delicious. The captain assured us that he had never felt able to accept promotion for fear of being parted from his chef.

In Greece the most memorable part of our journey was a visit to Bassae in order to see the temple at Phigalia. This involved a ten-hour mule ride, much of it on the edge of a precipice and at the end of it Agatha was unable to stand without support: her legs were in any case swollen as they had been bitten by bugs from under the plush cushions in the railway carriage on the way to Pyrgos. This was an early foretaste of the trials to which an archaeologist's wife was likely to be submitted. However we were encouraged by the reception from the innkeeper at Bassae, an enormously fat man with the name of Ombariotis. It was there that I read in a Greek newspaper of the terrible disaster to the airship R 101.

Unfortunately, towards the end of our stay, on a visit to the lovely temple at Sunium, Agatha began to feel very ill and on reaching Athens I had to summon a Greek doctor who told us that she was suffering from ptomaine poison, and for good measure he told Agatha in my absence that his last patient had died of it after four days; this gratuitous piece of information she discreetly hid from me, but I watched her progress with considerable anxiety.

After a few days she began to feel a little better and when there were only two more to go before my aeroplane was due to leave for Baghdad I had to ask the doctor to assure me if he could, as to whether she would live or die, because I had a vital assignment on 15 October and only her death would be accepted as an excuse for my not going. The doctor then proceeded to give me a lecture on the abominable brutality of all Englishmen. No one, he said, but an Englishman could approach the matter with such total inhumanity, and he could hardly treat me seriously. None the less I said I had to know, and fortunately on the night before leaving, both of us, that is Agatha and myself, pronounced her as a little better and felt that we might safely part. I therefore caught my aeroplane on the agreed date and left her to make her own way to London after spending no more than a couple of nights in Athens.

However, when I reached Baghdad I found to my disgust that the Woolleys had not arrived and were not expected for yet another week. I was extremely angry, and decided to leave post haste for Ur on the very next day accompanied by our foreman Hamoudi who had already arrived with his sons in Baghdad. On reaching Ur I ordered him to engage one hundred workmen and in a rage set out to build the new wing with all possible speed to my own plan; a spacious living-room with a handsome fireplace and chimney built on a grand scale with voussoir-shaped bricks and as miserable and contracted a bathroom as possible. The work was completed in five days and I then had the satisfaction of sending a telegram to Woolley saying that I had arrived in Baghdad as ordered, on 15 October precisely, and not finding him there had hastened to build the new wing to my own specification. As I expected, he was sent down post haste by Katharine and arrived in something of a panic, but had to admit that for his own part he rather liked the new living-room, though he thought that the bathroom was too small and would have to be demolished. Katharine herself arrived some days later and was gracious enough wholly to approve of the living-room but had the bathroom pulled down and enlarged. So ended that escapade.

I missed Agatha sorely during that first season of our marriage but there was only room for one woman at Ur and it was wise that she did not come out. I accepted that decision without grievance, but none the less I was determined now to seek work elsewhere at some site where my wife would be allowed to accompany me and I also thought it was time for me to acquire new experience, though Woolley naturally advised against it. Therefore when Dr Campbell Thompson invited me to go to Nineveh and assist him in digging a prehistoric pit through that great mound I accepted with alacrity, and so ended my sojourn of six seasons at Ur.

The final record of the work at Ur, mostly written by Woolley single-handed, consists of ten massive volumes which have taken fifty years to appear, delayed because many of them had to wait for the necessary funds before going to Press. Eight volumes of Ur texts written by various epigraphists have also been published.

It was not until 1933 that the record of five seasons in the Royal Cemetery and illustrating it was completed, about three or four years after the digging ended. The descriptive volume was over 600 pages in length and illustrated by 273 plates together with an end plan of the graves. Woolley had his helpers and was generous in acknowledging his debt to the late Miss Joan Joshua and myself. Miss Joshua was a dear old lady whose umbrella, adorned with a silver duck's head, we used regularly to redecorate with carnelian beads when she came to see us in the British Museum Research Laboratory. I am afraid that there were inevitable errors of detail in the final record, but had we checked and attempted to verify everything referred to on the site itself and in the many museums in which the objects were distributed, it would have taken another decade to produce and it is likely that many of the subsequent volumes would never have appeared at all. Woolley's methods were slapdash, but he had a sense of relative values and of what was truly significant. And although the pace at which he worked prevented him from observing every particle of evidence no one was more capable of accomplishing brilliant fieldwork.

I once watched him resurrect a long-vanished musical instrument by pouring plaster of Paris into some small holes which he had recognized as the shafts left by decayed wood. He has in *Ur of the Chaldees* (p. 36), recorded the episode: 'So too with wood; nothing of it survives, but in the soil there is left an impression, a cast as it were which with its effect of grain and colour might deceive the eye, although a touch of the finger obliterates it more easily than it dislodges the plumage from the wing of a butterfly.'

I used to see him in London at his house in St Leonard's Terrace, writing at incredible speed in English that was a model of lucidity, far into the night. The like of this prodigy we shall never see again.

CHAPTER 4

Nineveh

No greater contrast to Babylonia can be imagined than the land of Assyria which lies several hundred miles to the north above the bottle-neck where the Tigris and Euphrates rivers converge and are no more than thirty miles apart, in the latitude at which Baghdad stands today. In Assyria the capital cities, Nineveh included, were strung out along-side or near the swift-flowing Tigris whose ancient name Idiglat is thought to signify the 'Arrow' thus marking its distinction from the normally placid waters of the Euphrates, 'the river that flows gently down', *Purattu* in Akkadian.

Assyria moreover was hemmed in by the mighty range of the Zagros mountains on its eastern flanks and its frontiers were thus constantly exposed to invading hillmen, marauders from Iran, which caused the country to remain in a state of defence and to be per-manently at arms if it was to survive. Nor could Assyria exist in a state of self-sufficiency for it depended on the rich grain lands of Syria to the west. This situation inevitably encouraged aggression and an invigorat-ing climate easily bred a nation of warriors less naturally inclined to the sedentary arts. Although Babylonia was by no means immune to attack from Iran, its frontier was less immediately exposed, for entry from Khuzistan required a very long walk and the neighbouring Luristan was much more thinly populated than the Zagros which bordered Assyria.

To discover how far the inhabitants differed from the scholarly, religious and placid peoples of Babylonia was indeed a challenge to the excavator. For Herodotus had rightly discerned that the Babylonian was by nature a tradesman, or huckster. Moreover Babylonia was, as a rule, self-sufficient in grain which was there cultivated by intensive irrigation. A network of canals turned the country inwards on itself, and developed an introvert nation; the opposite of Assyria.

After the windswept dusty plains of Babylonia the green downland of Assyria was a paradise. We lived in a little house with a small garden at the foot of the Nebi Yunus where the prophet Jonah was buried, a big *Tell* which contained the remains of Sennacherib's armoury. From the house to the top of Nineveh or the mound of Quyunjik was a twenty-minute ride on horseback: there we surveyed a wonderful panorama of landscape and history. A hundred feet above the plain you looked over to the west at the steep banks of the swiftly flowing Tigris, and across it to the mosques and churches of the city of Mosul, passed by Xenophon on his epic march in 401 BC when he led his army of ten thousand Greek mercenaries from the plains of Cunaxa to the Black Sea: Mosul is perhaps an echo of Mespila, the name by which it was then known to the Greeks. A hundred miles to the north the homeland of Assyria led up to the frontiers of Turkey, past the lofty twelve-mile circuit of green turf embankments which contained within them the city of Nineveh and its Acropolis. To the east one gazed into Kurdistan and the snow-capped mountains known as the Jebel Maqlub and behind it at the Zagros barrier which separated Assyria from its dangerous enemy, Iran. To the south the plains ran towards the Zab rivers and distant Babylonia.

One can hardly imagine a greater contrast to Woolley than my new chief, the bluff, hearty, free-and-easy-going, Campbell Thompson, an epigraphist by training who had no high regard for archaeology. He had engaged me to make a deep prehistoric sounding into the mighty mound of Nineveh in order to discover what lay below the Assyrian levels. This I readily undertook as I had assisted Woolley in the digging of the deep prehistoric pit at Ur, and I think that Thompson was anxious to demonstrate that there was no such thing as a Flood at Nineveh. To me it was exciting to investigate the north after a six-year apprenticeship in the south and there was the added attraction of being allowed to take with me Agatha. Barbara, Campbell Thompson's wife, was a delightful, kindly and altogether unselfish character, whose life was dedicated to others. We always thought of her as a saintly person, as indeed she was.

Before being engaged to take part in an expedition Campbell Thompson made one pass through certain tests. One was walking through mud and bog, and the other was to be taken to the cinema, to which he was partial. Agatha survived the mud very well, and C.T. had warned me that one of my predecessors had failed the cinema test by making inane remarks. I was careful to say nothing, which he maintained afterwards was proof of my sagacity. There was however one much more serious hurdle to be surmounted and that was horsemanship. Fortunately, he did not test me in this before leaving but assured me that it was of the utmost importance that I should be able to keep my seat on a horse, because my unfortunate predecessor, R. W. Hutchinson, had lost prestige with the men by falling off in their presence, and this experience he said he could not afford to risk again. Although I had only ridden a horse twice on the open steppe at Ur, and on one occasion the horse had run away with me, I assured Campbell Thompson that I was a competent equestrian, and that I had never yet fallen off. He appeared to be satisfied with this assurance and I promised myself that throughout the summer I would take riding lessons. However, time passed and I did nothing. I therefore approached Nineveh with some trepidation and hoped somehow to survive. More than ever I was alarmed when I discovered that Campbell Thompson planned to buy me a horse in the bazaar at Mosul. As he was a man of the utmost parsimony, he was bent on buying the cheapest animal possible and found for the sum of three pounds a little pony that no one else would touch because it bucked, and this was allotted to me. We rode up to the mound on alternate mornings, and fortunately he was not there to watch me mount. I clung to the animal like John Gilpin and somehow survived the tarmac road and the steep and even more slippery slopes of the narrow track that led up to the top of the mound where I was immediately cheered by the men – an alarming reception for my horse which immediately bucked. Even more dangerous was the ride back as the horse slithered down the slimy path. But somehow I contrived to survive by clinging to the horse's neck, especially when it skidded on the tarmac. It was unfortunate that the only strip of road that was tarmacadamed was between ourselves and the mound and by good luck rather than by any skill, I gradually became more confident. Towards the end of the season I thoroughly enjoyed a ride and out-galloped Thompson on the plains. He paid me the compliment of saying that I then rode a horse like a centaur.

Perhaps something of my father's cavalry training had subconsciously survived in me.

The men at Nineveh were an unruly lot, not well disciplined as at Ur, and we were all on easy, familiar terms, but the Arab even in northern Iraq paid his respect to authority and there was never any great difficulty in managing them, though one had always to be alert and vigilant. However the start of my season with Campbell Thompson was not an auspicious one, for England in that year, 1931, had just come off the gold standard and C.T. was determined to reduce their pay. They were paid little enough already, 10d, 8d and 6d a day for pickmen, spademen and basketmen and I protested that it was hardly possible to make a further reduction. He insisted that we could not afford to do otherwise and that the wages must be reduced by 2d all round nor would any amount of persuasion on my part cause him to relent. On the first morning therefore we wandered up to the top of the mound, confronted the assembled workmen, announced that anyone engaged would have to come on the understanding of a 2d reduction all round. It was hardly surprising that this announcement was greeted with uproar, not to say tumult, and Campbell Thompson then proceeded to give an explanation in Arabic of why this reduction was necessary and of the meaning of coming off the gold standard. I am afraid that he had little success in his exposition and soon turned to me and said, 'I don't seem to be making much headway, you have a cut at it now.' My Arabic was in any case inadequate to embark on an academic thesis of this kind, indeed a thesis which I barely understood in my own language, and I therefore professed inability to co-operate, especially as I saw a worthy pickman with his pick balanced high over my head in a threatening attitude. None the less in spite of this opposition we went ahead with our determination and the men accepted the reduction. I doubt whether this has ever happened before, nor is it likely to happen again, but it says much for Campbell Thompson's strength of character.

It must be confessed that the work was conducted on rather disorderly lines and one of the arguments that Campbell Thompson used to the men was that they enjoyed coming up to the mound where they had a good gossip and that this was their club. He arranged things so that first the pickman did his stint and then after he had loosened his area of earth sat down, to be followed up by the shovelman and the basketmen, and the result was that it was impossible to tell who exactly should be working. Moreover to make matters worse we used to fill in every day as we went along and we were never able to see any long section of consecutive walling or architecture. It was extremely difficult to make the plans fit. The fact is that the work at Nineveh for the most part was a glorified tablet-hunt, and when nothing much appeared, Campbell Thompson put the basketmen to work in Layard's and George Smith's old dumps and we were invariably rewarded by finding additional fragments of the great Quyunjik library which already numbered 22,000 tablets. Thompson himself had a unique knowledge of this collection and in his time must have made many hundreds of joins. But he was indeed a curious mixture of talents for he was much more than a specialized epigraphist. He had an amateur interest in botany, geography and chemistry and by his specialized work on these subjects added much to these rare branches of knowledge in Assyriology. Moreover he was a skilled draughtsman, sketched rapidly and was a trained surveyor, having once worked for the Sudan survey though he did not last very long there and did not make himself popular, for as a young man he had been ordered to bring a brand new instrument out from England and succeeded in dropping it over a cliff. Always ready to save money and economize, for drawing survey he used a pastryboard that he had knocked down at an auction for half a crown on Boars Hill and his survey pole was a gnarled stretch of oak from the Turkish hills. None the less when he had completed his survey of Nineveh the drawings coincided with the air photographs and displayed only a minimum margin of error of no consequence to the archaeologist.

C.T. was, it will be gathered, a sportsman. On occasions he wrestled with the men, and if he threw an opponent was liable to accuse the victim of subservient cheating. He was a keen shot and we sometimes went out together to try and collect something for the pot, but not without a certain nervousness on my part as one of the barrels of his 12-bore gun was dented and he was too economical to send it to a gunsmith.

Sometimes it was difficult to decide whether or not to do a day's work in rainy weather during the winter. As the men lived some miles off, if they reached the work and there was nothing for them to do we had to pay them for part of a day. It was therefore necessary to decide in the blackness, at least an hour before dawn, whether we were going to risk a day's work or not. We used to hold a conference on the top of our roof, and having come to a decision, signalled by lantern yes or no to the watchman on the top of the mound a mile away and had sometimes to wait for a little time while the counterflash came back from the top of Quyunjik; we used to suspect that it was the watchman's wife, rather than the watchman himself, who relayed the message, incidentally accompanied by a dog called Washo.

As winter approached we had to buy wood to keep ourselves warm, and fortunately we had a fireplace in our dining-room. This was a difficult business and C.T. made it a practice to way-lay caravans of Kurds carrying down wood from the distant hills on donkeys. He used to accompany them all the way to Mosul bridge from the mound of Quyunjik trying to arrive at an economical price, and he hoped to reap the best advantage by offering them an acceptable quotation before reaching the bridge, where customs and municipal dues were imposed. But in the winter when I was his assistant, prices were exceptionally high for there was a dire shortage of firewood. He was therefore quite unable to arrive at an acceptable price. One day however, when C.T. was on top of the mound and I was working in the house, Barbara Campbell Thompson and my wife espied a caravan and urged me to rush out and obtain the wood at whatever price I could get it. This I did and very soon came to a settlement. I waited C.T.'s arrival with some trepidation, but his relief on seeing that I had obtained what was required was even greater than mine. He accepted the fact that the young whippersnapper had been done in, and not himself, and took it all with a grin. Although very close with money, he was on occasion exceptionally generous and many a time when a sweet vendor came up to the top of the mound distributed *helawa* all round to everyone in our employ, a generosity which met with some indignation on the part of Barbara, who said that he would not have done this for his own children. He was also a generous host and kept a good table. We ourselves had a small flock of turkeys in the garden which made for good eating and many a struggle there was to separate the fighting birds. Once or twice we entertained our landlord on the Nebi Yunus, an elderly gentleman called Sherif Dabagh with whom we were on good terms. With some amusement I noticed that on these occasions our house-servant went straight across to borrow all our host's plate and cutlery, for ours were not up to much, but this was accepted in good part by all concerned. The house itself was frugally furnished and C.T. deemed it a great extravagance when Agatha said that she wanted to go into the bazaar and buy a table on which to type her next book. This she did for £3 which C.T. thought to be excessive and was unable to see why an ordinary packing case would not suffice as a support for her typewriter. On it she wrote *Lord Edgeware Dies*.

On the mound he was sometimes rather exasperating, for he found it extremely difficult to make up his mind and decide where next to dig. We used to argue on this matter endlessly and having, as I thought, decided on a plot, he then used to say: 'I am going to be *advocatus diaboli*,' and start the argument all over again. I then used to walk away in despair, but I discovered for a time how to get round this, for he had two dear old foremen named Abdel Ahad and Yakub, a pair of old fools, whom he trusted implicitly since they had seen long years of service with him. I therefore used to go to these two worthies and say to them, 'Do you not remember that in 1904 Mr L. W. King advised you that this spot where we are now was a most promising place,' and I could be quite certain that they would relay this information in due course to my chief. This happened on two or three occasions until C.T., who was no fool, tumbled to what I had been doing, and accused me of being a young rogue, which indeed perhaps I was. I should mention that we used to go occasionally to be entertained by our foremen in Mosul, although with some reluctance on the part of C.T. and his wife, for their houses were not very well kept and tended to be insanitary. C.T. on the contrary was extremely keen on sanitation and all our water was pumped through a Bergfeld filter and suchlike precautions were taken. I well remember one occasion on which one of the children was passed from lap to lap and seemed to be whimpering. On C.T.'s enquiring what was the matter with the child, 'nothing,' said Yakub, 'it is merely suffering from chickenpox.'

From what I have said, I think it will be quite clear that Nineveh or the mound of Quyunjik was not a tidy one. Indeed it would have broken a professional digger's heart and it was fortunate that Campbell

Thompson was not of that ilk. The mound of Quyunjik, the top twenty feet of it had to be seen to be believed. It has been relentlessly plundered for more than 2000 years, the ground churned over and over again in an endless series of pits and dumps. Worse than that, generations of diggers had tunnelled through the heart of the mound and sometimes we worked through long tunnels with two or more of them above our heads. There was an element of danger in all this and risk of collapse, but none the less we survived.

The last series of levels, the top six or so, consisted of medieval houses and some of their contents were extremely interesting. They contained some remarkable pottery including imported Chinese wares, and some of the classic Samarran, but the houses themselves were in a piteous state; below that again we passed through Roman levels. Campbell Thompson believed that there had once been a Roman Castellum here, and we even found a Roman legionary's badge. Through them we passed through Sasanian, Parthian and Greek occupations until we got down to the Persian and the Assyrian.

Under such conditions it was therefore hardly surprising that C.T. himself never completely cleared a building. Indeed, there is only one good architectural plan on the whole of Nineveh and that is the great palace of Sennacherib, most of which was cleared by Layard, continued by Rassam and has recently been skilfully reopened and exposed by the Iraqis under Tariq el Madhlum. This great palace of Sennacherib had been described in detail by that king himself in his inscriptions and was deservedly named by him, 'the palace without a rival'. Elaborately adorned with scultpure and in part imitating Syrian palaces, it must have been the admiration of all at the time. Here it was that the larger part of the famous collection, known as the K collection of tablets, the great library of Ashurbanipal was discovered. C.T. reckons that the number of tablets complete and fragmentary amounted to about 22,000 in all; although 24,000 of them are registered in the British Museum, something like 2000 of them are joins, and as I have already said, he himself was instrumental in making scores of them.

The other part of the K collection was found in a building known as the North Palace quite close to Sennacherib's, but of this no coherent plan survives.

A word must be said about Sennacherib, who was one of the

greatest of all Assyrian monarchs, a mighty engineer and irrigator, whose works were well appraised by Campbell Thompson.

Campbell Thompson, a countryman, with a natural understanding of topography, was always on the lookout to discover traces of Assyrian remains on the ground whenever he took walks around Nineveh, and in about 1926 he brilliantly identified a great stone structure, 3000 yards north of Quyunjik, lying very close to the river Khusr, as the remains of a great dam which he was able to attribute to Sennacherib from one of the inscriptions which named it as the *agammu* pool where that king kept wild beasts, swine and other animals in a zoological garden and aquarium pleasing to the kings of Assyria. The remains of this dam which still girdles water consists of two great stretches of wall, one of them no less than 250 yards long, composed of blocks of ashlar masonry, limestone, sandstone and conglomerate, each block half a metre cube and one of them still standing more than nine feet above the level of the water. Much of the masonry is rusticated, that is, only the edges of the blocks, for reasons of economy, are completely dressed, the main portions of them are left rough. However that may be, this identification was proved correct by a remarkable investigation conducted by Jacobsen and Seton Lloyd on behalf of the Oriental Institute at Chicago in 1932, six years later than Campbell Thompson's discovery, when similar masonry was found in a great aqueduct constructed by Sennacherib not very far from Bavian at the headwaters of the river Gomel. This aqueduct which spanned a deep ravine led the water by a devious route a distance of something like forty-five miles all the way to Nineveh: the water had to be conducted across a bridge composed of three arches and of no less than two million blocks of ashlar which had been carried a distance of ten miles all the way from the quarries at Bavian, a gigantic undertaking. This achievement was a brilliant one which implied a technological understanding of the stresses and strains peculiar to hydraulics. In the summer when water was not flowing or was blocked at the Gomel riverhead, the Assyrian army or caravans could pass across the bridge dry shod when invading Iran and the aqueduct therefore served a double purpose. This great canal was one of a whole network of no less than eighteen, all of which Sargon (722–705 BC) re-excavated and cleaned. Such care and maintenance revealed the high regard paid by successive Assyrian monarchs to irrigation for the upkeep of orchards, gardens, and the promotion of agriculture.

The Assyrians, who have acquired an evil reputation on account of their propaganda extolling the cruel treatment of their enemies, were however very intelligent and understood the quality of mercy which they often judiciously exercised. They have thus acquired a reputation which does them discredit but is unfair inasmuch as they were no more cruel than the peoples of their time, and doubtless no more cruel than many great nations of our own day.

Thompson's investigations on the ground have thus taught us much about the wide-ranging energy of the Assyrian monarchy. He investigated the inscriptions always with the topographical element in mind and understood that a waterway constantly mentioned in the Assyrian Annals as the *Tebiltu*, was in fact almost certainly a canal, for there is no natural river that can be identified with it; this canal which was made to change its course on a number of occasions seems to have been diverted through one of the Assyrian gates. When it was in flood it was reported as raging to the extent of tearing down one of the Assyrian palaces, an impossibility for any natural waterway nowadays. Campbell Thompson's topographical interest also led him to attempt to make an identification of the fourteen or fifteen gates which the inscriptions recorded as giving admittance to Nineveh and although his solutions were not always on correct lines, his investigations did much to elucidate this aspect of the topography of the city. If his conclusions were sometimes erroneous he none the less inspired the Iraq Antiquities Department in our own time to conduct further work on the gates, some of which have now been brilliantly revealed by Tariq el Madhlum and thoroughly excavated and restored, an impressive sight to the visitor. On the ground however, the identification of the great dam at Ajila will remain permanently to the credit of Campbell Thompson.

As I have already explained, Campbell Thompson's main preoccupation at Nineveh was a glorified tablet-hunt and he added very considerably, year after year, to the collections. One single document seemed to me to be of outstanding interest, the discovery of a rare historical text dating to the reign of King Ashur-uballit, 1386–1369 BC, in which his own troops appeared to induce him forcibly to be led into battle against one of the Kassite kings and enemies of Assyria named Kashtiliash. This very difficult text attempts to give a description of the order of battle and to elucidate the composition of the Assyrian army. Another remarkable addition to our historical knowledge was a passage in a long text of Ashurbanipal, with a mention in it of the elder Cyrus, that is, Cyrus I, about whom we knew nothing whatever until this discovery. He is mentioned as a vassal of the king of Assyria to whom he gave his own son Arukku, which sounds very like the name Eric, as a hostage to Nineveh. Campbell Thompson himself did not realize at the time that he had identified a new Median monarch, and this was made clear to him by G. R. Driver.

In my opinion, however, Campbell Thompson's most remarkable discovery was one of which he made very little and surprisingly published in no more than a few lines and a quite inadequate photograph. This was a magnificent bronze head, life size, which is as I believe one of the finest pieces if not the finest piece in the Baghdad Museum today; a truly wonderful head of a Bedouin Sheikh, whom I ventured in one of the numbers of *Iraq* to identify as Sargon, the founder of the famous dynasty of Agade. He ascended to the throne shortly after 2400 BC. This brilliant head is solid cast, probably by the lost wax process, and illustrates a man with remarkable features, Semitic in character, heavily bearded and elaborately hairdressed in the style of one of the golden wigs at Ur. My reason for identifying him as Sargon is that his son, Manishtusu, was known to have erected a building called the E-me-nu-e in the precincts of the temple of Ishtar which endured down to the last kings of Assyria and, as this building is the only work of importance to be mentioned at a time when the head was probably made, I believe that it was set up by the son in commemoration of his famous father. Incidentally this monarch was never forgotten in the Annals of Assyria and there is an extraordinary stone head in the Museum at Turin carved in Assyrian times which appears to have modelled itself on this one. Our bronze head has the peculiarity of a divided beard which distinguishes him from the portrait of the grandson, Naram-Sim, who is always represented with a pointed beard, and gives me additional reason for thinking that this is a portrait of the founder of the dynasty.

I have never understood why C.T., who was not without artistic interests, did so little justice to this wonderful head, but I think there was the fear at the back of his mind that he might be thought to be searching for anything other than literary evidence, and that this might prejudice the then Director of Antiquities in giving him all the epigraphical relics to which he thought he was entitled.

Much as I was interested, indeed fascinated, by all C.T.'s discoveries at Quyunjik, my chief concern during the season which I was with him was the supervision of the deep pit with which he had entrusted me. Although he had no high opinion of prehistory he was well aware of the extraordinarily interesting discoveries which had already been made in Babylonia at Ur of the Chaldees, Kish, Warka and other sites, and had revealed the setting of the Mesopotamian stage at a very early date; for this reason C.T. thought that it was correspondingly important to try to establish what lay below the Assyrian remains down to virgin soil.

We therefore selected a spot at the top of the highest point of the mound and C.T. was confident that we would not have to dig down to a very great depth because he firmly believed that Nineveh had been founded on some kind of outcrop of sandstone or conglomerate, and that perhaps the maximum depth to which we would have to descend was 40 feet. Knowing how reluctant he was to spend money on a prehistoric excavation I firmly encouraged him in this idea although I had my doubts. Realizing that we were likely to have to descend to a very considerable depth we set to work on a surface area which measured no less than 75 × 50 feet, for it was obvious that the deeper we dug, the more our pit would have to contract in area and indeed by the time we got to the bottom it was no more than a very small chamber measuring about 12 × 12 feet.

It did not take us very long to penetrate down to the bottom of the Assyrian levels which we reached at a depth of about fourteen feet below the surface. Below that mark all the debris was prehistoric and very soon we reached a level which we could now date approximately to about 3000 BC. Day after day the pit became deeper and deeper and its sides contracted. C.T. began anxiously asking me when this frightening operation would cease, and I assured him that a few more days should see us through, and so it went on to a depth of 30, 35, 40, 50 feet with no signs of the debris ceasing. Indeed the potsherds turned up in ever increasing quantities.

After we had been several weeks on the job, he began to talk of calling a halt to this operation altogether. I then had to appeal to his sense of economy and parsimony and say that if we stopped now before getting down to virgin soil all our money would have been thrown away, a futile and truly wasteful operation. The point of this argument he took and we continued to descend to the bowels of the earth. It became truly frightening, for the men were by no means cautious and it was remarkable that we suffered no accident. We had, of course, cut the top thirty or forty feet at a slope, or batter, in order to be sure that we should not perish through the fall of some overhang, for some of the strata were much disturbed and I believe that if I had had engineering experience, or been less of a young hot-head, we would have suffered the most serious qualms from this dangerous-looking operation. In fact the vast weight of the superincumbent soil pressing down on either side soon meant that the consistency of the shaft at the side was really of stone and as we had taken precautions against overhang the operation was a safe one, except for the men themselves who were totally lacking in caution and used to jump across the top corners of this pit.

To cut a long story short, we had to dig through a depth of debris amounting to no less than 90 feet in order to reach virgin soil, and when we cast our empty baskets down from top to bottom of the pit the reverberation made the terrifying noise of a house falling in. In a contracted pit of this nature it was difficult to accommodate the stair-cases and very soon, instead of cutting ordinary shallow treads we had to make each step at least 3–4 feet high and station a man on each. The baskets were thus handed up in a chain and then thrown down again and this was the only practical way of getting them to the bottom with the minimum of delay. C.T. bravely insisted on coming down to the bottom of the pit once a day to see how we were getting on and young as I was, I was never able to understand the fuss he made about crawling up and down through this great depth. Only many years afterwards when I was of a more advanced age and had lost my head for heights did I realize what an exceedingly brave man he was to undergo this ordeal which to me as a callow youth meant nothing whatsoever.

By the time that six or seven weeks' digging were finished we had reached virgin soil into which we descended for some depth to make quite sure that it really was virgin; it proved to be a hard reddish marl, on which the original settlement had been founded, and to our amazement we perceived that more than four-fifths of this great mound were pre-Assyrian and prehistoric. This long succession of prehistoric strata was fascinating indeed and I shall have to recount these to give some general idea of what these sequences meant.

Of the total accumulation of just under 100 feet of debris which the great mound of Quyunjik consists, 72 feet is prehistoric and at the end of the work I was able to classify the strata into five main periods beginning with Ninevite I at the bottom, and ending with Ninevite V at the top. On a conservative estimate we can reckon that these five periods between them covered a range of at least 3000 years from around 3000 BC (Ninevite V), to at least 6000 BC (Ninevite I).

The stratum which contained Ninevite V was about twelve feet deep and of extraordinary interest. It consisted of the debris of ruined mud-brick houses which were partly filled with windblown sand, showing that they had been open and deserted for an interval after their abandonment. This stratum contained a remarkable painted pottery which has never been found elsewhere in such profusion, and before this time had hardly appeared at all. Great pedestal vases and big jars done in a black or a violet paint, carried both geometric designs as well as sketches of animals including a gazelle suckling its young, water fowl, and a series of long-necked goats, looking for all the world like giraffes, and reminiscent of the long-necked beasts sketched on vases in late Predynastic Egypt. It is quite possible that there was some stylistic connection between the two. This early variety of Ninevite V painted pottery must be related to the famous Jamdat Nasr of the south, and was the northern, independent version of it.

At this period, *c.* 3000 BC, metal was beginning to take pride of place and indeed metallurgy was implied by the late development of these painted Ninevite V vases which consisted of beautifully-made grey ware, obviously imitating silver and scored with designs which were a reflection of the chasing on silver. Subsequently on the dig at Chagar Bazar in N. Syria I found similar vases bound with a silver cord.

Ninevite V with its Sumerian-style cylinder seals was in close touch with Sumer or southern Babylonia, but was an independent northern version of it. To my mind the main attraction of Ninevite V is the probability that it coincides with the earliest appearance of writing in the north, that is to say in prehistoric Assyria.

Immediately below Ninevite V lay a deep stratum, Ninevite IV, which contained a sealing-wax-red ware, very fine in character, similar to a pottery found both at Ur and at Uruk, and towards the top there were some early southern seal impressions, the like of which also occur at Susa in Iran. In addition there were plum-red wares characteristic of the Uruk and Jamdat Nasr periods, and large numbers of extremely roughly-made bevelled bowls. These were found in hundreds all over Nineveh, overturned in the soil, and as a rule contained traces of vegetable matter. Some have thought that this very coarse ware might have been used for straining curds and whey, but I have little doubt that these were magical in character and used to consecrate the ground, in much the same way as in much later periods bowls inscribed with Phoenician and Mandaean magical inscriptions were buried under houses in order to avert evil spirits. Something of this concept must be associated with this remarkable bevelled ware which occurs all over western Asia; it has been found at Susa and even as far as Egypt at Armant, an amazing example of a widespread crude technology which fundamentally must imply a common magical superstition.

Deep down in the mound below Ninevite IV lay another big accumulation of debris no less than seven metres or over twenty-one feet in depth, Ninevite III, which contained predominantly a series of grey ware, some of it burnished. The pottery, unlike that of Ninevite IV, was made by hand, not on the wheel. This ceramic is partly contemporaneous with the period known in the south as Ubaid and should be dated somewhere between 3500 and 4000 BC. There was just a little painted pottery which could be interpreted as the extreme end of the Ubaid tradition. But proof positive of a southern connection was furnished by the discovery of clay sickles of a type exclusively used during the Ubaid period in the southern Euphrates Valley, a remarkable invention which must have coincided with an increase in the production of cereals, namely wheat and barley, and was perhaps devised at a time when there was a shortage of flint sickles. But baked-clay instruments were liable to excessive wastage and were abandoned at the end of Ubaid.

At the very bottom of this occupation we found a series of wet levels, fifteen consecutive strata of alternating mud and riverine sand, and this I interpreted as evidence of a well-defined period indicating an important climatic change. It is possible that this phenomenon observed at Nineveh corresponds with the Great Flood in the Ubaid levels discovered by Woolley at Ur, which I have described in the previous chapter. Thompson was frightened of the Flood and would allow me to say little about it, but this I believe is what it is, an index of a fluviatile period; Nineveh was of course too high to be affected by any great flood, but as a rule big floods have been associated with rain and this perhaps was the counterpart of the phenomenon observed at Ur in the south.

At last we come deep down in the bowels of the pit at a depth of about seventy-two feet below the top of the Ninevite V stratum to a very remarkable phenomenon, Ninevite II, which could be divided into three phases. The earliest yielded painted pottery with simple rectilinear designs, sometimes combined with incision on the same pot; there was a middle phase which we call Samarran, characterized by a very-well-known fabric found at the type site ninety miles above Baghdad on the river Tigris, and above that again a brilliant and gay pottery which we called Halaf ware. This beautiful fabric in which the designs, most predominantly geometric, many of them stippled, were often done in a shiny black paint; no other prehistoric ware excels it in quality and the discovery of its true, stratified place here made for the first time was thrilling, for though some of this had been found at the type site excavated by Baron von Oppenheim, namely Tell Halaf on the upper Habur, all the experts were at variance as to how to date it. Here we had the certain proof that it preceded Ubaid, proof which has been further substantiated by many other discoveries. We now have reason to believe that some Halaf ware was made as early as 5000 BC or a little later. Its assured place between Ubaid and following on Samarra was thus first ascertained in this pit at Nineveh.

Campbell Thompson himself had, on his previous walks round the countryside, observed the ware at the site of Arpachiyah about four miles east of Nineveh, and the men, while we were at work, also brought in specimens from Arpachiyah showing that the two wares were identical. It was this discovery that determined me eventually to initiate a dig at that site itself and this I shall describe briefly in the next chapter.

Of the bottom of Nineveh I need say little. We continued to dig down until we were on the virgin marl and in this contracted space, as I have already said, some twelve feet square, we found the beginnings of pottery in northern Assyria, very simple crude ware, together with a few sealings with string marks only. The same sort of pottery has cropped up on a good many other sites and it need only be said that here we were working in levels which were contemporary with the famous site of Hassuna, excavated by Seton Lloyd and Fuad Safar, and that antecedents of this same early period were eventually probed in the last few years at a site in north-western Iraq, namely Umm Dabaghiyah, by Diana Helbaek who has extensively illuminated an early phase of the same culture-sequence and found a series of primitive houses, far away in the steppe at a place where there was an abundance of game and wild animals. There it appears the early tribes migrated, apparently to gather hides and game, a source of supply for larger settlements to the east which were thus enabled to replenish their larders – with meat especially from animals such as gazelle and onagers.

To get to the bottom of this deep pit was no small achievement and we were all thankful to come out of it alive, except the workmen who thoroughly enjoyed the job and assumed that it was perfectly safe. I remember that Thompson thought that I would have great difficulty in finding volunteers to continue with digging because naturally as we got on with the job the number of men at the bottom of the pit was restricted, and he assumed that they would all prefer to go to the more rewarding digs in Assyrian levels where they obtained *bakshish* for every little inscription or tablet fragment that was discovered. However I countered that in a quiet way by giving tips for almost every painted potsherd, and as the men's eyes were screwed not to miss anything the task became great fun and they thoroughly enjoyed it, and so I never had the slightest difficulty in finding the volunteers to finish the job. Looking back on this pit, we remember it with some pride as a considerable achievement and it is certainly the deepest sounding ever made anywhere in western Asia. The like of it had never been done before, and is not likely to be done again. Of course the area of our dig was restricted and it was not possible to obtain more than a few fragments of architectural evidence which did however yield occasional scraps of walling both in pebbles in mud and in reeds, and strengthened the framework of our sequence dating which I think has stood the test of time.

After the dig at Nineveh was concluded, Campbell Thompson did not return to the East any more and we parted company as companions in the field, but he remained a dear friend so long as he was alive and I enjoyed my season with him enormously. He was not the highly skilled digger that Woolley was, but he was a robust Victorian, good company and good fun. A man of wide interests and vision, he had attempted an early decipherment of Hittite hieroglyphs by no means without value to which R. D. Barnett has paid tribute. He was full of interesting ideas and he it was who suggested that after 640 BC the Assyrian government may well have retired to Harran in the north, more than a possibility, for the Annals of Ashurbanipal virtually cease after that time. When the final struggle came with the Medes that is where they retired – this theory still deserves attention.

C.T.'s high standing as an Orientalist was recognized by the award of a Fellowship at Merton College Oxford, but he took little part in College Meetings, for he was intransigent in argument and opinionated. I am no good 'en comité' he used to say and had little time for what he called 'new fangled ideas'. I think that he was the most economical man on earth, for he contrived to run the dig at Nineveh at a total cost of £1700. At the end of the season he returned the change to Sir Charles Hyde, owner of the *Birmingham Post* who ran a racing stable, and a dig as a second string: the change amounted to 11d in stamps, conscientiously refunded to this Maecenas.

CHAPTER 5

Arpachiyah

In 1932 I was ready to conduct a dig of my own and the prospect of having a first independent command wholly free of servitude to others, however pleasant that might have been, was bliss, for I have never shirked responsibility. But there was the task of finding sponsors and that is never easy at the beginning. I was aged 28 at the time and remain eternally grateful to those who put their faith in me, for it is always something of a risk to entrust a young man with taking charge of a new enterprise where the expenditure of money is involved.

I appealed first to the British Museum of which the Director was then Sir George Hill, and I have not forgotten my joy when he said that the Trustees were prepared to have a go and to sponsor me, and I was no less grateful to Sir Edgar Bonham Carter, then the Chairman of the British School of Archaeology in Iraq, which also risked a stake amounting to £600, at that time a substantial sum of money. Another good friend to whom I am equally indebted for life was Sir Edward Keeling, the energetic and devoted Secretary of the School. Incredible as it may seem the whole enterprise including publication, cost a total of £2000 and was indeed well worth the money: the dig was published in the second volume of *Iraq* within six months of its completion, and that was something of a feat.

The staff consisted of no more than three persons, my wife, Agatha, who has since Nineveh joined me in every single expedition to the East, and John Rose, my friend who had served as architect at Ur. I remember inducing him to come with us by saying to him that this would be a glorious holiday – a phrase of which he was long to remind me, for I doubt whether we have ever worked harder in our lives, even at Ur. His eyes were hardly ever raised from the drawing board but this small expedition was a joyful one.

In those days the Director of Antiquities in Baghdad was a German, Julius Jordan. There was no difficulty in obtaining through him a permit to dig the site, although politically he proved to be no friend, for he was a paid Nazi agent, and did all he could to undermine British authority in Iraq. But personally he could not have been more charming; although violently anti-Semitic, he was an excellent musician, and sensitive; it seemed extraordinary that this artistic and cultured man could succumb to the new Hitlerian régime.

On arriving in Baghdad we stayed at the Maude Hotel, a primitive and simple establishment, but one in which good hospitality was given by that genial host Michael Zia, the Falstaffian manager to whom many visitors have been grateful for lavish hospitality. I remember that he had a barman who went by the name of Jesus, and it was strange to hear that invocation before being brought drinks.

We set out from Baghdad to Mosul in the early spring and it was just as well that we did, for there was much business to be transacted before ever we could set a spade into the ground. We stayed, to begin with, at a railway rest house in Mosul which was efficiently run by a Syrian Christian who answered to the name of Satan. It never ceased raining, and his prognostications were so gloomy that we thought we would never begin at all. However we put our time to good use, for we had to set about finding the owner of the land and get his consent to dig. This we did through enquiry both at Arpachiyah itself and with the help of an invaluable cavass at the Ottoman Bank, Majid Shaiya who had formerly been Campbell Thompson's servant, and did everything in his power to help us.

In order to get permission to rent the land we had however not only to trace the landowner but to find out to whom it was mortgaged, no easy task, for the mortgages, as is not unusual in the Orient, were numerous and seemed to increase daily. In the end we traced no less than fourteen of them and made superhuman efforts to round them up. Finally they were all distributed between two horsedrawn cabs and conveyed to the Bank in order to append their thumb marks on the contract; even then I believe that the numbers were incomplete but in despair we had to call it a day, and so in this way with many protestations we drew up a remarkable contract whereby the owner of the land was to pay the sum of £2000 if he in any way molested us; the whole affair was terminated happily for a comparatively small sum of money.

Another of our main preoccupations was to move from the rest house and find ourselves a suitable abode. Here we were fortunate in making contact with a landlord in Mosul who had a large empty house, not far from the old one in which we used to live with Campbell Thompson; it commanded a glorious view of the great mound of Quyunjik and the mountains on one side, and looked across the river Tigris to Mosul on the other. This big house was entirely suitable, for it contained large storerooms and good living-rooms, also a spacious flat roof, on which we were able to spread out our pottery in profusion.

The landlord was an old man named Daoud Saati – David the Watchmaker. He was well over ninety years old and described to me his remembrance of seeing an Englishman for the first time in his life – a little man dressed in a frock coat, staying in the Khan Rassam in Mosul, who used to walk across every day from Mosul to the mound of Nineveh which he was engaged in excavating, having no less than 800 workmen under his charge, an impossible number to control. I had no difficulty at all in identifying this little figure in a black frock coat with the great George Smith, who in 1873 had discovered the famous Flood Tablet in the course of his epic excavations, and it was fascinating to talk with an authentic witness who had known the little man in the flesh. This was not my only contact with a memory of that great man, for it chanced that some years later when I was in Aleppo, the British Consul came to see me and said that George Smith's grave which had been deposited in a Christian cemetery was about to be demolished and in danger of falling into oblivion; he asked if I would help to transfer it to more permanent ground. This I did, and it was satisfactory to have the tombstone set up again. Many years afterwards I had my reward when his grandson, Rowland Smith, who was a neighbour of ours in Devonshire, rang me up and asked if I had ever heard of his grandfather, to which I had the satisfaction of replying: 'Not only have I heard of him: I buried him.'

To return to Arpachiyah, we spent, of course, some time in arranging for the house to be furnished, and this we managed by engaging a gang of carpenters in Mosul, a headman and three others; every day they used to walk out from Mosul, the headman dressed in a high tarboosh, followed by his three assistants, who worked all day from dawn to dusk. New planks and the necessary woodwork were carried out by our lorry for an incredibly small sum. Within ten days we had furnished the whole house very comfortably from top to bottom with the additional purchase of a chest of drawers or two.

I remember that in the Antiquities Room we had a beautiful series of pigeon-holes carefully designed for the storage of stratified pottery as it came up, and it gave me great satisfaction to see the delight of the late Professor Frankfort who, on inspecting it, declared that it was the best method he had ever seen for storing stratified pottery on a dig. Very soon we were happily installed; moreover we enjoyed a big and lovely garden, filled with rose bushes which bloomed in profusion, although unfortunately every morning the owners used to come out and cut them for the Mosul market. Our last acquisition was a small gang of six mongrel dogs who were both guard dogs and good companions.

After all the preliminaries had been completed, some time in March, we set to work on the little mound, Tepe Reshwa, which lay in the midst of the cornfields about half a mile east of the village of Arpachiyah on the road to Bashiqah. We had no difficulty in recruiting labour, though we were not paying quite as high wages as the Americans; as far as I remember a shilling a day was as much as we could afford, but there was no lack of labour. The men flocked in from the surrounding villages and some of them tramped many miles. We recruited all the labour that we could in the adjacent village of Arpachiyah itself where we were on good terms with our landowner, Abdul Rahman. It was pleasant to be able at last to order the men to dig exactly where one wished without further consultation, and indeed there was little trouble at Arpachiyah in deciding what sector of the earth to go to, for the mound was not very large, the total area was not more than about two and a half acres although no doubt if further operations were undertaken outlying remains would be found.

Quite soon I experienced my first labour troubles because I had decided that one of the old instruments that Campbell Thompson had favoured, the *majrufah*, a gardening tool, a triangular hoe, should occasionally be discarded in favour of the spade in order to shovel away the earth, and this instrument I introduced to my labourers for the first time. Very soon there was a strike on behalf of the spademen who said that they could not work with such an impossible instrument. I dealt with this by saying that I did not wish to employ any except the fit and anyone who was not strong enough to handle a spade had better leave. Very few of them did so and I had no further trouble until the day came when I decided that a part of the work required the use of the old *majrufah*, and I then had trouble again because the men complained that they could not work with such an antiquated instrument!

In the first week or two the results at Arpachiyah were very disappointing and only mud-brick remains of the poorest character appeared. John Rose and I began to wonder whether we had not chosen a site that was a dud, an extremely primitive village with little left inside it. We, who had come from a site as rich as Ur were perhaps rather easily discouraged. We soon discovered that we were wrong. In a few weeks' time both the architectural discoveries and the small finds proved to be of a most exciting character. However, when we started at the top of the *Tell* we found rather a miserable mud-walled settlement with tiny rooms which contained potsherds of the Ubaid period. This discovery was of the greatest importance, for it established a well-defined connection with a developed stage of prehistoric culture in southern Babylonia, to be dated somewhere between 3500 and 4000 BC. Moreover as these Ubaid houses with their associated pottery overlay Halaf remains we definitely established once and for all the relation of this late version of Ubaid to that much earlier period when an entirely different pottery was produced.

Fortunately on the west side of the settlement we discovered a cemetery of the Ubaid period in which the inhumation graves were richly provided with pottery, and very fine specimens they were. John Rose preferred the spacing and economy of design and thought it more artistic than the minute and perhaps rather overladen designs of the Halaf pottery and he may in many cases have been right, but the fabric, and the baking of Ubaid was very much cruder and nothing could compare with the older Halaf in that respect. However some of the minuscule designs were beautifully produced and pleasing to the eye. Some of the larger bowls were economically decorated with big broad sweeping bands on the inside, great swathes round the bowl, a strange and rather attractive design which I have never seen elsewhere.

This is no place for a description of pottery which has been well illustrated in many handbooks including my original publication in *Iraq*, but one particular vessel I always found extremely interesting. It was a bowl, and round the outside of it there was a painting of what was obviously intended to represent three triangular sewn bands, the ends of which were fastened to a ring at the base of the bowl, almost certainly an imitation of a metal ring; it suggested as we now know from associated finds that metal was already in use.

It was interesting that of the 45 Ubaid graves not a single one overlapped another and therefore it was likely that all had been buried within living memory of the earliest. I suspect that originally there had been some kind of head-piece, a tombstone made of wood, which had long vanished, that had marked the spot.

There were not many small objects that we could definitely attribute to the Ubaid period, but a few beads and amulets were important because they were a hallmark of that time, especially some rather unusual incised beads and terracotta stamps which I thought might have been used for stamping cloth. I have already said that metal was beginning to be used and was represented by an open-cast flat copper axe of rare type which occurs also at Susa in Iran.

Below the top four levels of Ubaid houses we found a series of no less than eleven much earlier settlements, the bulk of which belong to the period known as Halaf. The fifth from the top, TT 5, may have been transitional, but below that ten more go back to at least as early as 5000 BC plus or minus. Here a remarkable architecture came to light, something in this part of the world then altogether unknown. It consisted of buildings on a circular ground plan, on stone foundations, namely *tholoi*, that is, domed buildings. There were ten of them in all, the earliest consisted of circular rooms, made of *pisé* or pressed clay, twelve feet in diameter, but as time went on they became progressively more elaborate and larger. The most imposing was the big north building in the seventh settlement, TT 7, where the round room measured 31 feet across, 10 metres high, and was approached by a long ante-room or *dromos* 60 feet in length. In seven of these buildings the stone foundations which consisted of large river boulders, pebbles, conglomerate and sandstone were intact. In no case had any of the later builders ventured to move or disturb the older foundations in spite of the fact that stone was not available on the site. The conclusion is that the foundations were deliberately preserved as an act of piety and that the buildings themselves were regarded as sacred.

The respect for foundations thus attested to the fifth or sixth millennium BC, reflects a practice which was still current in Sumer more than 2000 years later. We had little doubt that these powerful buildings must have served as shrines, for around the most important of them inhumation burials were laid directly up against the walls with extensive deposits of painted pottery and here obviously was the most desirable and sacred place for burial. No doubt they were heavily defended and could be used as fortresses in times of stress and the valuables contained within the settlement were probably jealously guarded within them. But internally all the evidence goes to show that the Halaf was a peaceful period, and weapons of war were rare or virtually non-existent, certainly very primitive in character. A few maces, arrows and sling bolts were the most bellicose objects of the time. There are various possibilities for the reconstruction of these buildings and our architect, John Rose, drew a number of them. It seems most probable that the ante-chamber was roofed, possibly even vaulted the importance of these rather elaborate buildings is that with one exception they were free standing, and not underground like the Mycenaean beehive tombs. They must be the prehistoric ancestors of the beehive villages of northern Syria which have survived in this primitive agricultural country until recent times.

If these handsome domed buildings were indeed shrines, to whom were they dedicated? To that question I think we know the answer, because in association with many of them we found numerous specimens in clay and just a few in stone of a figure that we called the 'Mother Goddess'. These were women, many of them with pendulous breasts, some were represented as if nude and others were quite elaborately dressed wearing belts and braces and the breasts exposed. Some of them were painted in the fashion of Tell Halaf pottery. Although we called these figurines 'Mother Goddesses' they may not have represented the Mother Goddess in person, but were perhaps dedicated to her by women in the expectation of the favour of the goddess during childbirth. Some were women of a certain age, others maidens, and a very interesting collection they were. It is also odd that many were very simple pieces of plastic mud, only just recognizable as women, but the breasts and the female markings were always clear; particularly prominent were the steatopygous buttocks, primitively associated with successful child-bearing. Several figures were represented as squatting, the natural position in primitive childbirth and although these figurines had been variously interpreted, the most reasonable explanation is that they were for the most part intended to hasten parturition by sympathetic magic and that they also served as charms to bring fruitfulness to barren women. The vulvar region was often, but not always emphasized and this together with the protuberant navel suggested the imminence of delivery.

Some of the more elaborately painted specimens represented women wearing a tightly fitting, perhaps diaphanous, scarlet dress; the breasts were sometimes emphasized by stippling. The head was never more than a peg or stump, and there was evidently a horror of representing it realistically, perhaps on account of some kind of taboo or fear for the person thus captured. Similar figurines have been discovered, also in close association with *tholoi*, at Yarim Tepe in the Sinjar, where a Russian expedition has found long sequences of Halaf burials and dwellings. It was interesting that at Yarim Tepe there was considerable evidence of burning in and around the *tholoi*; traces of burning were noted in only one of the outlying *tholoi* at Arpachiyah, but not in the middle of the site.

In contrast to the goddess at Arpachiyah the masculine element was personified by the bull, of which again there were numerous representations. We also found models of horned heads of bulls and two superb little amulets, of a bucranium in limestone and a bull's hoof; many other specimens displayed the skill of the Halaf people in miniature stone-carving of all kinds, including a number of beautifully made stone bowls. Painted representations of the bull's head or bucranium was common on the pottery and ranged from rather crude naturalistic or realistic representation to geometrically-stylized drawings and elaborate convolutions of the horns.

Obsidian was found at Arpachiyah in profusion and consisted predominantly of knives and scrapers worked on the spot, for large cores were found alongside the finished implements. The knives were sharp and capable of being used as razors. A unique discovery was a tall obsidian vase which must have been extremely tedious and laborious to grind. There were also many obsidian links, perhaps used as girdles, and a necklace containing big lozenge-shaped beads of the same material alternating with cut cowries, thus indicating distant trade relations with the north on the one hand, and the Indian Ocean on the other. All this volcanic glass comes from the shores of Lake Van in eastern Anatolia and involved return journeys over several hundred miles and indicated an extensive trade. We know that the obsidian was Vannic because there are three varieites of it including a tortoiseshell; all of them occur together both at Arpachiyah and at the source of origin, Shamiram Alti.

Numerous clay models of cattle, oxen, sheep, some birds as well as steatite ducks and a painted hedgehog display not only the interest of the inhabitants in the animal world but also their readiness to model their own livestock. Also remarkable are little steatite models in the shape of a double axe, symbolic of what we do not know, but they may have been associated with a cult of the dead. Cruciform designs also appear commonly as centrepieces on the pottery in elaborate forms.

I must also mention among the amulets miniatures which we thought might be representative of winnowing fans. Model sickles were not uncommon and there is one remarkable little pendant which, as it represents a house with gabled roof and bending ridge-pole at the top, gives us some idea of the appearance of domestic homes less elaborate than the domed shrines.

Flint knives and scrapers were common and one house contained models of finger bones in stone, curious objects, the like of which is known at the prehistoric Almerian site of Almizaraque in Spain. There was a single limestone mace head, perhaps a ceremonial piece, a basalt axe, and four pieces of pumice doubtless used for polishing and possibly for abrading obsidian. Plain stone axes or celts and chisels were commonly used and there were numerous bone instruments – skewers for eating meat.

This summary description of the small objects, a very rich collection, will have to suffice, before we consider however briefly, the very beautiful series of Halaf pottery and its significance. Many varieties of this Halaf ceramic ranged through a long series of occupations which spanned several centuries and overlaid specimens of Samarran ware and the early Ninevite in the bottom levels.

The classic Halaf ware which came out of the mound in a rich profusion was most attractive to the eye, very gay in its decoration and
some of it probably reflected the designs on every-day wearing ap-
parel. The designs were almost exclusively geometric in character,
even when the bull's head or bucranium was represented. The remarkable feature of the best of this pottery was its beautiful finish, the purity
of the clay, and the high glaze of the paint. Many of the dishes were a
polychrome and stippled ware; the most attractive colour was apricot.
The paint, which was often lustrous, ranged through black to brown
and red. In its most developed phase, between the eighth and sixth
settlements before the top, that is TT 6–8, some of the dishes were very
large and elaborately decorated with centrepieces of many-petalled
rosettes as well as cruciform designs.

On the finest specimens I concluded from ocular observation that
the clays were ferruginous and carefully refined. It has therefore been
no small satisfaction to me to discover that recently a young archaeologist named Thomas Davidson, trained in neutron activation analysis,
has with the aid of the microscope and the necessary apparatus, detected scientifically what was the result of my own ocular observations.
This archaeologist has through chemical analysis detected stages, at
least three main stages in the development of pottery which correspond
to the typological analysis set out by me in the first publication. It is
clear that the potters obtained their clays from some special source,
probably not very far from Arpachiyah and spent considerable effort
in the washing and refining of it; in addition the baking must have
been very carefully controlled.

Such early experiments in the control of pot-firing undoubtedly led
to developments in metallurgy which followed not long after the
Halaf period was over, though I suspect that already they were beginning to make primitive experiments in metallurgy. In this respect, one
of the most arresting types of pots was what we have called the Arpachiyah cream bowl. Some of these vessels were made with very thin
walls, little more than egg-shell ware in thickness, and all of them had
bevelled bases, which enclosed a deep channel round which milk could
be swilled, exactly similar to the metal milk cans used in the village of
Arpachiyah today, and this suggested to me that even at that early date
they might have been based on some metal prototype. The finest of the

Halaf wares have very rarely been found elsewhere; even at Yarim Tepe where a USSR expedition has dug through an accumulation between seven and eight metres of Tell Halaf, very little is of the exquisite variety made by the Arpachiyah potters who obviously catered for some privileged community as well as themselves – I suspect Nineveh itself.

The climax of our discoveries in the Tepe of the Halaf period was reached in the very centre of the mound in the sixth settlement from the top, TT 6, and I will quote the original account of it first published in *Iraq*, vol. II, p. 17. 'The workshop contained in all more than 150 objects, the stock-in-trade of the potter and stone worker. Polychrome pottery, stone vases, jewellery including an obsidian necklace, cult figurines and amulets, flint and obsidian tools were lying in confusion in a single room which also contained thousands of cores and chips characteristic of the debris in a stone-carver's shop. Many of these objects, in particular the pottery and the jewellery, lay close to the walls of the room, on carbonized wood, suggesting that they had originally rested on shelves or more probably furniture, perhaps tables.

'That the occupant was a potter and not merely a collector is proved by the discovery of a large lump of red ochre and of painters' stone palettes lying on the floor associated with the pottery.

'These remarkable finds had been preserved for us by the fortunes of war: this house had been sacked and burnt by an invader, presumably the al Ubaid inhabitants of the subsequent settlements. Fortunately the enemy had been content to destroy and had not bothered to remove the objects, which were found in a rich hoard lying under the roof which had fallen in the fire.'

It has been suggested to me by a Russian colleague from Yarim Tepe, Dr Munchaiev, that perhaps this discovery in TT 6 may have represented a deliberate breakage of the occupant's goods, but I do not think so because of the evidence of what followed afterwards. The subsequent settlement TT 5 was, I think, transitional in character and may only have represented a temporary reoccupation, for it seems to have been pre-Ubaid as was suggested by the large size of the rooms. I think that here was a deliberate destruction due to an enemy – the enemy most probably the Ubaid peoples who were seeking *lebensraum* and were later to extinguish the Halaf peoples in the north, or to make them subservient. It is true that elsewhere at Arpachiyah as also at Yarim Tepe we did find evidence of deliberate smashing of vases and beside them deposits of animal bones. This apparently was a regular practice in the Halaf period, but I do not think that TT 6 was an instance of it.

However that may be, the pottery found in the house at TT 6 was unsurpassed; there were some gorgeously decorated plates and bowls, one of them a lovely piece in black and red displayed a most striking centre which consisted of what has been described as a Maltese square. And another great plate was embellished with a magnificent centre-piece consisting of a 32-petalled rosette. This was done in trichrome, black, red and white; very fragile in character, it had sharply angled ridges and its form was more appropriate to metal than to pottery. This plate had been smashed into 76 pieces, every single one of which was recovered. That I think was not the deliberate work of the owner but the work of an enemy, as I have already explained.

Looking back, I think that one of the most impressive sights was the network of cobbled, stone roads which converged on the centre of the mound, radiating outwards from TT 6 and all the *tholoi*, an impressive witness not only to the original wetness of the place, for they were obviously intended for the pack animals to get a grip as they unloaded their cargoes at the most important building on the site, but also of central authority.

One has to reconstruct in the mind's eye a series of very high, domed buildings, impressive landmarks in the broad, open cornfields, not only at Arpachiyah itself but in the villages elsewhere, as far as the Jebel Sinjar, rather like the conical mud-brick villages that still strew the plains of northern Syria today. We can judge from the base of the biggest of them at Arpachiyah which was no less than 20 feet in diameter, that it may have risen at one time to a height of 25 or 30 feet and have dominated the plain. This great mud-plastered building was stone based, but the whole was covered with mud.

These elaborate domed buildings lead one to reflect on the eventual transmission of this architectural style to Crete and the Mediterranean, in far distant Mycenae, something like 3000 or more years later. What the connection was we do not know, and obviously the links

with Arpachiyah were so remote that we may never discern precisely
what they may have been. But there can be little doubt that from this
part of western Asia a style of architecture once common in the rural
districts was never altogether forgotten and who knows if it may not
have been basic to a reinvention perhaps in Greece and at Mycenae
itself. Thus the great domes of Arpachiyah which cast their long
shadows over the surrounding plain, also cast in a mysterious way,
those same shadows over a far later Mediterranean world, thus never
forgotten. And it is also remarkable that at Arpachiyah we found
evidence of the double axe and of the cult of the bull, exactly as at
Minoan Knossos where the same two elements of religious symbolism
play a prominent part in the Cretan Pantheon.

To return to the dig, I must recall yet another amusing episode. We
found that the men were salting their collections of antiquities with a
number of sun-dried clay figurines, mostly of animals and some of
human beings, rather skilfully carved, for many of these peasants were
able modellers, but it was clear that the technique was wrong, and after
a very little while we became suspicious because they were cut and
finished with a knife, a technique never used on any of our prehistoric Halaf or Ubaid figures. As I paid tips for these things, the men
thought I had been taken in, and became more and more extravagant
in the range of their models which caused us much amusement and
enjoyment. However, at the end of a week, having selected a number
to keep for the sake of interest, I lined up the remainder and arranged
an exhibitionist demonstration on the dig. Having made a speech and
told the perpetrators that these things were forgeries, I deliberately
smashed them with a pick in order to impress them. Unfortunately in
doing so I have to admit that I also smashed a small bitumen spoon,
which at the time was unique and the like of which had not been seen
before, but I now believe that this was genuine, for shortly afterwards
two or three appeared at the site of Gawra in an early context; thus are
mistakes occasionally made.

We celebrated the closing days of the season at Arpachiyah by
organizing a cross-country race, open to all who had taken part in the
work. This was a tremendous to-do. The rules were announced to all
would-be competitors on the dig, and it was decreed that the race
should be run from the Nergal gate at Nineveh on the Mosul side of

the river Khusr, thus involving a river crossing, over a length of about three and a half miles, the finishing point to be just below the *tholos* in Arpachiyah. We offered substantial rewards to the competitors, the first prize to consist of a cow and a calf, second prize a sheep and a lamb and the third prize a goat and a kid and the fourth, as far as I remember, was a substantial sack of dates. The fifth prize was a hundred eggs and after that in descending denominations, there were nine more prizes of eggs in all; moreover, every competitor who finished and did not fall out of the race was to be rewarded by a presentation of as much *helawa*, that is as much sweetmeat as could be covered by the span of two hands – a generous ration. Our cook was kept busy for many days organizing the purchase of these goods in the market at Mosul. He was an Indian; 'Too much work, Memsahib,' he said to Agatha, and I think did not particularly enjoy collecting the prizes, which on the day of the race were motored out to Arpachiyah in our lorry. A glad sight indeed to all the would-be competitors.

Unfortunately the river Tigris was in full spate at the time and the pontoon bridge to Mosul was cut, but we invited the No. 30 squadron of the RAF at Mosul to witness the spectacle from the skies. As this was held shortly after sunrise nobody bothered to attend. None the less on the site itself and on the day we had many referees posted over the length of the course, to see that nobody cheated; apart from a tripping or a ducking or two in the crossing of the river the race was cleanly run and we were kept amused by a large crowd from the countryside which turned up to witness it; heavy betting on the winners was organized on the site.

The punters were all wrong in their prognostications and the race was won by a very poor countryman with no possessions at all. The winner proved to be a born and stylish cross-country runner; and it was good fun to see the competitors come up one by one, breast the tape, right up to the last puffer, the hundredth man. It was rumoured that one man had died in the effort, but this cannot have been true for no claims for compensation arose; altogether this was a most enjoyable and satisfactory spectacle. Great was the feasting at night and I fancy that all the prizes were consumed with rapidity in a very short time. Many were asked to partake in the feast.

We returned to Baghdad, I think not far from the beginning of May, to take part in the division, which was something of a strain as the temperature at the time was rather high, I remember 106 degrees Fahrenheit, and I think we wore down the Director, Julius Jordan, in the execution of a task which lasted for over two or three days. Unfortunately, at that time nationalism was gaining ground and while we were operating under a clear-cut law there was a determination on the part of the Iraqis to allocate to themselves a more heavily weighted share of the finds although they were already accorded objects considered to be of national importance. We were operating under a generous and rewarding arrangement, but this was shortly to come to an end.

When we asked for our signed share of the division to be allocated to us there was a hitch and we suffered an unwarrantable delay of no less than five months until finally the permit was issued. The matter went to a vote of the Iraqi Cabinet and we were awarded justice, it was said, by not more than one vote, and we are still grateful to those who saw fair play for us. Thereafter the law was amended and I fancy that we were the last expedition to Iraq to be accorded this favourable treatment under the old law. None the less, as I have previously stated, the publication was completed in record time. I do not think anything has been more expeditious, but as far as we are concerned this was the end of our excavations in Iraq for many years and we deemed it thereafter judicious to move to Syria where, in the next chapter, I shall describe three or four years of very successful operations before the beginning of the 1939 war.

Since Arpachiyah I have led many other expeditions or have been closely connected with them in the Orient over a period of 50 years, but this, my first independent dig in which Agatha and John Rose alone took a main share, stands out as the happiest and most rewarding: it opened a new and enthralling chapter and will for ever stand as a milestone on the long road of prehistory.

CHAPTER 6

The Habur Survey

After Arpachiyah there were cogent reasons for moving to another part of Mesopotamia. Syria, which was then under French Mandate and offered generous terms to the excavator was an obvious attraction, for the officers responsible for administering the Service des Antiquités made all archaeologists welcome, and licences for digging were granted with a minimum of fuss.

The first step in the new venture was to decide where we were to concentrate our efforts, but this was not difficult for I was desirous of working in a part of Syria closely related to Iraq where I had already spent ten years; in this way I could widen a horizon with which I was already familiar. Western Syria and the Lebanon was already the scene of intense archaeological activity, but much less had been done on its eastern flanks. I therefore selected as the field of my survey the Habur Valley of N.E. Syria, much of which was *terra incognita*, for apart from some brief soundings at Tell Hamidi by Maurice Dunand, only Baron Max von Oppenheim had worked on a large scale at the big site of Tell Halaf near the headwaters of the Habur.

At the time my special interests were prehistoric and I knew that here I would be able to widen them, but I was no less desirous of discovering written, historical information in a part of Syria where texts inscribed in cuneiform could then be counted on the fingers of the hand. To me the prospect of filling in blank pages of history was a powerful incentive as it always has been throughout my professional life. In determining the scope of my new activities I was guided by the wise advice of my friend Sidney Smith who was Keeper of the Department of Egyptian and Assyrian Antiquities, as it was then named, in the British Museum. He himself had for a time acted as Director of the Iraq Antiquities Department in Baghdad and was anxious to promote excavations and was desirous of helping me, a young archaeologist who had served his apprenticeship. Sidney Smith was a good friend and a good enemy; all who had relations with him needed to tread warily. I was glad that I managed to avoid the pits into which many of my colleagues fell.

Agatha and I were thus bound for Syria, in order to conduct a survey, in November and December 1934 – propitious months because sherds on every mound were easily discerned in the comparative absence of vegetation, though towards the end of that time we were beginning to be driven out by rain. But before we reached our goal much planning and many things had to be done. Once again I had good reason to be grateful to the British School of Archaeology in Iraq which gave financial aid and its blessing on my proposals.

The preparation for our expedition inevitably involved a longish stay in Beirut where we stayed at a modest little hotel named Bassoul with a delightful terrace overlooking the waterfront. The food may be described as Oriental and the service primitive. I remember that the waiter in the dining-room regularly summoned us to a meal by knocking at the bedroom door and sticking his hand in his mouth, a sufficient sign that the food was prepared.

Whatever trials we had to endure in making our arrangements were thus lightened by the society of our friends in Beirut and most of all by Henri Seyrig. Director of the French Institute as well as being Director of Antiquities for Syria, he was unsparingly helpful in enabling us to overcome all difficulties in the course of the long and tedious preparations which are an indispensable preliminary to archaeological survey and excavation. After those first cordial relations he remained a lifelong friend. He and his wife entertained us liberally in their flat which was artistically furnished and contained a series of *mobiles* as well as a good library.

Seyrig had the gift of making friends and his high learning was widely respected; he became a great authority on Greek numismatics, especially in the identification and arrangement of the vast bulk of the coinage of Alexander the Great and of the other Hellenistic kingdoms into which it broke down. He had a profound and original understanding of Palmyrene religion and, in order to publish the *tesserae* of Palmyra, familiarized himself with Aramaic.

He was, in France, in his own field, the leading Orientalist, but this did not prevent him from taking endless pains over excavators, French,

Syrian and foreigners. No matter in how remote a spot one was digging he was sure to pay a visit and conducted the divisions that took place at the end of the season in the fairest manner possible.

His wife, Miette, was vivacious and high-spirited. As a student at the French School at Athens she had sailed the Mediterranean in a small craft which established cordial relations with the Flagship of the British Commander-in-Chief, Admiral Sir Roger Keyes, who ordered her and the two other girls that composed her crew to be piped aboard and be entertained while a naval party repainted and refitted her little ship. The incident I do not doubt long remained a favourite yarn of the Admiral as well as herself.

High praise is due to Seyrig for his organization of the Antiquities Service in Syria between the First and the Second World Wars. This he was able to achieve thanks to the authority of René Dussaud, the powerful Secrétaire Perpétuel of the Académie des Inscriptions et Belles Lettres, and persuaded the French Government to vote lavish funds towards the preservation and restoration of Syrian monuments and buildings.

Our first and most difficult task in Beirut, was to obtain a vehicle suitable for the rough ground over which we intended making our survey and as nothing immediate was available we had to obtain a four-cylinder Ford with a very sturdy engine for the sum, as far as I remember, of not more than £150. For a little more money in a local workshop, we had the chassis built very high, and rather top heavy, but the best that could be done in Beirut. It was painted lavender blue, and on account of its height and dignity, indeed majesty, we rather impertinently nicknamed it 'Queen Mary'. This remarkable small lorry which could be seen from afar served us well, and we managed to get it out of many an apparently inextricable *wadi* or watercourse; it was light and six to eight men could pull it out of almost anything. It had to carry some four tents, two for the European staff and a third to serve as a cook-house and for our servants, the fourth was a small lavatory tent.

On leaving Beirut we headed for Homs and then crossed straight to Palmyra, so beautifully described by Gertrude Bell as the white skeleton of a town, standing knee deep in the blown sand – a good start to our tour.

At Palmyra we stayed in a hotel which went by the grand name of Zenobia, the famous queen who was eventually made to bite the dust by the Emperor Aurelian. The sanitation was poor and the smell of drains in the bedrooms appalling. I remember complaining to the proprietor that the smell was evil and unhealthy, to which he replied, 'mauvaise odeur oui, malsain non.'

Thereafter we made a long trek to the banks of the Habur which were to be the scene of our peregrinations for the next weeks to come, and established our camp near Hasaka, at the junction of the upper and lower Habur and one of the *wadis*, *wadi* **Waj**. We were at first obliged to use this centre for administrative convenience, and found it an exceedingly unpleasant place. There seemed to be a perpetual wind and the town was covered in dust. Therefore after paying our respects once again to the French military and to the post office which we had to suffer for the sake of our communications, we went a few miles south and pitched our first camp at a place named Meyadin in the courtyard of a big khan where we set up camp for the first time.

The pillar of our expedition was a young architect named Robin Macartney, a man endowed with a cast-iron stomach and few words, assets that I have always regarded as indispensable on a survey.

In those days before operating I made it my practice to go to the Architectural Association in order to induce some young architect who had just completed his training to come out for a period of some months to the East at our expense for the joy of the trip and for a holiday of a kind which he would never again experience. This worked extremely well and it was at that time fairly easy to persuade young men to come out on these terms. Macartney's father had been Sir George Macartney, a famous character, who spent between thirty and thirty-five years in Kashgar and ended with the rank of Consul-General, our sole liaison in those days between the governments of India and China. Macartney had inherited something of his father's talents in his capacity for hard work, his ability to come to grips with detail, his perseverance and persistence. He was an extraordinarily silent man, silence and horses were to him more important than anything else in life, and my wife at first found it hard to get him to speak at all, but his apparent superiority and superciliousness were really due to shyness. As he was as shy as my wife it was not easy to break the barrier between them, but it happened in the long run, for familiarity in mud, water and difficult situations will eventually break down anything.

The event that led to a new relationship happened when we had returned to camp at Amouda after examining a wonderful mound named Mozan. A gale was blowing and we had the greatest difficulty in holding up our tents at night. We were all concentrated on one of them when the main tent pole snapped and Macartney fell flat on his face in the mud. This mishap which occurred when struggling against the height of the wind in the small hours of the morning proved too much for his natural reticence. He let fly a volley of oaths and from that time onwards became human.

Macartney was a competent draughtsman and his plans gave the professional architectural touch to our drawings. He was also a quick surveyor, but he never succeeded in learning the vernacular and communicated with his tape-boy and pole bearer by a series of whistles, a system which amused the Arabs and was surprisingly effective.

After establishing our first base camp at Meyadin a few miles to the south of Hasaka we were well placed for conducting the first part of our survey, that is for examining the mounds on either side of the lower Habur between Hasaka itself at the apex and Circesium, where the river joined the Euphrates: the latter, an interesting site riddled with mosquitoes, contained remains of Roman and other occupations which were beyond our objective, but contrary to expectations we found no early settlement at this southern latitude. None the less it is probable that one awaits identification for the Habur has without a doubt changed its serpentine course, frequently; but we did not have the time to prolong our search.

However on either bank of this stretch of the lower Habur we examined a number of formidable mounds riddled with Assyrian potsherds: especially Ajaja (Arban); Shaddadi, Shamsaniyah and Markada on the right bank, Fadhgami and Tell Sheikh Ahmad on the left, 40 miles south of Arban. These are massive accumulations which one day will repay excavation: the Assyrians who had as good an eye as the Romans for positioning their strategic centres clearly established themselves there on older bases for convenience of defence and administration along a river line, a natural frontier. The aim of the Assyrians in the ninth century BC was no doubt to reinforce trade links with the rich granaries which lay on the upper Habur and to provide a bulwark against the troublesome Aramaean tribesmen who infested the steppe on the western confines of Assyria proper.

Without a doubt the dominant site along this stretch of the river which pre-eminently demands further excavation is the one partially excavated by Layard in about 1850, namely Tell Ajaja – the dusty mound, known to Arab geographers as Arban, a flourishing medieval city. Much earlier however, it had been an Assyrian provincial capital of considerable importance under the name of Shadikanni. Here in a tunnel overlooking the river we caught sight of the inscribed, winged human-headed bull or *lamassu*, one of a pair; illustrated by Layard in *Nineveh and Babylon*, p. 276. The inscription, a single line, bore the name of an independent prince known to have held authority here in the early ninth century BC. Layard, who excavated for three weeks, also discovered a second pair of bulls which had once flanked the doorway of a palace nearer to the centre of the mound, and in addition he found a bas-relief illustrating a warrior and a stone lion of the same period. I commend the excavation of this magnificent site to some future digger who will surely make some wondrous additions to the legacy of Assyria as well as to earlier and later periods of history.

But in 1934, attracted as I was to the place, which would now be a most interesting pendant to Nimrud, there was too much to discourage me from making the attempt. First there was no evidence of anything prehistoric, or of the links I required to establish with the earliest periods of Mesopotamian civilization; next there was an enormous overburden or top layer of medieval and Arab remains which would have required many years of excavation, and lastly and the most formidable objection was the fact that there were large numbers of Moslem graves overlying the site. I leave that task for some stout-hearted hero.

Arban, the biggest settlement, was also the furthest north and the nearest to Hasaka beyond which we traced very little evidence of Assyrian occupation. As I have already stated the sites along the lower Habur were primarily military bulwarks, only secondarily agricultural, though designed to cement trade links with the north. The landscape was that of a dry steppe.

We therefore decided not to linger on the lower Habur once we had taken leave of its limits, for we wished to measure ourselves against a wider spectrum of history which we rightly suspected lay further north, and we took regretful leave of Arban, a mound pregnant with history and enriched by the memories of our predecessors who had an inspired appreciation of ground that covered significant remains of the past.

Our base near Hasaka had been well chosen; it was conveniently situated for the exploration of the upper Habur as well as its lower reaches which we now abandoned. In the course of this survey we were careful to report to the French military authorities who had been warned of our arrival by Seyrig and they were invariably helpful. In Hasaka we called on the officer in command, who received us in his windblown dusty office. He made a vivid impression on me, a wizened grey-haired little man, the Colonel Tracol, for he wore as he sat, a black skull-cap and looked like a learned professor; I suspected that he was a Normalien and a man of academic calibre.

With the encouragement of Colonel Tracol we travelled northwards up the right bank as far as the great mound of Tell Halaf and then back to Hasaka on the opposite side of the river. Each of these journeys could be achieved by a hard day's driving in our sturdy transport, but we lingered over various mounds examining potsherds for many days, and with the exception of Tell Halaf itself the results were disappointing, for prehistoric remains were not in evidence beyond about twenty miles south of it, and as far as we could judge the mound of Abu Hajar the 'stony one' represented approximately the limit of their dispersion.

Later we concluded that a line drawn eastwards across the map at approximately that latitude terminated at Tell Brak and it became apparent that the users of prehistoric painted pottery were reluctant to extend their settlements beyond the area of intense winter rainfall, or below the zones at which the *wadis* or little river valleys tended to run dry. The lower two-thirds of the upper Habur thus appeared to fall outside our immediate objective but I noted with interest that a number of mounds, Tell Ruman among them, concealed remains of the Romano-Byzantine period which probably overlay traces of Assyrian occupation and we may conclude that a more thorough examination would yield evidence of Assyrian stations on which, in the ninth century, they may have established themselves, albeit on a small scale, in the course of their raids up as far as Guzana, the name they used for the ancient site of Tell Halaf.

Of Halaf itself I will not speak in detail for its remains are well known through the publications of von Oppenheim and Hubert Schmidt. But this huge mound on the west bank of the river was a beacon of light urging us onwards to discover more about the contemporaneous settlements in the eastern reaches of the river valley and to ascertain whether some of the finer quality of their ceramic which we had discovered at Arpachiyah was also to be found in this part of Syria. The later periods of Tell Halaf are also of interest, for they are illuminated by elaborate buildings and the crude basalt carvings associated with a local prince named Kapara whose authority was brought to an end by the incursion of the powerful Assyrian monarch named Adad-nerari III shortly before 800 BC.

After our rapid survey of the upper and lower Habur we felt free to examine that wonderful triangle of territory bounded on the west by the upper Habur from Ras al Ain to Hasaka, on the east by a small river with the improbable name of the Jaghjagha, and on the north by the railway line which demarcates the frontier between Syria and Turkey. In this area, hundreds of ancient mounds, an archaeological paradise, clutter the plain: the majority contain remains of agricultural settlements which flourished in the fifth millennium BC and lived on the fat of the land. This triangular area is intersected by numerous *wadis*. The *wadi* Waj contains the mounds of Tell Saiqar and Tell Baindar; the *wadis* Khanzir and Dara contain Tell Mozan and Tell Chagar Bazar; the Jaghjagha contains the mounds of Tell Hamidi and Tell Brak.

Every one of these sites would yield, as some of them have already yielded, rich rewards to the digger. The reader who is archaeologically interested in this region must examine my account of it and of the ensuing excavations in the Journal *Iraq*, vols. III, IV and IX, which retrace our steps. Suffice it to say that we made brief soundings on the frontier at Tell Ailun and Tell Hamdun which a German expedition examined profitably later; there we were greatly attracted by Mozan, a site endowed with magnificent masonry walls, and then we were puzzled by the circular or oval shape of the great mound of Baindar.

It was however, the trial soundings at Chagar Bazar where rich evidence of the gay Halaf ware was overlaid by remains of the second millennium BC that appeared to be the most tempting, rewarding and practical prospect. This became our immediate objective before making the attempt on the grandest settlement of all, the mighty mound of Tell Brak, which together with Chagar Bazar will be the subject of the two subsequent chapters.

CHAPTER 7

Chagar Bazar

After our survey in the closing months of 1934 we used the intervening months for making all the necessary preparations to excavate Chagar Bazar. The site itself was conveniently situated for, in Kamechlie, 40 kilomtres to the north, we had at our disposal a useful shopping centre, a bank – succursale of the Banque de Syrie et du Grand Liban – and a post office.

During our first season, however, while building a house of our own on the site we rented a large mud-brick residence with spacious court-yard in Amouda near to the frontier. This town was inhabited mostly by Christians and our temporary home was at first far from comfort-able. We were infested with a plague of mice which ran all over us after dark, and the first three nights proved so unnerving that Agatha threatened to go home, but fortunately we were saved by the acquisi-tion of an intelligent cat who defeated the lot, and by introducing some sheep to the house and putting down cement floors we also got rid of most of the fleas, and at last settled down happily having acquired some furniture which was to be used when the main expedition house was put up at Chagar Bazar itself.

Amouda was not without its excitements, for on some nights raids occurred from across the Turkish border and there was a considerable amount of random firing through the streets. There were attempts to seize women and carry them off. Rarely were they successful, but some-times burglaries and some damage was done. But we were never in serious danger, for the French military was well in control of rather an unruly part of Syria and of the frontier at the time, and we knew that any raids were likely to be rapid and sporadic.

Our staff for this first season in addition to myself consisted of Agatha, of Robin Macartney and Richard Barnett and the number of men that we enrolled ran approximately to one hundred and forty.

They were a mixed gang of Arabs and Kurds, with a sprinkling of Yezidis, the mild devil-worshippers from the Jebel Sinjar and a few odd Christians. In addition some of our best men proved to be Turks who had smuggled themselves across the border and entered the country illegally, but as they were strong and eager for work we had little hesitation in employing them. They crossed the frontier in Arab head-dress and having reached us safely immediately put on their Turkish caps. We never regretted having taken them on. There was considerable illicit crossing of the frontier in both directions but nobody worried much, though occasionally some unlucky trespasser managed to get himself shot. As will be readily imagined it was not always easy to control so many variant nationalities, for a babel of tongues was to be heard on the dig, but in spite of this cosmopolitan crew there were surprisingly few interruptions to our progress.

Our policy for the first season was to try to obtain a broad con-spectus of what lay within the great mound itself and for this purpose I selected a plot of ground about twenty by twenty-five metres in area, not on the highest part of the mound, some seven and a half metres below the surface top, at a point where a certain amount of denudation had occurred, and where we would do the minimum of damage to the buildings of the latest period near the surface. By the end of the season we had dug a great chasm some fifteen metres deep, and in so doing descended down to virgin soil through a tremendous range of history and prehistory.

The topmost level contained architectural and other remains which, as we afterwards ascertained, belonged to the centuries between about 1900 and 1600 BC: fifteen metres or just under fifty feet below them on virgin soil, there were traces of the earliest occupation of the Habur, as we now know, running back to about 6000 BC. Down at the bottom of this huge pit, more or less corresponding with the earliest remains at the bottom of Nineveh in Assyria, the first settlement was not more than a camp site, as at the mound of Hassuna west of Assur where the earliest pre-Assyrian remains have been found.

At Chagar Bazar the earliest level with traces of mud-walling in it at a depth of fifteen metres below the surface contained the remains of what is known as Samarra ware, rather a striking painted pottery, named after a type site on the Tigris ninety miles north of Baghdad and here we found some very good specimens of that class. There were painted designs illustrating not only the typical step pattern of Samarra and its characteristic shapes, but also specimens of human figures painted in primitive form on the pottery itself. It was interesting to find that these painted fabrics of Samarra had preceded a long series of the brilliant and variegated Halaf culture, the attractive pottery which we have described in the previous chapter.

In this post-Samarran occupation stratum we found no less than six superimposed settlements of the Halaf covering a depth of just over four metres which comprised a considerable chunk of the Halaf period, a long one, as has subsequently been proved at the site of Yarim Tepe in the Jebel Sinjar. We found many specimens of the bucranium or bull's head design and a number of comparatively realistic or naturalistic drawings of it elaborately set amid stipples, and growing vegetation on its head, and this makes me wonder if the bull does not also go with the power to bring rain. The bull design was superceded in the end with the design of the sheep's head, or mouflon, in which the horns were turned down instead of up, and we also found the many different convolutions which mark the later stages of Halaf. In the ninth level from the top we found remains of an elliptical wall, not circular as in the *tholoi*, but certainly implying that elsewhere the occupants must have constructed the *tholoi* or domed buildings that are commonly found on Halaf sites and are more than six thousand years old.

Perhaps the most interesting discovery in the Halaf settlements was a series of figures, some of them in terracotta painted, some in sun-dried clay, and they were for the most part seated, very simply modelled and wearing turbans (see illustration on p. 124). The head was no more than a stump and never realistically represented. All of them were women, and they were seated. Two specimens were associated with little cylindrical discs and found in position thereon. There is little doubt that these seats were intended to represent birth stools: in the Sudan such stools are used to assist the female in the act of parturition. It was not easy to interpret all the markings as some appeared to indicate dress and others tattoo marks. That some of the markings were dress seems to be proved by the fact that a few of the figures wear braces and that one or two were veiled, as women very properly should be in the

East. We now have a most remarkable series of these figures which run back to at least as early as 6000 BC and have been found at Samarran sites, notably the settlement of Sawwan, which has been very well excavated by the Iraqis and has revealed the fullest sequence of the development of that early culture. These figures must have been tokens of a magical fertility cult in which the subject begged the god or the appropriate goddess to protect her in the dangerous process of bearing children. No doubt the infant mortality rate at the time was very high.

In the later Ubaid series so common in Iraq some of these women are represented as suckling infants. We have now a full series of such figures from many different sites in Iraq, Syria and some striking ones in Persia which have been fully illustrated by Edith Porada and are well worth a glance. The tattoo marks consisted as a rule of the dot-stipple and stripes familiar to primitive tribal societies.

It is possible that the Halaf period at Chagar Bazar lasted rather longer than elsewhere for there were no traces there of any of the next culture known as Ubaid, but eventually they were driven out. It would indeed be extremely interesting to know why this long period of Tell Halaf occupation came to an end and what was the cause. Elsewhere we have evidence, particularly at Ras Shamra on the Mediterranean coast, that their extinction was due to the onset of Ubaid peoples. Here perhaps they were driven out in the same way but not supplanted by them, for there is no evidence of Ubaid. Even more intriguing is the length of the gap between the end of Halaf and Ninevite V, the next period of occupation, and I think it is likely to have been not far short of a millennium, a very long period of time for desertion of this once prosperous site.

At all events there is in the top of the Halaf a barren stratum filled with the collapse of mud-wallings and over this waste ground eventually some newcomers were to lay a cemetery, for as is usual in the Orient, waste ground was selected for burial, and there we come to the famous Ninevite V people with their not unattractive painted pottery and elaborate metalwork. There are two successive settlements of Ninevite V and we found here the early style of their painted pottery followed by the usual incised and grey ware imitating silver. One remarkable find was a grey bowl with a rounded base, tied with fine silver wire by which it was obviously suspended, for the pot was never intended to stand independently on its own.

This next sequence, the cemetery, had been dug into house ruins of the earlier period. A number of graves were found in a layer of clean soil and sand and the sequence seems to have been at first painted pottery and then later, corresponding with level IV, the incised, imitating silverwork, a phenomenon that I have already mentioned.

Superseding IV and therefore probably after 2900 BC, during the period known in Mesopotamia as Early Dynastic II and III, comes a sequence of an entirely different pottery which is a grey ware, rather well made and as I believe sometimes imitating silver but more often leather, for many of the pots have rounded bases and were not meant to stand but were either for suspension or when not in use were turned upside down. It would appear that this ware has rather a long easterly extension into northern Iran and there are certain pot types at a site called Shah Tepe in the Elburz mountains which are similar.

The use of metal was steadily increasing but did not become pronounced until we reached level I, the last of the long series of occupations at the site. Here we found the remains of mud-brick houses and numerous graves as in level III, which incidentally had contained a number of child burials; certain houses seem to have been devoted to infants.

At the top of level I, we reach an entirely new and altogether different phenomenon in the long history of the pottery of the site, characterized by rather a well-made ware consisting of big jars, decorated exclusively with geometric designs, hatching, triangles and the like, and we were puzzled for long to know where this came from and its origins. Very soon I dubbed this pottery Habur ware, and it has been known and recognized under this title ever since. It now seems probable that it was invented in the Habur Valley itself, the widest centre of its dispersion and productivity. Nowhere else has it yet been found in such large quantities. Specimens of this pottery have been found quite far afield, at Mari, some at Atshana, and in a very late and rather degenerate form at Hama in the Orontes Valley; in northern Syria, at sites in the neighbourhood of Carchemish particularly at a place called Hammam. Some specimens of it also appear in Assyria, not far from Nineveh, at Billa.

We were long puzzled to think out where this pottery had come from and what its sudden appearance signified: we now know the answer. The contrast between the frequency of its appearance in the Habur Valley and the rarity outside it is striking. Even at Mari not very far south there are a few specimens, but they are rare. All this points to a sudden resurgence of native talent in the upper Habur Valley, at a time when metalwork was in full production. Many of the pots were intended probably for the drinking of beer which was amply drunk at Chagar Bazar. Little conical copper strainers were frequently found at the bottom of them.

We also have evidence that the Hurrian native horse-copers in the Habur were users of this ceramic, for there are numerous specimens of bridled horses' heads, some of them painted, in other cases the bridles are appliqué. We know from a cuneiform text at Mari that it was bad form for the king (Zimrilim) to be seen riding a horse in Akkad. This was a new barbarism which had been introduced by the Hurrians, whose presence is also attested at Chagar Bazar by the appearance of a Habur ware painted spoked wheel which made for much easier and lighter traction.

Coinciding with the appearance of the painted Habur pottery in about 1800 BC the increase of metal objects indicates some pressure from the north, where the metalsmiths were by this time highly experienced and near the true source of ores. The nearest known copper mines are situated at Ergani Maden some way up the Euphrates from Diyarbakir. It seems that there was a coincidence of native potters and Anatolian smiths.

At all events the long history of the Habur reveals evidence of the extraordinary pressures that were exerted on this naturally very fertile region from almost every direction, north, south, east and west, though dominant at all times was pressure from the direction of the Tigris. The presence of Habur ware however, indicates a period of great prosperity and we have evidence that more than one city was fortified with a town wall at this period.

All through our first season we worked at considerable inconvenience from our base at Amouda, 25 kilometres away, and sometimes had to make the journey in our top-heavy lorry 'Queen Mary' in such appalling conditions that at times we skidded through 180 degrees on the wet and slithery track, and it was by no means easy to get over the *wadis* or watercourses, which intersected the road between that place and Chagar Bazar. Others suffered similarly and I remember a bus being stuck in a *wadi* and unable to get across for ten days during which time all the passengers sat patiently on the banks of it, eating bread and onions and apparently not one bit perturbed. Such is Oriental resignation. However, that determined us all the more to build our residence and in due course towards the end of the season we set about erecting our mud-brick house.

We designed the new house with our architect Robin Macartney and a very attractive plan it was. A five-roomed house with the addition of kitchen and dark room, a big common-room, working-room in the middle, and two rooms at either end. We had intended to build a cloister on one side, and the central hall was domed. None of us had built a dome before and we had no good notions of how to set about it. We had thought of a heavy spherical cupola; by the time we had finished this turned out to be the shape of a sugar loaf: we went through agonies trying to get it done. In building the dome we fitted together a wooden centreing which was rather a heavy and clumsy contraption and as our workmen were no less clumsy they contrived to drop it: through the machinations of the Armenian carpenter it fell down on one of the Arab workmen and did him no good. An infernal row and fracas broke out in consequence between the Armenian and the Arab; the Armenian who was on the point of running away had to be forcibly restrained in order to complete the work.

In the course of these operations we had between 10,000 and 20,000 mud bricks lying out in the rain for many days. There was little chance for them to dry and it was doubtful whether the house would stand up at all. None the less the core of it was built in ten days and in fourteen, finished, a solid jellied mass which glued itself together and looked beautiful when it was done. An attractive sight on the landscape – we were very proud of it, but we were not a little annoyed when Sheikh Ahmad bespattered all four corners with the blood of a newly-slain sheep, propitious magic which spoiled the appearance of the freshly-plastered brickwork. We never got round to completing the cloister which remained an open passageway, but had an alluring aspect, with its buttressed arches leaning up against the main body of the house. I think the whole job cost us not more than £150 including all the woodwork fittings: the furniture we already possessed.

We look back on this house with affection, for we lived on a green sward; a kind of paradise, the plain was all the way between us and Kamechlie, where hollyhocks grew wild and in profusion. The vegetation that year was marvellous and we lived on lovely sheep's *lebn* and better sour milk I have never eaten, brought to us every day from the Sheikh's house.

The house itself, of course, was also an attractive prospect to the Sheikh as we had promised him that one day it would become his own. Indeed after three or four years when we left the Habur this desirable residence brought him prestige, though I doubt whether he ever lived in it. We had been careful to warn him however, that the longevity of the house depended entirely on replastering it and drainage and that it would be dangerous not to devote care and maintenance to it, otherwise the dome might fall in and kill him. I understand however that this shrewd old man turned the situation to good advantage and quickly sold the property and his small village to some other landowner before moving elsewhere. He thus reaped a rich reward from a house on which he had spent nothing and doubtless he told the new owner that we might yet return and enrich him also. I believe that the house, once a resplendent building of ecclesiastical appearance, miraculously survived for about twenty years before dying a natural death.

Our shrewd Kurdish Sheikh, like the Armenian settlers on the Habur, was a living reincarnation of an extremely ancient connection with the north, perhaps best illustrated by some of our metal finds. In the course of our first season we made a remarkable discovery in a grave of the fifth level belonging to the period of Ninevite V. It was a fragment of an iron dagger hilt, possibly as early as 2900 BC, and when submitted for analysis was discovered to contain over 50% of ferric oxide corresponding with 35.95% of metallic iron. The specimen contained no nickel, and therefore could possibly have been of meteoric origin.

This latter specimen was therefore a most important counterpart to the discovery made by the late Dr Frankfort at Tell Asmar in the Diyala Valley, a tributary of the Tigris, of a fragment of a dagger blade of terrestrial origin, made not later than 2700 BC. The discovery of iron at Chagar Bazar illustrates a long-standing Armenian connection. Iron is native to Armenia and the first iron-masters probably were probably born there. The name Demirdgian, the son of an iron worker, is common in Aleppo in the blacksmiths' shops today, or was at the time, and iron working I should think has been in the hands of Armenian smiths from time immemorial.

Belonging to the same period in contemporary graves of Ninevite V we found a beautiful little copper pin surmounted by a pair of doves, some good copper weapons and a silver bugle bead with splayed ends, rather similar to beads discovered in the Royal Cemetery of Ur.

Looking back on our first season at Chagar Bazar we should not forget a copper bead of exceptional purity without trace of nickel, tin, zinc or sulphur at a great depth in a level following directly after the Samarran period, and here we were clearly near the beginnings of metallurgy. This confirms the evidence from Arpachiyah where a fragment of lead was discovered in the early levels and justified the contention that some of the fine milk or cream bowls with sharply-angled bevelled bases were imitating metal. This discovery of primitive metal makes sense, for it is clear that the Halaf potters were beginning to experiment with their kilns, and were increasing their ability in fire control, as well as making experiments in pigmentation. They found that a light application of a red pigment on the bowl yielded that colour, when a heavier application more highly fired turned black. Moreover, even more remarkable, they found that a cream slip when more heavily fired turned an apricot colour, one of the most attractive features of this early pottery. At first therefore, the vessels were poly-tone rather than polychrome, but this eventually developed into a true polychromy. All this was due to these early experiments in pot baking which led eventually to the advances in metallurgy. These advances were perhaps retarded by the advent of their successors, the Ubaid peoples of southern Babylonia, who had to recover some of the ground that had already been trodden on by their predecessors.

The extraordinary competence of the Halaf potters who preceded the Ubaid has, more than forty years after the excavation of Chagar Bazar, been confirmed and established through scientific analyses of the ceramic by Hugh McKerrell and Thomas Davidson who have submitted numerous sherds of this fabric to the neutron activation process while the last named has conducted soundings on the *wadi* Dara where Chagar Bazar is situated, in order to test and analyse the clays of which this pottery was compounded. The conclusion is that the clays and silt carried in suspension by these *wadis* have not changed in 7000 years and the same elements including chromium, iron, cobalt and others may still be detected as in the sherds themselves. It has thus been conclusively proved that the fine clays here used for Halaf ware were derived from the local *wadi* beds of which the shrewd Chagar Bazar potters took advantage and traded their pottery over considerable distances. The clays of the *wadi* Dara were of a superior quality. This has also been confirmed by examination of other sites such as Tell Aqab situated on the same *wadi* where there was an accumulation of no less than ten metres of Halaf deposits. By these recent scientific experiments the Halaf potters have been established as the wise men of their craft.

These early finds of metal were no less remarkable than those in level I, the top level of all, wherein we made a most interesting discovery, in a grave which contained a small crucible which was of exceptional interest. The crucible consisted of an open box which held a cup in suspense at the top, and a fireplace in the bottom. In this same grave there were deposited some good specimens of big painted Habur ware wine jars together with a beautifully-cast copper pin, square in section and engraved with linear designs. This pin had a circular disc head, the upper part of the shank was pierced to contain a ring so that it could be attached perhaps to the cloak as a toggle. I believe that this was the grave of a wealthy coppersmith and I wondered if he had not come from somewhere in the Caucasus or in the Caspian region where similar pins had been found by de Morgan a century ago; in the next season we found not only more crucibles, it is true of rather a different character, but also big basalt moulds for the casting of weapons, and there was no doubt that even before 1800–1600 BC, this important activity was pursued at Chagar Bazar and earned the smiths considerable wealth.

We made many other small finds of interest in the course of our first season and anyone who wishes to see them can do so by consulting the third volume of our Journal *Iraq*. It would be inappropriate for me to discuss them further here but I must not omit to mention two more discoveries, one a beautiful seal impression illustrating a hare, stamped in about 2900 BC and belonging to the period known as Ninevite V.

It is interesting that only the hare occurs, never the rabbit, which appears to have been indigenous to Europe; why they chose to imprint a hare on this particular sealing I do not know. The second find was a purchase, an amulet, carved in the shape of an equine head, bought in the village of Amouda. It may have represented a horse, more probably an onager, a beautifully carved piece of brownish stone, a very early specimen of an equid, clearly of the Jamdat Nasr period. It was one of the most attractive things that came to light in the course of this season though not actually from the dig.

Finally there was the architecture. We found the time to dig out one spacious house with mud-brick walls and rather small rooms. It was approached by a big open courtyard and was in plan related to private houses familiar to Assyria rather than to Babylonia. The date of this one fell between 1800 and 1600 BC. It must have had two storeys; at any rate there were steps leading to the roof; the place was evidently as muddy then as it is today, for in one of the internal courts the floor was covered with small pebbles. It was interesting that two kilns were attached to the house and there were traces of corbel-vaulted mud-brick roofs. In the kitchen there was a variety of the usual domestic and kitchen utensils, querns, grinders and the like. All these and other discoveries made it quite clear that we were working at a site well worth digging on a larger scale and we therefore resolved to come back again at least for a second season in the following year before proceeding to something bigger and more important. Our intention was to discover more architecture, not to go deep down to the prehistoric but to dig the upper levels on as extended a scale as possible and in the hope of finding tablets. This required yet a third season to bring to light and what we found in the next year fully justified our resolve.

We thus had every reason to feel well satisfied with our discoveries during the first season and were to return with great expectations. not least of which was to be the joy of residing in our new mud-brick house with its handsome conical dome and unfinished cloister, which we hoped one day might be completed, but in the event never was.

We returned to Chagar Bazar for the second season in the spring of the year 1936 and a pretty wet season and a most enjoyable one it was. We then had the joy of residing in our lovely airy and light house, with its central common-room under the dome, which thank heavens did not show any signs of collapsing upon us. My two assistants in addition to Agatha that season were a retired Colonel from the Indian army, A. H. Burn, an amateur archaeologist with a sense of humour and very good with the men, for he was accustomed to handling the like. He was inclined to be a trifle military and expect them to keep orderly ranks and line up in columns of four for their pay, but this they seemed to enjoy and looked on with amused tolerance. He was a good friend to all of us. His company was also much appreciated by our young assistant Louis Osman who has since made a name for himself as an architect in this country. I remember that he was nicknamed 'Bumps', because on the journey to Kamechlie on the Simplon Orient Express he referred to all the hummocks, that is the ancient *Tells* which litter the plain, as bumps and was astonished to hear that they represented the inhabited places that we were out to dig as part of our mission, but Bumps he was to be called thereafter, and he was a cheerful companion also gifted with a sense of humour, that indispensable asset on any archaeological expedition.

These two good companions helped us bring our excavations at Chagar Bazar to a happy conclusion which was achieved in our third season together with the faithful Robin Macartney. At long last in 1936 not twenty feet away from our first trial trench dug two years previously we struck the goal of our search, it was at the extreme end of a mud-brick building, in a small chamber which contained 70 cuneiform tablets, mostly written within a single year, dated by the Assyrian *limu*, or magistrate, about a decade before 1800 BC when Shamshi-Adad I was king of Assyria and his younger son Iasmah-Adad was in charge of the district. These tablets gave us a chronological orientation beyond price and established the dating of our painted Habur pottery, for they rested on little potsherds of it which served as trays.

C. J. Gadd, who deciphered the lot in the British Museum with his customary skill, believed, and probably rightly, that they enabled us to identify Chagar Bazar as the modern name of an ancient township called Til-sha-annim meaning 'the mound whose answer is yes', appropriately named because it contained a *bit bari* or 'house of diviners':

its antique reputation had been preserved by our Kurdish Sheikh Ahmad who was still a magician of repute in the district. It is indeed possible that the building in which we found these records was the *bit bari* itself, but it is more likely that it was some other temple, of the Sun god (?) mentioned on the tablets, or even a palace.

We have left a simple and attractive task to some other digger – the recovery of the rest of the archive which undoubtedly remains to be found in the same building. It is interesting that the tablets mention fodder provided for the upkeep of stags kept in the shrine, as also of gazelles so frequently illustrated on the cylinder seals associated with trees as part of the temple scene.

The connection of Chagar Bazar with the royal house of Assyria, as attested by the tablets, is of extraordinary interest and justifies our choice of the site for excavation. These tablets also refer to another royal Assyrian city, Ekallati, to which supplies were often dispatched. There is more than one mention of Shubat-Enlil, the capital of the king of Assyria at the time, and some scholars prompted by my friend, the late Professor Goetze, have believed that Chagar Bazar must be identified with it. But in my opinion this is wrong, because one tablet records the dispatch of supplies to Shubat-Enlil – not received by it, and moreover our site seems insufficiently massive and important and not strategically placed for the Assyrian capital which probably lies somewhere in the district not far off. Its proximity is proved by the close connection with Chagar Bazar of the king's younger son. His name occurs several times on these tablets and establishes the fact that he kept here teams of horses, asses, oxen and a yoked chariot in charge of five grooms and a trainer, thereby preceding by several centuries the practice of the Indo-Aryan royal house of Mitanni which has left the record of a famous horse-trainer named Kikulli. Iasmah-Adad, the Assyrian king's son, made generous provision for his horses, and justified the reproaches of his father who in the Mari records accused him of being a spendthrift and wasting his substance on women. His father dubbed him as effeminate – without hair on his chin – and compared him unfavourably with his elder brother, a brainless soldier who soon lost the throne. Iasmah-Adad the younger, who acutely realized the danger to the kingdom of Assyria when his father died, is my favourite and reminds me vividly of Yahya the scallywag eldest son of our foreman,

Hamoudi, who preferred the stability of his less able, militarily inclined younger progeny.

The remainder of the tablets give us a picture of a community engaged in agricultural pursuits, the rearing of sheep and the growing of barley. Wheat is never once mentioned and the ground, perhaps over-irrigated and inclined to salinity, was not favourable to its cultivation. Barley, still the staple crop in our time, was used according to the ancient records not only for provender and for bread but as the main constituent in the brewing of beer: good ale and the equivalent of 'small beer' are mentioned.

The townships referred to in these records included a city named Kahat, which may now be identified with the big mound of Tell Beri, thanks to an inscribed brick found there – a few miles N.E. of Chagar Bazar near Nisibin, to which a special kind of *magaru* bread was sent. Most interesting were generous gifts expressed in measures of bread and beer dispatched to the city temple on the day of purification by over 2770 inhabitants of Qir Dahat, a city which I suspect lay to the north and is a token of the high esteem in which Chagar Bazar was once held as a holy city. Incidentally the standard measures were recorded in *Homers* and *Sutu* familiar to Assyria, proof of the dominance of its culture.

The core of the city as we learn from the texts were farmers of every kind, shepherds, gardeners, cattle men, fullers and weavers, priests and scribes, boys and girls including some who were blind. It is surprising that there is only one mention of metal as payment, and none of smiths, but this lacuna will doubtless be made good when the remainder of this once large record is discovered.

There is ample evidence that trade was widespread – on the west it embraced the district of Yamkhad around Aleppo, and to the S.E. there is mention of a town in Elam. Other places to which there are references include townships on the Tigris and the Euphrates and the Diyala Valley – Kish, Akshak and other cities, as well as the district of Hana in Palmyra.

Thus we conclude that on this site there once lived a vigorous and prosperous community half of whom spoke a Semitic tongue, either (Mesopotamian) Akkadian, or (W. Syrian) Amorite. About a quarter were non-Semitic Hurrians, native horse-copers and soldiers who as we have seen were later incorporated as the nucleus of the Indo-Aryan dynasty of Mitanni. There was yet another important element whose names ended in 'AN'; we do not know who they were, but I have sometimes wondered if the massive and obviously rich mound of Mozan, a few miles N.E. of Chagar Bazar is not an echo of it.

After the discovery of the tablets we felt free to move and concentrate our labour on the great mound of Tell Brak, much the most important centre in the Habur and one that cried out for excavation. At Chagar Bazar we had found our bearings and begun to understand the main sequences within the district. We were now equipped to undertake the more complicated and formidable task which confronted us at Brak.

Although eager to embark on our new and exciting venture, we left Chagar Bazar with regret. I have a happy recollection of a visit by Ernest Altounyan together with his wife Dora; they spent a few days with us and tended the sick, especially our sick foreman Abd es Salaam, who, like many others from the district of Carchemish, was tubercular. Dora's contribution was an oil painting of Agatha, seated in our dining-room, mending the pottery and looking a picture of happiness. I still possess this lovely souvenir of the year 1936.

Seated mother figure.

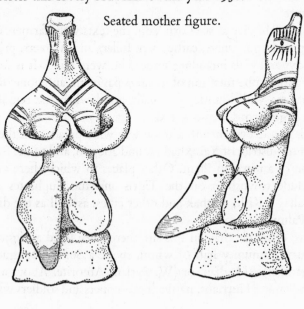

0   5 cms

CHAPTER 8

Excavations at Tell Brak

We first saw the great mound of Brak in November 1934. It was the dominant personality at the lower end of the Habur triangle just as Tell Halaf was the dominant one at its top end. From the first moment of vision I made a resolution that one day I would dig it. It took a long time to get down to business, for as I have explained we had first of all to get our bearings by excavating the lesser but important mound of Chagar Bazar.

We contrived to make a start at Brak in the course of the spring season of 1937 and our first efforts confirmed my determination. We therefore returned to conduct two full-scale campaigns in the spring and autumn of 1938 while we were making our final efforts at Chagar Bazar and the moment that we discovered the collection of tablets that I have described in the previous chapter we felt free to leave Chagar and concentrate exclusively on Brak.

This mighty mound cannot fail to impress, for it looms over the plain and dominates it. Standing 300 miles east of the Mediterranean and 130 miles west of the Tigris as the crow flies, it is from the Tigris that it seeks inspiration. The two nearest towns are Nisibin, just over twenty-five miles to the north, and Hasaka, about the same distance to the south where the river Jaghjagha joins the lower Habur. Brak is within easy reach of water as it lies only four kilometres from the west bank of the river and its confluence, the *wadi* Radd, on which Chagar Bazar itself stands. The mound, the largest in the district, is roughly oval in plan and has maximum dimensions of about eight hundred by six hundred metres. The total area is something under fifty hectares or about a hundred and twenty acres in all.

The highest point stands 40 metres above the level of the plain, that is to say it is more than ten metres higher than the great mound of Quyunjik or Nineveh. The cubic capacity of the site alone made it a certainty that it must conceal within it remains of the highest importance of almost every period from the prehistoric down to at least the middle of the second millennium BC. Many years before our visit, Father Poidebard had identified the site of what he believed to be a Roman camp lying at some distance in the plain and David Oates subsequently ascribed this to the Byzantine period, roughly to the fifth century AD.

Topographically the site divides itself into two halves, each of which is separated from the other by a low-lying and spacious Maidan or campus, through which all traffic had to make the approach after the time of its fullest development. The highest and steepest part of the mound is the north-western flank which is separated from the south-eastern by the comparatively low-lying ground or broad ravine. The difference in height between the two flanks can easily be accounted for.

The north-western flank was mainly a residential quarter reserved for houses whereas the south-eastern was chiefly occupied by temples and public buildings which accumulated less quickly because they were more solidly built and kept in better repair. Moreover the south-east flank appears to have been abandoned shortly after 2000 BC whereas the opposite side was continually occupied for at least another six centuries. Thus after 2000 BC the inhabitants had to undertake a steep climb before entering their houses and there must have been very great difficulty in getting their water up so far above the plain. Even with the use of wells this would have been highly inconvenient, for some cartage was inevitable. But this inconvenience was perhaps compensated for by the greater security which the residents enjoyed against the incursion of casual raiders from the north.

I have already explained that on the Habur we ourselves experienced small-scale raids from the Anatolian hills and in most of the villages nightwatchmen were employed to give warning against such contingencies. From the top of Tell Brak one looked out into the far distance at the purple hills of the Jebel Sinjar, a part of which lies in Syria and a part in Iraq, and this situation too made it obvious that Brak lay on an international thoroughfare. Much nearer lay what the Romans called the *Lacus Beberaci*, which one can but think must refer to the lake of Brak and some day when the name of the ancient site is discovered perhaps the name Brak will be found to be at the root of it. The rather saline waters of this lake lay less than a dozen miles away and were a very suitable place for a picnic on our days off. Another great landmark which was clearly visible was an extinct volcano, the Jebel Kaukab, which, however, must have long been extinct by the time that the earliest inhabitants thought of occupying the land.

On reaching Brak, Agatha and I at first took lodgement in a high tower at the entrance of the khan. The tower was at first infested with bats and we used to have to spend quite a large part of the night beating them down, first ourselves, then Colonel A. H. Burn and Louis Osman, who took duty on alternate days with us and thus took it in turn to suffer the rough twenty-mile journey between Chagar Bazar and Tell Brak.

As far as our own lodging went we were extraordinarily fortunate to have at our disposal a great empty khan or caravansarai at Tell Brak, for it was ideally suited to a visiting expedition with its ten rooms, servants' quarters and kitchen and thus provided us with all the accommodation we needed in addition to a huge courtyard into which our lorry could empty itself and where we could even disperse our potsherds and had ample space for that purpose. I don't think I have ever been more generously accommodated anywhere. In due course we erected a huge wooden doorway with two leaves and a wicket gate, and put the fortress into a proper state of defence and security, heavily bolted and barred as in the ancient palaces. When we finally left the dig we stacked all our furniture into two rooms at one end of the khan and I sometimes wondered what happened to it, for the war intervened and we never again recovered it. I expect that it is somewhere waiting still in the village, perhaps might yet be of service to any expedition fortunate enough to return to this magnificent site, but this valuable accommodation is, I understand now put to good use as a police station.

In the early days of digging Brak and Chagar Bazar, one of our major problems was to obtain sufficient silver coins to pay the men at the end of the week, for paper money was not then in circulation. I therefore used to make the 40-kilometre journey into Kamechlie, and as silver was often unobtainable at the Bank, go down the bazaar with a cheque, collecting the required sum of money, usually a few hundred pounds, from the highest bidder. This operation was rather an amusing one: I walked down the street, holding the cheque high in the air, and shouting the amount of silver I required. I closed after a short time with the highest bidder. This was a truly appalling business for the coinage consisted of the mejidie, a big silver coin the size of a cartwheel, and really worth more than its face value, about 1/10d, and the little coins consisted of what they called the big and the little *bargoudh*, that is the big and the little fleas, and these all had to be counted out and poured into two great suitcases which I then carted home on the lorry without any guard at all, but never did I suffer any attack though we were fired at on one occasion. To begin with I used to cart the money home to our lodgings in Amouda and spend a good part of the night counting out the coins from the suitcase on my wife's bed. I remember her indignation when I left her once for twenty minutes; I forgot all about it. 'I might have been murdered,' she said when I came back, but fortunately there she was, still alive.

The discoveries that we made at Tell Brak in the course of two and a half seasons' work were of extraordinary interest, archaeologically, historically and artistically, and fully justified the effort that we expended on it. Not only was there treasure trove in abundance, gold and silver, to whet the appetites of the amateur, but two grand buildings dating from before 3000 and about 2300 BC respectively. There were also architectural monuments which now take their place in the record as memorable landmarks, and historically there was the satisfaction of finding a few documents, though unfortunately the name of the place has not yet emerged, but we may now hope that this will take place soon for Professor David Oates is about to resume the excavations (1976). If we are to single out the monuments, I should select as pre-eminent a limestone head of the Jamdat Nasr period, dating perhaps to a little before 3000 BC, that has been declared to be a classic piece by one of the leading German authorities, Dr Moortgat, who has expatiated on it at length and praised it for its extraordinary aesthetic values. Some of the small amulets of approximately the same period, were of astounding beauty and remarkable finish and they too take a classic place in the history of small carving comparable to Chinese jades although made mostly of soapstone and other soft stones. Outstanding too was another wonderful find, an altar-front decorated with gold, silver, shale and limestone, a classic form of decoration for a temple façade, here uniquely found *in situ*; two of the panels we completely restored to their pristine condition.

Two buildings of outstanding importance have to be added to the architectural record. The first is a temple which I have called the Eye Temple, which I shall describe in detail later in this chapter. The second major discovery was a great Akkadian palace which we named the Palace of Naram-Sin, who was the third in succession to the founder monarch of Agade, Sargon. This great palace was unearthed over the southern flanks of the eastern wing of Tell Brak and was an astonishing discovery, for it was possible to recover the outline of the entire ground plan in the course of little more than a fortnight, simply by tracing the tops of the bare foundations, although in some places the chambers still retained their brickwork to a considerable height. The mound had been so much eroded that only one chamber retained a floor within it.

The plan consisted of four courtyards, the biggest of which had dimensions of more than forty metres square and around them was built a series of magazines which were intended for the storage of cereals. There was only a single entrance, almost certainly flanked by a pair of towers; this building confirmed the historical truth of a long-standing tradition that these kings of Agade had indeed established their sway in Asia Minor over vast distances and it was self-evident that this fortification had been erected as a heavily-defended blockhouse to cement the long lines of communication between the capital of Agade which lay near Babylon and the outlying empire which extended as far as Cappadocia in the centre of Asia Minor.

Subsequent discoveries, however, by an Italian expedition at the important site of Ebla near Aleppo have proved that Naram-Sin's immediate intention was to make himself the paramount overlord of central Syria, for in the course of his military campaigns it seems that he destroyed that city state which was then dominant on the upper and middle Euphrates.

The architecture of Naram-Sin's palace or 'Great House' as he styled it on his bricks, was purely functional and admirably designed for the purpose intended. This huge edifice covered a superficies of over one hectare or about two and a half acres of ground and is the largest building of that period, *c.* 2300 BC, ever to have been recovered. The intention was to use it as a gigantic storehouse for the grain which was collected as tribute and taxes in the region and it would have served as a supply base for the armies of the Agade dynasty on their northern campaigns.

It was evident from the enormous thickness of the walls that Naram-Sin realized that his fortress was situated in hostile territory and that so rich a granary must be made theoretically impregnable. The outer walls therefore were built to a thickness of ten metres or 32 feet and even the inner partition walls were proportionally solid. Since the greatest depth of wall foundations was about five metres we may, bearing in mind an ancient formula of the relation of depth to height, reckon that the total height of the building could have been fifteen metres or just under fifty feet, a calculation not likely to be much exaggerated when we compare it with late Assyrian palaces.

There was only a single entrance to the fortress which was defended by a heavily-buttressed pair of towers originally two storeys high and so designed to enable a watch to be kept over the distant plain from the battlements where the king's archers could take up a position of vantage against attack. The single entrance was flanked on either side by quarters which were the only residential ones within the building; each consisted of a courtyard with flanking chambers and it is not unlikely that they supported an upper floor. A part of the plan has been reconstructed, and thanks to the presence of a high ridge which circumscribed its periphery we were able to determine the extreme limits of the building.

The discovery of a bitumen model of a human foot, obviously once overlaid with sheet copper, to be dated *c.* 2300 BC, attests the high skill of the Agade dynasts as bronze and copper workers. In a previous chapter we have admired the magnificent bronze head of Sargon discovered at Nineveh, and as recently as 1975 a report has come of part of a once magnificent life-size, or nearly life-size, copper statue inscribed with the name of the monarch Naram-Sin and discovered in the district of Zakho, in northern Iraq, beyond Mosul.

There is no need to discuss the Brak palace in any detail for this has already been done in the primary account of its discovery, *Iraq*, IX, 1947. A great courtyard served as the main distributing centre and was capable of receiving massive cargoes and numerous pack animals as well as their drivers. We may imagine an army of clerks at the receipt of custom under the close supervision of the Residency in the two wings of the entrance.

No evidence of internal finishings remained but the walls must have been plastered with *jus* (cement) and mud. In some of the magazines traces of roof timbers survived and these were examined by the Forest Products Research Laboratory at Princes Risborough. There it was possible to identify ash, elm, oak of the red oak group, plane and poplar; pine of the hard pine group was found in the later houses not far away. How many of the trees named grew in this district is doubtful – probably only the oak and the plane which still exist there today; the remainder would have been imported from North Syria and Anatolia. We know that in antiquity much timber was shipped down the Euphrates for export to Mesopotamia. Osteological remains of the lion, *Panthera leo* were found in the palace together with *Canis* sp.; *Sus* sp.; *Capra* sp. (small and large); *Bos* sp. (medium to large); *Bos* sp. (small); *Equus* sp. (small); and there were remains of a typical Mamber goat with twisted horns.

All the magazines must have been covered by flat roofs to protect the grain, and numerous traces of barley and some of wheat were observed. As expected a few grain receipts were found in the principal courtyard which surprisingly yielded some fragments of beautifully engraved bone inlay illustrating a bearded and hairy hero of the 'Gilgamesh' series, a five-pointed star and a lion's head. These must have been parts of a box belonging to a high officer of the guard. A finely engraved serpentine cylinder seal depicts lions and horned beasts rampant in the heraldic style of the period.

We were disappointed at not finding any trace of metalwork in the palace itself, for we know that metallurgy was extensively practised at Brak where not only did we find an abundance of copper tools and weapons but also a big basalt mould for casting ten different types of implements and elsewhere on the site there was much treasure trove, namely gold and silver jewellery. Brak served as a blockhouse for the Agade dynasty on its northern campaigns against Asia Minor and a major objective of these campaigns must have been to secure the valuable metal ores which were situated there, as well as grain from western Syria. It may be that elsewhere at Brak some other buildings designed as a metal store remain to be found, but it is not unlikely that any surplus found its way directly into the capital of Agade, and that what was retained at Brak was rapidly distributed among the resident smiths and quickly utilized.

This great fort remains as a permanent testimony to the effort Naram-Sin's government made to consolidate his conquests in the north. The success of this enterprise, however, was not destined to last for long. In the courtyard and the chambers we found extensive traces of black ash: the place was destroyed by enemy incendiaries and the walls were razed to ground level. When that had been achieved another foreign dynasty filled the vacuum left by the defeat, that of Ur Nammu, first monarch of the powerful Third Dynasty of Ur, whose name was found both on a tablet and on a sealing. The place was apparently rebuilt and the floor level raised by at least three metres. But the new work was poor in comparison with the old, for Naram-Sin's bricks had been well compacted with ample straw temper and well laid in headers and stretchers. The replacement was second-rate in comparison and the walls were narrowed by nearly a metre and set back over the old foundations. Probably the new control lasted for not more than a century and a quarter, and it is likely that the final destruction came from Amorite pressure, for it was against the Amorites that Ibbi Sin, the last of these monarchs, built a mighty wall in a vain endeavour to save his dynasty which succumbed to double pressure, the Amorites on the west and the Elamites of southern Iran who finally carried him away captive.

More puzzling is the question who destroyed the palace of Naram-Sin, but there must have been pressures both from the east and the west. We know that after his death his successor Shargali-sharri had to conduct a campaign against the 'Amorite in Basar', that is against the Syrians in the district of Mount Bishri which lay between the Habur and the Balikh rivers in the heart of Amurru where the Agade dynasty had secured a foothold as we discovered when excavating a circular walled town at Jidle in the Balikh Valley. Another not less likely candidate is the dynasty of the Gutians, the powerful kingdom in the Zagros mountains which was primarily responsible for the disintegration of the Sargonid empire.

The difficulty of deciding whether it was the east or the west that destroyed the palace illustrates the danger of the thrust to which any régime on the Habur was exposed. The identity of the enemy who destroyed the city may only become known when we are able to establish the ancient name of Tell Brak and by good fortune discover a historical reference to it in some contemporary record. We may yet be rewarded by such an accretion to knowledge, provided that the thrust of archaeological research continues.

It is interesting that at Ashur, the religious capital of Assyria, there is a building which must be genetically related. This was excavated by that great German archaeologist, Walter Andrae, who recovered the plan of what he described as the 'oldest palace at Ashur'. When the plans of the two buildings are laid side by side at first sight they appear to be very different, but the difference is illusory. What remains of the Ashur palace consists only of its deepest foundations and these are riddled with multiple criss-cross walls, which served only to distribute the weight of the superstructure. Above foundation level the two buildings would appear to be not at all dissimilar by comparison, and to a large extent in plan. Moreover as near as makes no difference the overall dimensions of these two huge buildings are the same: Ashur palace about 112 × 96 metres, Brak palace about 111 × 93 metres. They could have been erected by the same architect. Further, the brick measurements at Ashur conformed with a brick size used in a private house of the Agade period at Brak. Finally it needs stressing that the Ashur building was excavated by tunnelling and that in one of the tunnels an inscribed cuneiform tablet with rounded ends typical of the Agade period was discovered.

Walter Andrae attributed this building to the period of Samsi-Adad I, the end of whose reign, shortly before 1800 BC, overlapped with Hamurabi's, partly on account of the depth at which it was found, partly because of its alleged resemblance to early Babylonian buildings, and because of the appearance of the size of its bricks, 34 square by 10 cms. None of these reasons provide proof for ascribing it to that Assyrian monarch (Samsi-Adad I) – would that I could call up the shade of Dr Andrae and discuss it with him, for what is as I believe a readily understandable error has been perpetuated in the textbooks. In my opinion the old palace at Ashur was probably built in the Agade period and confirmation of this comes, as I have said above, from the discovery of an Agade period tablet found in the precincts.

The evidence from the palace was supplemented by the discovery of mud-brick houses in other parts of the mound. These provided ample testimony to the wealth of its inhabitants, both in the Agade period and during the century or more which followed the destruction of the palace and its rehabilitation under the Third Dynasty of Ur.

In one of the Brak houses which contained a treasure-hoard of gold and silver rings there was also an inscribed clay tablet which included a list of small cattle, sheep, goats and a pot of wine noted as coming from various places. The owner was a man of property; in his hoard of jewellery a miniature silver bead-amulet with four coiled spiral ends can be closely matched at Troy II which many scholars believe is contemporary with the Agade period. Much of the metal was probably cast on the spot since, as we have seen, metal-moulds have been discovered both at Brak and at Chagar Bazar and there was also an active industry in bead-making for which many articles of equipment were devised. A few well-written clay tablets were found, typical of the period with rounded ends, neatly inscribed; all of them referred to agricultural products.

After the Agade period under the Third Dynasty of Ur c. 2100 BC, the private houses continued to be occupied and reflected Sumerian influence. An altar or offering table with a decorated empanelled front and a scalloped top was very similar to mud-brick pedestals discovered in contemporary chapels at Ur, 800 miles down the Euphrates. Vases decorated with snakes and scorpions, probably used in connection with some chthonic ritual were Babylonian in character, as was the contemporary pottery of the vaulted graves, but these belong to the period that succeeded the Third Dynasty of Ur, about 1900 BC when the new peoples who introduced the painted Habur ware were in the ascendant.

The houses on the highest portion of Brak, that is on the high eminence which crowned its north-west flanks, were of a much later date and ranged between about 2000 and 1450 BC. Architecturally they were not informative but a thorough excavation is bound to yield more interesting results. Here the excavations produced some beautiful fragments of the white-painted ware which as I believe were prized by aristocrats of the Indo-Aryan dynasty of Mitanni whose horse-breeding nobles known as *Mariannu* may well have exercised their sway here.

The delicate pot types carrying these attractive designs were at the time of excavation skilfully restored by my step-daughter, Rosalind Christie, who was persuaded to undertake a task which she began reluctantly and ended by enjoying. These attractive designs are done in a white paint on a black and red ground and often consist of spirals and twists which may be a reflection of metalwork, as well as dotted circles, spirals and triangles, and birds on the wing. It is not unlikely that the royal residences of the period were decorated with similar, gay-painted murals.

One more find on the top of the houses deserves illustration. It is a painted cup of the same period, about 1450 BC (see illustration on p. 147). This illustrates a mock-king wearing a crown, his eyes and beard vividly painted and the vessel was no doubt used for quaffing merry libations of wine or beer, perhaps by that celebrated figure of antiquity – the substitute king, who was allowed to pose as the monarch for a short period of time, but he afterwards sometimes suffered the death penalty at the end of his assumed reign.

It is now time to return to the Eye Temple which was superimposed above a series of buildings of a much earlier period, erected between about 3900 and 3500 BC. These were embedded in a huge mud-brick platform consisting of no less than six metres of solid brickwork.

One of these buildings, the second from the top, we were able to excavate completely. We called all these buildings the Eye Temples because associated with one of them we found hundreds of little eye-images of black and white alabaster which I shall describe below. These little idols left their imprint on all these buildings and indeed in the principal temple there was evidence that the walls had been overlaid with copper panelling decorated with designs of eyes in repoussé. We are therefore confident in the use of our title, the Eye Temple.

It was both interesting and disappointing that we found the remains of a double-compartmented alabaster box, smashed and discarded, which must certainly have contained the original foundation tablets of the king who ordered its erection. What would we not have given to know the name of the responsible monarch and, how illuminating it would have been, had it been possible as at Mari, to associate his name with the Sumerian King list. Perhaps further excavations will provide an answer.

The sequence of Eye Temples, counting them from the top, consisted first of the plano-convex Eye Temple in the topmost stratum, below that came the second or principal Eye Temple which we could assign to the late Jamdat Nasr period, that is, to the end of the Uruk period, let us say round about 3300 BC, though it may possibly have lasted a little longer. Below that, third in sequence from the top, at a considerable depth we found traces of a white plaster foundation and flooring of a building which we therefore named the White Eye Temple, and below it, four buildings down, grey brick walls of a Grey Temple of the earlier Jamdat Nasr period, and finally in the bottommost depth of all, that is, six metres down, the fifth and earliest building, the red brick walls of a Red Eye Temple which may belong to the Uruk period proper, and reach back let us say to about 3500 BC. We may be thought presumptuous in suggesting that there were five superimposed temples here, but I do not think so, indeed there may even have been more if we count sub-phases. It is my devout hope that one day someone will turn back to this wonderful spot and excavate the entire series, which would enable us to tie these northern temples within the great succession that has been found at Erech itself in the south.

The plan of the principal Eye Temple is a landmark in the history of early ecclesiastical architecture. The walls were made of mud-brick and whitewashed, the floors were of mud overlaid with bitumen and reeds and, as I have already explained, copper panelling with repoussé representations of the eye had once adorned the walls of the sanctuary.

The most important room in the building was the main sanctuary which was eighteen metres long and six metres wide. There were two entrances in the short wall at the north end, and at the opposite end projecting from the short wall stood a whitewashed clay altar or podium three feet high. Here a wonderful discovery awaited us, for the greater part of the valuable frieze which had once adorned the three sides of the podium was still in position. Two panels were practically intact, only a part of the third had been torn away. Never before or since had the decorated front of a temple altar been recovered. This one consisted of three panels, all identically executed; each one was three feet long and four and a half inches wide, carved in fretted bands of blue limestone, white marble and green corrugated shale. The surround to the panel was

Above: Max and workmen at
[...]rak, about 1935.

Right: Agatha on the bank of the
[...]ver Jaghjagha, 1935.

Above: Gertrude Bell and Lionel Smith at Eridu, 1926.

Left: Landscape at Brak.

Above: '*Queen Mary*', the expedition lorry, on the ferry at Raqqa.

Right: Hiyou, the family at Chagar Bazar and ak.

Driver Michel, Colonel Burn and Max at Chagar Bazar.

Expedition house at Chagar Bazar.

a gold foil casing and the entire frieze had a wooden backing. The stone portions were held in position by copper fastenings and the golden bands by gold-headed nails with silver stems. One of these panels completely reconstructed, and restored with certainty, is in the Museum at Aleppo, the second in the British Museum. The form of the decoration is purely architectural and reflects the external appearance of contemporary temple façades. The topmost band is clearly a copy of the typical Jamdat Nasr cone mosaic which once decorated the façades of Sumerian buildings on the lower Euphrates at the period and the corrugations can be matched in the architecture of Erech. A cylinder seal from Brak depicts the entrance to a shrine with much the same aspect: on the southern outer wall of the temple a strip of brightly-painted cone mosaic was still found in position. The walls at this time were also adorned with sets of eight-petalled rosettes in blue, white and pink limestone which were affixed to the plastered façades of the temple: we recovered two examples intact.

The main sanctuary of the building was flanked by two wings; on the eastern side there was an elaboration the like of which has never been found before. I now surmise that there were four sanctuaries perhaps devoted to four separate gods, approached by a courtyard. Immediately adjacent to the sanctuary on the east side there were storage magazines, and on the west a series of much larger chambers which must once have served as treasuries; some of the chambers on the east side were probably for use by the priests.

By the time that this building was planned we may be certain that the architects had many centuries of experience behind them, a long tradition of ecclesiastical design which probably originated in the south, but a surprise may yet await us when we come to dig in the deepest levels of all. The problem to be solved is to discover who conceived the original plan, but it is my belief that this remarkable type of ecclesiastical architecture was dispersed very rapidly throughout the Tigris-Euphrates Valleys at about one and the same time.

The plan inevitably makes one think of the Christian church, indeed the Christian cathedral, and there is even a cruciform transept at the top end of the nave which brings the parallel home very closely.

One intriguing feature of the temple was that the clay altar which stood in the middle of the southern wall was composed of miniature baked bricks of which we found many examples loose in the soil else-where; the use of such miniatures must therefore have been a regular practice in constructing such altars, and perhaps the building of the god's altar in this way had some magical, esoteric significance. However that may be it is certain that the canon of proportions used in the sanctuary, which was exactly three times as long as it was broad, also reflected southern Sumerian architectural tradition which can be matched in a number of other buildings there.

The building, like all others, was in due course sacked and destroyed by an unknown enemy, and eventually had to make way for a suc-cessor after being mainly stripped of its contents, but fortunately the fall of the roof, a result of the sack, so effectively buried the altar that the enemy had not the time to uncover the golden panels which have thus survived of us as a witness to its former glory.

However, in due course this was to make way for a new building – the plano-convex temple in the layer above it. But before its successor was erected, the older building was packed solid with mud-brick, hard and compactly pressed down, for the land which had been devoted to the god was the god's in perpetuity and woe betide anyone who at-tempted to make other use of it. This was consecrated ground and only finally abandoned when the city itself was deserted.

It was no easy task to excavate the Eye Temple for the brick packing was hard as stone and it bruised, battered, blistered and damaged the men's hands: only by great perseverance against much resistance on their part was I able to persuade them to finish the job, but how well worth while it was to recapture this wonderful building. Some inkling of what it had once contained we obtained from excavations in the deeper levels below.

By the time that the main Eye Temple was built this part of Brak had been transformed into a very high mound, artificially elevated over its great platform: it probably dominated the plain from afar. Eventually these sacred buildings, successively abandoned and replaced each at a higher level than before, led to the deliberate construction of the ziggurats or temple towers which emerged at a comparatively late stage in the proto-history of Mesopotamia.

Probing the deep levels of the Eye Temples was a wonderfully re-warding experience, and we were led to do so by eight plunderers' pits which had been dug at various places from the surface by temple robbers who no doubt reaped a rich reward at a much later stage, after these temples had been abandoned. We ourselves explored the depths by using the same ancient shafts and were amazed by the quantity and quality of the small treasure which we recovered in a short space of time: much still remains behind worth the pains of exploration. As far as we could judge most of the deposits which we unearthed were associated with what I believe to be the fourth temple from the top, the Grey Eye Temple, for they were largely associated with the stratum of grey bricks. These deposits consisted in the first place of dozens of beautiful amulets which I shall describe in a moment, lovely little pieces reanimating for us the animal world with which the people had once lived, smooth and pleasant to handle like Chinese jade, and in addition there were the hundreds of Eye idols which I have already mentioned, in black and white alabaster.

Before taking our leave of Brak we must mention beads which were found in quite extraordinary numbers – hundreds of thousands I have noted in my original report, and I did not exaggerate. The ground was sown with them, and many had been puddled-in with the clay used for the mud bricks in the temple foundations. The greater number of them were of glazed faience and of glazed steatite, and some rarer segmented glazed beads appear to be the earliest known specimens of the type.

This massive bead-sowing was obviously part of a religious ritual practised at the time when the early Eye Temples were founded. None of them is likely to have been made much later than 3200 BC. Dr J. F. S. Stone, a bead expert, who examined a segmented faience bead noted that: 'Further afield, we have such large, highly developed faience specimens from the Indus Valley,' – these beads we may now, in my opinion, date to about 3000 BC. 'The Brak bead is not unlike the specimen from Harappa. Both are of soft white faience, and both were originally coated with a light blue glaze . . . It is not impossible that both have a common origin. Without question, therefore, this bead from Brak is of very great interest. It is not only the earliest faience segmented bead so far discovered, but it exhibits characteristics which are normally associated with beads of a very much later date, in particular the highly developed technique of manufacture.'*

* Note. *Iraq.* ix, p. 255.

It may well be that these similar manufactures occurred at the same time and that a common technology was diffused through southern Iran, perhaps through the district of Kerman, at some site such as Tepe Yahya where a trade route by sea or by land, ran through the Indus Valley on the one hand, and to the Euphrates on the other, as has been demonstrated by the discoveries of Lamberg Karlovsky and others. It remains only to be said that at Brak, as in India, glazed steatite was by no means uncommon and that at Brak most of the faience beads were once covered by a blue glaze overlay in addition to black.

Most of the shafts which gave us access to the underground chambers were on the south side of the temple, though one or two were situated elsewhere and one even as far away as the courtyard of Naram-Sin, but when we dug down near the bottom of the platform we entered a warren or maze of underground chambers, 32 in all we examined: the task of grubbing about in them was difficult and not without danger for these ancient mines were airless and one could not remain underground for more than twenty minutes or half an hour at a time without becoming exhausted. We had to work in relays by the light of hurricane lamps which occasionally went out. It was impressive to see a mass of brickwork over our heads – the brickwork of the Eye Temple which lay above us – and what we achieved was really a tribute to the builders of the Uruk and Jamdat Nasr period whose work was so compact and tenacious that we were able, with a minimum of risk, like our predecessing robbers, to work underground and suffer no loss of life or casualty.

In this hallowed, consecrated ground, we found Eye idols by the hundred and they must originally have been deposited in thousands (see illustration on p. 147). The normal type of figure consisted merely of a flat biscuit-like body surmounted by a neck and two eyes which had originally been in-filled with malachite paint. There were many examples of four-eyed figures which looked like representations of a pair of individuals, and there was also a three-eyed figure and a few had six eyes. Among curious variants there were idols with large numbers of eyebrows superimposed over the eyes, and other variants in the shape of one figure standing on top of the other. These were the principal varieties of what I call the naturalistic form of Eye idol.

Many of these images had markings in the front of the body and some of them had a feminine appearance, for they were clothed in long gowns with 'V'-shaped necks, decorated by punctuations which might have been simulating jewellery. There was also a unique example which was engraved with a stag and a bird. I believe that this one must have been associated with the Sumerian goddess, Nin-Harsag, who was associated with childbirth and it is simplest to believe that many were dedicated to secure her favour. This interpretation is reinforced by the appearance of numerous idols with little ones on the front, clearly mother and child, perhaps mother bearing child. A supplication for offspring was to be expected in a community which required an increase of population for the expansion of its agricultural and pastoral activities. Many of the figures were adorned with a high hat or *polos*, a special form of turban. Those which had more elaborate head-dresses obviously represented the upper strata of the hierarchy.

We have already noticed that at Chagar Bazar there were instances of rich contributions from communities outside the actual city and that from one of them named Qirdahat there were contributions on the occasion of a religious festival of barley for making bread and brewing small beer from no less than 2770 people. These massive numbers of Eye idols at Brak suggest that similar offerings were made on certain occasions in this holy place and that large numbers of people came not only from the city itself, but from afar, to subscribe to a god or goddess or both who were probably highly venerated beyond the district. Every one of these little eye-images was easily portable and obviously made for personal presentation to the gods or goddesses in the temple. Not one of the many hundreds that we found was larger than could be held in the open hand, and one or two were minute, but generally speaking they fitted comfortably into the palm of the hand. There must have been some centre probably in the city itself, if not in the vicinity, devoted exclusively to their manufacture. Their presentation reminds one of the lighting of a candle by a devotee in a Roman Catholic church, that was more or less the equivalent. The form and appearance of these little idols give rise to many questions and much speculation. Who is it that these images were intended to represent? At first we thought that they represented an eye god, for there are many eye diseases endemic in this part of the country, opthalmia and others, and that perhaps the sanctuary at Brak had some special sovereign healing property for those so afflicted, but I think it is unlikely that this is the answer. It seems more probable that the eyes were intended as reflection of an all-seeing god and that the representation of the face and the human form was taboo; this kind of inhibition was not uncommon in primitive communities.

Perhaps the clue to the meaning of these idols lies in an engraving from a contemporary seal, round about 3000 BC, which was found on the Diyala, a tributary of the Tigris, at a mound named Tell Agrab. This unique seal illustrates a typical shrine of the Jamdat Nasr period flanked by a pair of poles on either side, designated in the texts as *urigallu*; in the sky above the temple there is a stylized face, the prominent feature of which is a pair of eyes disproportionately large: the eyebrows, nose and mouth are summarily sketched. Accompanying the eye face are eight-petalled rosettes, also in the sky, closely associated with the temple as they were at Brak and at Uruk on the façades of religious buildings. On this seal the temple appeared to be dominated from heaven by an all-seeing god and this I would surmise was the intention.

We have already noticed that one or two exceptional idols are represented as wearing crowns and therefore would seem to be upper members of the hierarchy. One in particular is of special interest because it is represented as wearing a most elaborate form of crown, and this is the only example for which I have been able to find a close parallel, though of a very much later date. It is to be seen on a Kassite boundary stone of about the ninth century BC dedicated by a governor of the Sealands of southern Babylonia to one named Gul-eresh: the same stone illustrates many symbols of the gods and some of them represent the temples or shrines themselves. This boundary stone invokes no less than ten gods and we therefore cannot associate the crown with any one in particular, but four of the great gods are twice mentioned in the text, namely Anu, Enlil, Ea and Ninmakh, the Great Lady. It is tempting to associate the feathered crown represented on this stone with one of them. On the boundary stone this crown is set on a high pedestal which may represent the shrine itself or a podium within it. I am inclined to trace its ancestry far back to our image at Tell Brak.

Closely relevant is another set of images, this time in the shape of what I have called Spectacle idols. The body is once again plain, but surmounted by a pair of loops with perforations, usually open circles; rarely they are infilled with paint. These images are as I believe, older than the standard type of Eye idol and probably go back to the earliest temple of all. There is one beautiful little specimen in soapstone where the image is set on a pedestal and is clearly represented as it once stood in the temple. The front of the image is engraved with parallel stripes and there are nicks on the pedestal base, no doubt representing an ornamentation such as we found on the temple altar. Andrae would have interpreted these as hut symbols, made of reeds, but I myself can see no strong reason for this suggestion. There is one extremely interesting example of a soapstone gable-seal from the north Syrian Hogarth Collection in the Ashmolean Museum, which represents a pair of pedestals or altar bases with looped idols upon it. Intermediate between these looped idols and the Eye idols are other specimens in which the perforations are not carried right through, instead there are simple circles probably once infilled with paint, and this leads me to believe that we can discern here the earliest stage from which the Eye idols were evolved. We also found fragments of very big Spectacle idols made of terracotta and these I do not doubt were images which were set up in the temple for worship. The Spectacle idols have a wide distribution and have been found as far afield as Ur, at Susa in southern Iran, in Babylonia and in Syria.

In summarizing our conclusions I would repeat that the eye form was merely intended to emphasize the all-seeing nature of the god and that there was some taboo against representing the divine face. There is no doubt that we are confronted with family dedications as well as individual ones. Variants of alabaster idols are also known in the district of Marash, but nothing is exactly comparable and we may say that their distribution ranges from northern Syria to south-eastern Iran.

Apart from the Eye idols the discoveries which pleased us most were numerous seals and amulets. The typical fauna of the district and the adjoining mountains is fully illustrated. Lions, bears, sheep of the domestic and wild variety, goats, monkeys, hares, pigs, foxes, hedgehogs, frogs, ducks and eagles are common; antlered stags, scorpions, felines: various cryptic signs are engraved on square stamp seals. The best of the amulets, those which represent animals in the round, are superb *objets d'art* in variegated stone and because of their luxurious touch and delicate economy of form are the Mesopotamian counterparts of Chinese jades. The best of these amulets are miniature masterpieces of their kind and their makers had a keen awareness of the vitality and poise with which their animal models had been endowed. These miniatures were produced by craftsmen accustomed to observe wild and domesticated animals in their natural surroundings; they possessed the artistic powers of selection which enabled them to disregard what was inessential; they achieved their effects by building up a series of boldly contrasted planes, a simple stylization combining plastic power with a natural rhythm. Especially interesting are the representations of the monkey, including the cynocephalus, or dogheaded baboon, the only beast out of the whole repertory of animals which was not at home in this part of the world, but was perhaps then familiar in Asia Minor.

We may assume that the lion was common in these parts at the time, for osteological remains of the lion *Panthera leo* were found as we have already reported in our account of Naram-Sin's palace. We may conclude with certainty that lions were common both in Babylonia and in the north much earlier, before 3000 BC, for at Uruk-Warka the German diggers found the skeleton of a young lion in a foundation box of the Jamdat Nasr period (*UVB* VIII, p. 31).

Another type of amulet which occurred very commonly were kidney-shaped objects mostly in soapstone. On the flat side they were engraved either with horned animals or cryptic signs. The idea occurred to me that they might have been used for divination. One square amulet was engraved with a pair of objects represented *tête bêche* which looked like a pair of human feet with a snake between them: the like of it has now been found in southern Iran by Lamberg Karlovsky at the famous site of Tepe Yahya which he is digging in the province of Kerman, where tablets of the Uruk Jamdat Nasr period have been found. This discovery now establishes a link between Brak and S. Central Iran before 3000 BC. A lovely little circular stamp seal was decorated on its flat side with a representation of five squatting does, a beautiful seal which displayed real artistry and a good sense of spacing. Another rarity was a seal and impression which depicted a vertically-set line terminating in four spiral ends. This was evidently a symbol with a high magical potency, for on a seal impression of the same period there was represented a seated male figure in front of this magical spiral and above him an antelope preceded by a seven-petalled rosette. It would not be surprising if magical emblems of this kind had been set up in the temples and placed there for worship.

Returning to the amulets we found large numbers in shape of bears, beasts which of course frequented the mountains, were certainly extremely common at the time and survive today in Kurdistan. Much highly-skilled carving was executed in bone, both ducks and lions and a wonderful representation of a ram (*Iraq*, IX, pl. XI, no. 3). The position of the horns suggests that it is a wild species of Armenian sheep, as opposed to the domesticated variety which is also represented. A certain number of these specimens as I now believe were made of ivory, that is, probably boars' tusks, although I did not identify them as such at the time. We need not discuss this remarkable variety of objects in any further detail and I hope that readers who are interested may refer to our Journal *Iraq*, vol. IX (1947), where numerous plates illustrating them amply repay the effort of laying hands on this volume.

It may seem surprising that so many amulets were deposited in the temple and one wonders why. I think the answer is simple enough. There was no current coin, no money available in those days, and the dedicant who presented petitions to the gods had to bring a gift of some kind. This was not money to subscribe to the church, but the most valuable offering available in the shape of semi-precious carved stones, which doubtless filled the temple treasuries, and these together with the many thousands of Eye idols were personal dedications within the temple. It is also interesting that the animal amulets are in style very similar to those discovered at Erech and elsewhere in Sumerian cities down the lower Euphrates: but although Uruk in particular has hitherto been considered to be the source of the finest little animal carvings they do not exceed in quality those that we discovered here in this northern capital at Brak.

The artistic relationship of many of the finds at Brak to those at Uruk was such, including the architecture, that one is led to believe that the two cities were then under a conjoint authority and that southern Babylonian writ may well have felt itself as far north as the Habur Valley. This is pure speculation, but the relationship between the two architecturally, artistically and domestically is so remarkable as to imply something more than a parallelism in the art products of the time. It implies the very closest form of trade and personal links between these two great cities, of which of course, Uruk was the larger.

Not the least of the many remarkable discoveries in the deep levels of the Eye Temple was a magnificent alabaster head about seventeen centimetres or nearly seven inches in height, which seems to have been associated with the Grey Eye Temple. This extraordinary figure with the large eyes, summarily treated ears, big nose and pursed mouth is represented as wearing a cut-down Oriental hat, the type known as *tarbush* which was probably affixed on the head through two holes perforated through its sides. A deep and wide groove all the way down the back shows that the figure was once mounted on wood and we have to think of a wooden body perhaps overlaid with metal. This head has won the highest praise from a leading German archaeologist, Professor Anton Moortgat.

We may well be content with such appreciation from an archaeologist who is the doyen of the authorities on Oriental art and architecture in Germany. His account of the beginnings of this development written in a book entitled *The Art of Ancient Mesopotamia* is replete with stimulating and provocative thought. In my opinion this wonderful head which stands as a lone monument at the portals of Syrian sculpture is a blend of abstraction combined with an attempt at natural form which is revealed in the rotundity of the face and the fleshiness of the neck. But the disproportionately large eyes, the enormous nose conjoined with the eyebrows and the fleshy lips together with the two ears, each of which consists of a pair of concentric ovals, is an effective formal convention adopted by the early ecclesiastical carvers. This head when mounted on a wooden body which was probably overlaid with sheet copper must have commanded attention as a dominating personality in some temple sanctuary. Three other smaller heads display similar characteristics.

Contemporary sculpture in other parts of Syria is extremely rare but there is an exceptionally interesting head discovered by Harald Ingholt at Hama (western Syria), a site in the Orontes Valley (*Sept Campagnes de Fouilles à Hama en Syrie*), which is likely to have been made at approximately the same period and is evidence that this level of sculpture was widespread at the time.

The Hama head was life-size, made of limestone, and at one time covered with painted plaster (there were traces of black and of red paint); it wears a high *polos*, has a big nose and a little slit mouth, also cavities for the eyes. Sculptors were in travail at the time and struggling to find expression. I have little doubt that the big Hama head no less sophisticated was approximately contemporary with those from Brak and it was found in a stratum which contained a Spectacle idol and a crude bevelled bowl of the type which was common in the Uruk Jamdat Nasr period. These parallel discoveries in western and eastern Syria respectively show that much more remains to be found of the beginnings of monumental sculpture in western Asia.

Underneath the lowest Eye Temple lay the prehistoric debris of even earlier stages. Among the potsherds were some fine examples of sealing-wax-red jars with rims which were clearly imitating metal; they belong to an early sequence of the Uruk period and can be nearly matched at Uruk itself, at Ur, and at Susa in Iran; these sherds are further indications of the richness of the prehistoric levels that await probing deep underground.

It still remains to be determined how much of the Ubaid period, fifth millennium BC, has left traces of itself at Brak, though we know that Ubaid sherds have been observed on other mounds in the neighbourhood. But sherds of the preceding Halaf period, especially of the late part of it which saw the production of polychrome and white-painted ware, were abundant, and when we left off digging we had tapped a level not much later than 5000 BC. Much more of this remains to be discovered, not only under the Eye Temples but at the base of the lofty mound which flanks the opposite side of Brak, where four or five decades of digging would barely suffice to get to the bottom of it. This task I bequeath to posterity.

Eye idol.

Mock king.

CHAPTER 9

Excavations in the Balikh Valley

We decided to curtail our excavations at Tell Brak because of the blackmailing pressure of the Sheikhs of the Shammar tribe who were obviously bent on inducing our workmen to strike. Anticipating this trouble we thought we had better leave the site in good time, for time was money to us and we dare not be caught by such tactics. Having accomplished as much as we could in the Eye Temples of Tell Brak, we therefore made all arrangements to pack up.

I remember that just before we left the village we summoned our good Sheikh of Chagar Bazar, the Kurdish Sheikh Ahmad, to give him a parting present. Of course the most valued gift was the mud-brick house which we had built on his site, but I had promised him a horse and this I gave him. Somehow I was never lucky in my presents to this good man for the horse had one white fetlock and as we parted he said, 'A white fetlock – death – the kiss of death', and that was the last I saw of him.

After that we moved over a hundred miles westwards to the Balikh Valley, into marshy country which however remote is really a paradise for the archaeologist. Masses of things remain to be discovered of all periods, some of them entirely unknown, others that can be linked historically and prehistorically with what has been done elsewhere, both to the east and to the west, and all the more interesting for that.

In the Balikh Valley we selected as our headquarters the village of Tell Abyadh which lies at the top end of it, just below the Syrian-Turkish frontier, and from there in the distance you can see, on a clear day, the magnificent mound of Harran where many have worked, most recently Seton Lloyd, and how often I wished that we could have been allowed across the frontier to examine it.

The importance of Tell Abyadh is that just a few kilometres below it there is a spring called, 'Ain al 'Arus, 'the well of the betrothed', from which it is generally thought issue the waters of the Balikh; this well stands at the river's headwaters and although some claim that there are more distant sources to the north situated in Turkey, as these turn out to be a mere trickle in the summer, I think that 'the well of the betrothed' may be credited with the honour of being the true origin of this river. Here was the traditional meeting place of Abraham's servant and Rebecca and also that of Jacob and Rachel. The river itself takes a winding course through marshy country and must have changed its channel many times. The main track along the western bank measures about sixty-five miles to the Euphrates junction, that is from Tell Abyadh down to Raqqa, a name which means the morass. The river can never have been navigable and only the overland route was used. This was good pastoral land for much water was available, but the marshy nature of the country was not favourable to the growth of capital cities. Whilst there is some evidence of ancient materials and objects typical of western Syria and the Orontes Valley it is clear that throughout its history the Balikh fell on the whole within the orbit of Mesopotamia – connections were dominantly with the east and to a lesser degree with the north. The five sites examined by us we shall describe very briefly hereafter.

Our excursion into this comparatively unknown territory was interesting, but by no means painless, for although we lived in a commodious little house, it had been built on a marsh and I used to get up in the morning crippled with rheumatism and often find it difficult to get out of my camp bed. The village itself must have been highly insanitary for the main sewer ran through the high street, or what one may call a high street, and often enough the women of the household were seen to be washing their domestic dishes in the middle of it. When on occasion I remonstrated with them, they said it was true that sickness prevailed in the town, but somehow they survived, and so did we.

We were fortunate to be served by a sweet-natured man in the shape of our Syrian cook Dimitri who came from Antioch, or its neighbourhood, and we thrived on his fare. A charming character, he was oppressed with domestic worries and through the Levirate supported the entire family of his deceased brother, who had left him a wife and I should think a dozen children. The other impressive character on the staff was our head servant, Subri, a Christian who had once lodged in Turkey but had been driven out under the régime of Mustafa Kemal for whom he had no love. He was a wild man who often slept with a knife between his teeth. Trained by Colonel Burn he proved to be a model valet, butler and house servant, whom I would gladly have taken to England. I am sorry to say that in Tell Abyadh he got himself into trouble by enticing away the head prostitute of the brothel and thereby incurred the displeasure of its keeper who incidentally was a devout Christian. I gathered that because of Subri's infatuation, she had lost her best girl and I suffered a somewhat embarrassing interview when she came to the house in order to protest at the unseemly conduct of my servant and to request me to make amends for his dastardly conduct. Agatha has given a masterly account of that interview in her book, *Come Tell Me How You Live*, and I would advise readers to consult it. I remember that at the interview my ingenuity was severely taxed, for this was to me a novel experience, and I did not know how to cope with the situation. But in the end I had to agree with the rectitude of the brothel keeper and decided to fine Subri an appropriate amount of money out of his wages, and hold this as surety against his entering that brothel again. But I remember the devout piety of this good Christian woman and her extraordinary dignity at the interview. I have thought about it many times.

In Tell Abyadh we were joined by my good friend John Rose who had been with me at Ur and Arpachiyah and I commend to the reader his beautiful set of surveys and drawings of the various mounds which we examined; done extremely quickly in the course of six weeks, they are masterly appreciations of the sites that we visited. Nothing could have conveyed more information with greater clarity and sense of style, a model for all such surveys. The tract of territory bounded on the west by the Balikh forms a rough parallelogram with two rivers, the Balikh and the Euphrates, Harran at the northern end and Raqqa at the southern. In antiquity it was known to the Romans as the province of Osroene and appropriately was next door to the province of Adiabene, which literally means the impassable, or the land of no thoroughfare, and difficult indeed was the thoroughfare in these parts, through this fearful marsh. None the less it attracted an outflow of population from the more prosperous regions, perhaps wild men, who could not find a home in more civilized metropolitan cities. But this was extraordinarily rich country and practically all the periods which we had noted further east on the Habur were represented in it, and in addition a very rich legacy of Hellenistic, Roman and Byzantine remains; to a medievalist this would be wonderfully rewarding. Some of the *Tells* were mainly medieval in content and of a great height. Would that I had yet another two or three lives left me in order to examine them. When I think of what lies underfoot and above ground to be historically and archaeologically tested I stand amazed and can but be aware of our very small contribution to knowledge of the past by comparison with the far greater amount still awaiting discovery.

I would not be justified in making more than a brief reference to the five mounds which we examined and I shall say just a few words about each of them.

First comes the mound of Aswad which lies about fifteen kilometres south of Tell Abyadh on a river which is a branch of the Balikh, a very high mound which stands more than twenty metres above the level of the plain and covers an occupied area of about thirty acres. It is extremely ancient, for we found numerous specimens of Neolithic chert arrowheads as well as remains of extensive occupation of the Halaf period and earlier sequences. At the top of this extraordinary mound we were successful in extricating the ground plan of a little prehistoric temple. There was a long room which must have been the main sanctuary and adjacent to it a smaller chamber on the threshold of which was lying an ox skull, a magical sacrifice in the doorway. There had been a flat roof made of reeds and mud weighted down with pebbles and in and around the building, animal bones identified as pig, sheep, goat, ox and a small *Equus*, all apparently domesticated. It is clear that mixed farming including animal stockbreeding was practised by these early communities in the Balikh Valley as well as the cultivation of wheat and barley, many specimens of which were found at another mound called Mefesh which I will describe next. I thought that the building at the top of the mound named Aswad was probably of the Halaf period, but I may have dated it too early, because I am not sure if the associated sherds were really contemporary. However that may be, great accumulations of Halaf have now been found elsewhere; if this association is correct, then the mound itself must be of immense antiquity and a long sequence of that period lies below it. It may be that this temple was rather later in date than I had estimated, but here again is an attraction to some prehistorian who must go and revisit it one day.

After Aswad, which consisted mainly of a concentration of the early Halaf period, we looked for a mound which was likely to give us samples of the next sequence and we lighted on a place named Tell Mefesh, a word which in Arabic means gushed, and the place was doubtless so called because it was situated close to a *wadi* which is now usually dry, but during the winter rains is quickly filled with water. It is possible that when the mound was last occupied in the Ubaid period, this *wadi* may have been a river of some importance, and it is said to be traceable to the north-west as far as Arab Punar whence it runs down in a general south-easterly direction to the Balikh. This settlement lies about twenty-five miles south of Tell Abyadh and seven and a half miles west of the river Balikh within easy reach of the modern track to Raqqa. The mound is fifteen metres high and the area of occupation about eight and a half acres, quite a formidable small provincial settlement but one that again could be made to yield very much more information than we could extract in the five days that we allotted to it, and that was all the time that could be spared.

When I look back on those days I realize how carefree and easy they were, for all we had to do was to show that we were competent excavators; then ask for permission to make soundings in the district of our choice. We were then allowed to proceed without let or hindrance provided that we had nominated the sites on which we wished to concentrate and had promised to give a written account of them when we had concluded our operations. The men too found these excursions both interesting and exhilarating and there was much competition to join the small lorry-load which morning after morning left our headquarters in Tell Abyadh for various sites in that river valley, sometimes not inconsiderable distances. Their enthusiasm, however, tended to evaporate in the cold black dawn and on wet days, especially in the month of December, and long before we had reached the site of our destination they looked like a party of frozen ducks: but work with a pick and a spade soon thawed them and in the end they enjoyed these little excursions as much as we did. In the five days that we were able to devote to sounding Mefesh, it was not possible to recover a coherent ground-plan, but the excavations did reveal a range of four small rooms built of mud bricks which were much larger than the little ones used in the Halaf period: it was usually easy to discern the difference of period in walling of these two successive phases for that reason alone. In the courtyard which flanked the rooms we discovered a number of circular corn bins and these contained large quantities of barley, *Hordeum vulgare* or *H. Hexastichon*. One of the rooms contained remains of the fallen roof which had consisted of wooden poplar beams, oval in section, and as they spanned the full width of the room they must have originally been more than two and a half metres long. There were also traces of the reeds which overlaid the wooden beams. It may be assumed that poplars, willows and reeds were growing freely in the Balikh Valley at this period. Both barley grains and the houses revealed the action of fire, an observation confirmed by Miss D. M. A. Bate who examined some of the animal remains, which also showed traces of burning. As all the associated pottery was of the Ubaid period it may be assumed that these occupants who followed the Halaf inhabitants were burnt out and came to an end. We do not know who the enemy was. Among the animal remains we observed the remains of a large goat with a spiral horn, a large ox and a small *Equus*. The pottery discovered in the house was particularly interesting because although unmistakably of the Al Ubaid period it revealed characteristics of the earlier Halaf phase of culture and indicated that the Ubaid period occupants at Mefesh were in their ceramic considerably influenced by their predecessors. The painted pottery types exhibited bowl forms, the use of a black paint, and the practice of painting a ring round the base of the bowl that can be closely matched in the contemporary Ubaid pottery found at Arpachiyah. There was an example of an Ubaid pot in the Halaf tradition and there was a sherd of the Halaf period with a double-horned bucranium design and stipples. We have, therefore, no doubt whatever, that these two sequences of development are to be found in this mound which would be a little paradise for explorers interested in those particular periods, for there they would also discover many specimens of animal and vegetable remains and so be able to produce very useful data on the ecology of the district. It is unfortunate that at the time of our excavation the method of determining chronology by the carbon 14 method, had not yet been invented, for here at Mefesh was a vast supply of organic remains. A future excavator now knows where to go for more of it.

Lastly one would not like to take leave of Mefesh without drawing particular attention to an interesting fragment of a sun-dried-clay mother goddess figurine discovered in the house debris. This figure appears to be represented as wearing a high hat though it would also be possible to interpret it as an antlered head, surmounting a body in human form, and this I think is in fact what it is. The general conception of this figure is reminiscent of the high-hatted mother goddess figurines with quasi-animal heads, discovered in the Ubaid flood pit stratum at Ur, an interesting example of the confused mixture of forms on such prehistoric representations of primitive gods or goddesses.

Gathered from a mound on the slopes of Tell Shuwaikh, a prehistoric mound in the near neighbourhood of Mefesh, there was an admirable example of the earliest type of Halaf pottery, a big bowl, rather crude, with three horizontal bands of hachured lozenges. One of the Ubaid bowls was illustrated with panels of long-necked birds, heads down to the ground, feeding, and I think that these possibly may have represented bustard, perhaps the greater bustard, which were probably at that time, as today, not uncommon in the neighbourhood. No more need be said about Mefesh itself except that it is a typical example of the rich potential of this part of the Balikh Valley for the discovery of the early prehistoric sequences and that enemy action at the end of the Ubaid period has preserved for posterity numerous samples of the handicrafts of the time which were evidently of no value to the attackers.

The third place that we examined was Tell Sahlan which lay in very marshy country on the west bank of the Nahr al Turkman, a tributary of the Balikh, about half a mile upstream from Tell Aswad which, as we have already noted, is not a great distance from Tell Abyadh. Access was very difficult and we could not spend more than two or three days there. The workmen often had to get there by swimming and we ourselves found it by no means easy to reach. Sahlan is the most massive of the mounds surveyed by the expedition and stands no less than 40 metres high. The occupied area covers about 26 acres. I estimate that the enormous series of sequences contained within this mound must belong to a range of occupation which exceeds 6000 years in all, and there is therefore material for almost every kind of expert to examine, for it began in the early prehistoric and ended in our own era. Perhaps the most significant discovery was a fragment of a cuneiform tablet, unfortunately illegible, which I picked up on the slopes of the mound and this leads one to suppose that there must be more documents to be found somewhere in the middle levels of it.

The upper levels of Sahlan contained Roman, Romano-Byzantine and Islamic debris through at least ten or fifteen metres of accumulation. On the opposite side of the mound overlooking the river, at the 8-metre contour, we exposed the face of a stone wall at least four metres wide composed of rough gypsum blocks ringing the mound. A fragment of a painted clay bottle with a red band of paint on the shoulder was found embedded in the stones and was evidently part of the rough filling between the blocks. As this was a piece of Habur ware we may say that the terrace wall cannot have been built before the period of the First Dynasty of Babylon; we may date it to *c.* 1800 BC.

Summarizing the results obtained at Sahlan we may say that it was a site with a very long history, not easily accessible owing to its marshy surroundings, and that at some period during the second millennium BC, there was a heavy terrace-wall providing it with a strong defence. We are uncertain about the date of the earliest settlement, but it is probably subsequent to the Halaf period when the neighbouring site of Tell Aswad was last occupied. Sahlan may then have first been settled at a time when Aswad had become inconveniently high and possibly completely ringed by marsh in the closing stages of its career. The question arises as to why Sahlan continued to be occupied after it grew to so great a height. The answer may be that under the Roman *Imperium*, when it became a part of the *limes*, a high and derelict mound such as Sahlan was considered to be a most suitable site for a small *castellum*, difficult to storm, and commanding a wide field of vision. For similar reasons in Turkish times, ancient sites such as these were often selected as police posts. Thus does history repeat itself.

The fourth site which we excavated was named Tell Jidle, a word which I believe means roots, and was conveniently situated for us, for it lay only two and a half miles south of the headwaters at Ain al Arus, on the west bank of the river. I have rarely seen a more delectable and beautifully situated spot. It was a compact mound with steep slopes, standing to a height of fifteen metres and it covered about four and a half acres in all. The top of the mound directly overlooked the crystalline-blue waters of the river which were transparent right down to the bed and teeming with fish; the banks were lined with a few willow trees and the only presence of human occupation was a small house which belonged to a lonely miller who ground wheat and barley brought to him by people in this district. How devoutly I hoped that this mound would turn out to be a good one. We could happily have settled down here for several years in delectable surroundings. But it was not to be. Although we extracted much information the architecture was disappointing, some settlements were more or less derelict and filled with windblown sand, but the sequence was valuable and one of the levels, the fifth from the top, contained interesting evidence of defences of the Sargonid period, let us say about 2400 BC.

Within the top metre there were Romano-Byzantine remains, probably about AD 300–600, and the walls were constructed of rough blocks of gypsum and mud-brick. It was evident that in the near neighbourhood there were considerable sources of a not very good gypsum building-material which occupants could quarry. Contents of this level consisted of cremation-pot burials with children's bones, a few fragments of clay lamps and some unidentifiable bronze coins. A solitary clay jug found in this level complete, has been illustrated by me in *Iraq*, vol. VIII (1946).

The next two levels descending in sequence from the top were Jidle 2 and 3. Jidle 2, the foundations of which stood no less than thirteen and a half metres above river level, is to be dated somewhere between 1450 and 1350 BC and was the tail-end of a prosperous occupation. Here we found fragments of a painted pottery decorated with white paint on a red or a black background characteristic of the Hurrians; it died a natural death and marked the terminus of the Hurrian period. The Hurrians, a northern peasant folk, were also warriors and had been organized as a coherent group by the Indo-Aryan dynasty known as the Mitanni, and in this part of Mesopotamia prospered for several centuries before 1400 BC. Some outside pressure, perhaps from the east, reflected the rising power of the Middle Assyrian kingdom which was beginning to squeeze out the inhabitants. But probably the Assyrians did not think it worthwhile to expend their efforts on this distant region potentially inclined to disturbance.

The most prosperous hamlet, however, was represented by the level below 2, namely Jidle 3, where we also discovered some characteristic Hurrian pottery. The interesting feature of this settlement was that it had been completely destroyed by fire and ransacked by invaders, as was proved by the extensive traces of ash all over that level. The same fate had befallen the contemporary settlement of Tell Hammam only half a mile upstream on the opposite bank of the river. The relative situation of Tell Hammam and Tell Jidle with the river Balikh flowing between them has been very clearly illustrated in John Rose's simple contour survey. We do not know precisely at what date Jidle 3 was sacked or what were the causes, but its end may have been due to some pressure on the dynasty of Mitanni either from Syria or from some other part of Asia Minor. On archaeological grounds about the middle of the fifteenth century BC appears to be a reasonable date for the end of Jidle 3. Much of this settlement was filled with windblown soil and proves that the site was abandoned for a few years before the foundation of its successor, which as we have seen, marked an unsuccessful attempt to renew links with its predecessor. The hiatus between the two settlements need not have been much more than a decade and there were certainly no very great intervals because of the strict continuity of the pottery. In Jidle 2, the buildings were very poorly constructed and had all the signs of a degenerate and somewhat decadent reoccupation. The date of the beginning of Jidle 3 is an archaeological problem with which I need not weary the reader here, but it is likely to have begun not earlier than about 1700 BC. A few interesting objects were found in this settlement: a terracotta figurine of the mother goddess suckling a child, and a cylinder seal of Cypriote type indicates an extensive and far-flung trade.

Below Jidle 3 lay the wall foundations of Jidle 4 at a depth of about eleven and a half metres below the top of the mound, and the floor of a chapel stood at twelve metres above river level. All that remained of this shrine were three mud-brick walls of an oblong room and a mud-brick altar standing to a height of over three feet against the long side of the room. In the precincts of the shrine we discovered a remarkable painted 'Ishtar' mother goddess figurine decorated with red paint and probably not much later than the Third Dynasty of Ur, let us say about 2100 or 2000 BC at which period Mesopotamian figurines were being naturalistically modelled. Some sherds of Habur ware were discovered and an unpainted bowl type similar to pottery associated with the Third Dynasty of Ur at the city of Ur itself. Extensive use of rather rough-hewn gypsum rocks again indicates the availability of this material in the neighbourhood. We need not go further into the evidence which suggests an overlap between the First Dynasty of Babylon on the late side, and on the early side of the Third Dynasty of Ur. There was probably a break for at least a hundred and fifty years between Jidle 3 and Jidle 4 and tentatively I would date this fourth settlement to a period between about 2100 and 1800 BC.

Much the most interesting stratum in this settlement however was Jidle 5. The foundations were not at a constant level but followed the contours of the mound and were contained by a great oval town wall which rises gently as it swings round and away from the river. The town wall was at its lowest against the spring on the eastern side of the site and by the time it reached the river Balikh on its opposite western side, had risen by at least four metres. This 350-metre circuit of defensive walling, never less than a metre thick, was a strong bulwark against attack. Any enemy who attempted to storm the city would have been obliged either to breach the walls or to cross the river which provided a natural obstacle on its northern and eastern sides. The quality of building was better than at any other period of Jidle's occupation: the walls were faced with whitewash and a kind of *jus* cement plaster; the sizes of brick were reminiscent of brickwork used in the Sargonid period at Brak. Some sections of the town wall were reinforced with rough gypsum blocks and on the east side some lengths of the wall were composed entirely of gypsum. There was a stone pavement at the 10½-metre contour.

The main entrance to the city at this period appears to have been through a gap on the south side of the mound. At this point the wall may have been composed entirely of stone and there were perhaps flanking towers which would have been stripped by builders of a subsequent period. It is probable that there was a raised causeway running for some distance beyond the main gate over the marshy ground in the immediate vicinity of the town wall.

The evidence of the pottery proves that the town wall was in exist-ence under the Agade dynasty, probably during the reign of Rimush or Naram-Sin who built a palace at Brak, thereby consolidating the conquests of Sargon, founder of the dynasty, as we have already seen in a discussion of that site. The discovery of strong defences on the Balikh at this period is therefore exactly what we should expect from our knowledge of the extensive building activities at Brak under the Sargonid dynasty and provides a further link cementing the lines of communication with Asia Minor.

Against the inner face of the town wall on the S.W. quadrant of the mound there were the remains of a disturbed Sargonid inhumation-grave containing a necklace composed of faience duck amulets and carnelian ring beads similar to jewellery discovered in the Sargonid levels at Chagar Bazar in the Habur Valley. The great oval town wall illustrated by Jidle 5, probably follows on a sequence of Early Dynastic circuits indicated by cushion-shaped plano-convex bricks which were typical of the more ancient era that had preceded it. From the available evidence it is likely that Jidle 5 covered a considerable part of the Agade period in round figures about 2400–2200 BC and that this settle-ment fell into disrepair during the anarchic times when the Guti invaded Mesopotamia, an invasion which had obvious repercussions and disturbances in Syria itself owing to a relaxation of the strong central government control which had been so successfully exercised for 200 years in the Agade period.

In levels 6–8 which preceded Jidle 5 we did not find anything earlier than the Uruk period and it is quite possible that the first foundation of Jidle occurred not long after the final abandonment of Tell Mefesh, in which we had observed nothing later than the Ubaid period. We may assume that Jidle was first occupied in the last quarter of the fourth millennium BC, during the Proto-Historic age.

The last subject of our examination was Tell Hammam. The top of this compact mound which capped an inhabited area of about three acres in all, rose to a peak no less than eleven metres above the level of the plain and beneath it were contained all the main sequences that we had discovered elsewhere. The site was first occupied in the Halaf period, probably even earlier, in the Neolithic, for there were some well-made flints, lanceheads, arrows and the like as well as ob-sidian gathered together from the sides and base of the mound includ-ing one blade of the greenish, Vannic variety which came from Asia Minor.

The situation of Tell Hammam is made very clear by John Rose's contour map which shows the two mounds, Jidle and Hammam, standing on opposite sides of the river, the upper one, Hammam, on the north bank, and Tell Jidle on the south. These two settlements were complementary and must have been jointly defended, each guarding their particular bank and reach of the river, and this was particularly clear in the settlements at Hammam which corresponded to Jidle 2 and 3 fairly high up in the mound.

Underneath the last Romano-Byzantine occupation at the summit of Hammam, as at Jidle, there were house sites of the middle of the second millennium BC and we were able to draw up a plan of a mud-brick house which included four chambers and some bread ovens. The rooms which were found to be covered by a band of ash immediately above this level indicate that after the destruction there was another brief period of reoccupation corresponding to Jidle 2, rapidly abandoned and deserted, for the remains were filled with windblown sand. In these levels we found fragments of shallow bowls of a deep pinkish clay, bordered by a wide band of bright red paint, a type of pottery which also occurs in the palace level IV of Alalakh in the Orontes Valley excavated by Leonard Woolley; a few fragments of this same ware were also found in the corresponding settlements at Jidle. These discoveries demonstrated the importance of finding a distinctive pottery associated with a particular level, for it enabled us not only to correlate the occupation of these two mounds in the Balikh Valley but also to relate them to an occupation far to the west at a well-known site, Alalakh, in the Orontes Valley where history has illuminated the sequence of events.

Further evidence of the date of the house site which we excavated at Hammam was supplied by the discovery of a faience cylinder seal with two registers, the bottom one depicting a row of gazelles or possibly goats, and between pairs of them a star planted on a pole, a religious symbol, while the top register was decorated with con-centric circles and a star in the field. I believe that these were pictures of animals kept in the temples at the time, for we have at an earlier period, evidence from the tablets at Chagar Bazar that gazelles were attached to the sanctuaries.

The record of our excavations in the Balikh Valley demonstrates that there was a scarcity of metal implements, a sure sign that the hard, wet and marshy conditions of the Balikh attracted more primitive, less wealthy and less urbanized settlers when compared with the installations in the Habur Valley. Correspondingly, however, some of the chert and flint implements as well as the obsidian were of high quality and deserve more attention than we were able to give them.

Our excursions into this valley which lasted no more than six weeks proved to be an exciting and pioneering episode for little was known about this region before we went there, although the late Professor Albright, in about 1926, had examined one prehistoric mound named Zaidan at the bottom of it. But no archaeologist, to the best of our knowledge, had sojourned there for more than a few days and appreciated its extraordinary potentiality. W. F. Albright's brief excursion was recorded in *Man* (1926) p. 25f. But two pioneers had taken a theoretical interest in the valley and we should not forget in this connection R. Dussaud, that great Frenchman, who in his *Topographie Historique de la Syrie Antique et Médiévale*, especially on p. 481, has a most interesting discussion on the source of the Balikh. Secondly, references to the Roman *limes* on the same river will be found in the comprehensive account written by Father A. Poidebard entitled, *La Trace de Rome dans le désert de Syrie*.

In my opinion however, one of the most interesting aspects of the mounds in this valley is the evidence that they can produce of the Romano-Byzantine occupation, very extensive evidence hitherto untested and we should remember the provocative opinion of Fr A. Poidebard who said that 'Toute politique d'avance en Mésopotamie, à partir de Trajan, visa à établir le limes au Habour. Toute politique de retrait le ramena au coude de l'Euphrate', a principle which is illustrated by the eastern campaigns of the emperors Trajan, Septimius Severus, and Julian and the temporary abandonment of the eastern front after Julian's death.

I should like to see some archaeologist who is interested in the Romano-Byzantine period investigating this district and giving us his conclusions on how the occupations of that period entered into the establishment of the wonderful *pax Romana* which endeavoured to follow the principle laid down in the dictum, *parcere subjectis et debellare superbos.*

We were lucky to extricate ourselves from the Balikh Valley towards the end of the year for the tracks in that district become impassable once the winter rains set in. However, fortune favoured us and we set forth from Tell Abyadh to Aleppo without mishap although in using one of the little-known tracks across the steppe we were hopelessly bogged down and, as it happened, on rather a hot day without too much water to spare. We were happy eventually to reach the bank of the Euphrates, ferry across on a rickety bark and to call in at our foreman's house in Carchemish at breakfast time altogether famished.

Although we had hoped for a frugal repast off a few flaps of bread, perhaps washed down with tea or coffee, our host, one of Hamoudi's sons, said that such a thing was unheard of, and refused to allow us to go until the family had prepared a sumptuous meal. That meant going out into the village, killing a sheep and preparing it. We were reluctant to disappoint them and to have refused to be entertained would have been churlish. After sitting for at least six hours an enormous meal was finally brought with a whole sheep stuffed and a mound of rice. By that time we were so far famished that we could hardly eat, but with loud protestations of gratitude and friendship to our generous hosts we eventually left on the 70-mile journey to Aleppo where we arrived in the evening in time to be entertained at the Baron's Hotel by the hospitable Koko, an Armenian whose proper name is Mazloumian, from whom I have received a Christmas card regularly ever since the early days when we met him some forty years ago.

Koko was *plus anglais que les anglais* and had served in the Air Force for a time. Koko Baron has always been most hospitable, especially to all visiting archaeologists who sojourn at Aleppo and we have good reason to be grateful to him for his generosity, his friendship and his kindness. A character who has weathered many storms. Koko was married to an English woman.

The other great character in Aleppo was our dear friend, Dr Ernest Altounyan, part Irish and part Armenian, who was married to the sister of the Oxford philosopher and historian, R. G. Collingwood. Ernest Altounyan's father was a remarkable old man, who became a brain surgeon of world renown. Brought up in his youth as a bottle-washer to some American missionaries in Marash, his natural brilliance attracted them to him and they sent him to be educated in Istanbul. Thence he graduated to Paris and thereafter founded the once-famous hospital in Aleppo which survived through his son. Alas it is no more. The old man would never attend patients unless they first crossed his palm with gold, and every man in Syria if he could, would find the coin in order to be attended by this man whom they believed to be a wizard and likely to be immortal. A very remarkable fellow who at the age of over ninety, married an English woman some sixty years younger and successfully operated on her for some tumour on the brain which no other surgeon dared touch.

PART II

The War
1939 - 1945

CHAPTER 10

London and Cairo

At the end of 1938 after our third, prolific, season at Brak, we had piled up a mass of information which had to be prepared for publication. It was therefore archaeologically fortunate that the time was not propitious for further digging. To the meanest intelligence it was obvious that we were drifting towards war, and in the summer of 1939, I declined an invitation to attend an archaeological Congress in Berlin for that reason: the Congress indeed came to a sudden end before its scheduled conclusion.

During this last year of peace I made good headway with writing and for this I am immeasurably indebted to the principles dinned into me by Leonard Woolley who year after year had inculcated the maxim that to dig without publishing is a heinous crime.

In preparing the written account of Brak and Chagar Bazar, I was favoured by fortune for Agatha, partly at my urging, had decided to sell Ashfield, the Torquay house in which she was born in order to buy Greenway, a Georgian house in an idyllic setting four and a half miles from Dartmouth, up the river Dart, on the left bank opposite Dittisham.

How well I remember listening in the kitchen there to the proclamation of war over the radio in September 1939 – the silly Mrs Bastin whose husband lived in our picturesque thatched ferry cottage on Galmpton Quay, wept into the vegetables, though she, of all people, was least likely to be affected.

During the first year we contrived to spend one glorious summer in the peace and calm of the phoney war, although momentous things were happening. At the evacuation of Dunkirk in 1940, the entire Belgian fishing fleet was anchored below the house for a time, a picturesque mass of rigging the like of which had not been seen in the Dart since Elizabethan days.

With us at the time was Dorothy North whose son Lord North, a lieutenant in the Royal Navy, lost his life when his ship was torpedoed at sea. Those were the days when Winston Churchill had the courage to proclaim to the nation: 'The news from France is very bad', an admission which gave us trust and confidence in him for the rest of the war. Whatever Winston's failings he was one of the giants, the personification of England's hearts of oak: his denigration comes from the mouths of small men by comparison and he remains of venerable memory.

Also associated with those early days at Greenway is the memory of 'Tanks' Chamberlayne, who sailed his own Brixham trawler and castigated his wife for lamenting the outbreak of war – 'at last,' he was reported to have said, 'the joyful day has arrived for us to get to grips with the Germans.' Tanks Chamberlayne I first knew as the commanding officer of No. 30 Squadron RAF in Mosul; he flew me over Nineveh and Arpachiyah when I wished to examine the ground from the air and so revealed to me that it was the northern end of the former mound that still yields high promise for a digger.

Gnawing at me was the desire to play my part in the war effort, but so unprepared were we that none of the services wished to make use of any of my qualifications, such as they were, least of all did they require any Oriental expertise. In 1940 I obtained some comic satisfaction by serving in the Brixham branch of the Home Guard.

So short of weapons were we that we had at first no more than two rifles for distribution between ten men, and how effective they would have been in case of invasion is doubtful, for one of our patrols was found supine and dead drunk on the road at 3 a.m. outside our guard hut at Windy Corner. When the red invasion alarm was in force and one of our yokel farmers was ordered to take up a point of vantage he exclaimed: 'No fear, my dear, I've got to go and milk kuh.'

Early in 1940, I found at last some scope for a more active life. Some time in the summer the town of Ercincan in eastern Turkey had practically been wiped out by an earthquake, and those of the inhabitants who survived found themselves destitute in the countryside. This country's reasons for coming to the rescue were both humanitarian and political: it was important for the British people to find favour in Turkish eyes because we desperately needed their supplies of chrome for which practically no other source was available at that time – this is an essential component of steel. But the ordinary man was genuinely moved to compassion, as he always is for suffering, when an appeal is made to him.

It happened that Professor Garstang, an archaeological friend, knew that I might respond to a call for help. He was a renowned friend of Turkey who had founded the British Institute of Archaeology at Ankara and he immediately set about forming an Anglo-Turkish Relief Committee with a powerful body of patrons of whom Lord Lloyd of Dolobran was President and Sir George Clerk, one-time Ambassador in Ankara was Chairman. I was invited to hold the office of Hon. Secretary and this I avidly accepted, though I had but a remote idea of what I might be letting myself in for.

Garstang had a splendid nose for scenting promising sources of aid, but little foresight of the sea of trouble which would threaten to submerge him. His first effort at securing a small back room in the Royal Institution, Albemarle Street, was ingenious, but rapidly led to that unfortunate office being hopelessly encumbered by our secretariat which soon occupied a big room on the ground floor.

Shortly after joining as Secretary I was asked by Lord Lloyd to prepare the outline of an appeal to the nation for gifts in money and in kind. We drew a grim picture of the sufferings of the Turkish people during their winter season, and I remember including for the broadcast, an extract from a letter which we had received from a poor woman in the suburbs: 'I have only two coats – I send you one.' The response to the appeal might be described as fantastic. The General Post Office found itself flooded-out with parcels which overflowed into the street and there was nowhere else to receive them.

Many amusing episodes were associated with the Anglo-Turkish Relief. Our Public Relations officer, a sportswriter and well-known journalist, provided some of them. He told the public about the howling of the wolves in the Turkish countryside and sent shivers down the spines of the ignorant. At the outset, Lord Lloyd decided to hold a big meeting in the Mansion House, attended by half a dozen ambassadors, and instructed me that this affair was not to be a flop.

In those days it was possible to fill a number of charabancs with impecunious gentlemen dressed in frock-coats, and for the sum of £1 a head, one could reckon on swelling an audience if necessary. We organized a reserve of this kind, and our journalist, Wentworth-Day, volunteered to recruit some attractive lady programme-sellers. This he did by enlisting the help of a bevy of ladies of easy virtue from Leicester Square. They were hastily ushered to the back rows by Esme Nicol who was always resourceful on such an occasion.

The meeting was an unqualified success, and I remember that Neville Henderson, our ambassador to Berlin, one of the High Table guests, then said, 'Only a fool would prophesy, but I venture to say that the war will not last for more than six months.' In spite of this prophecy, or perhaps because of it, our Anglo-Turkish Relief set off to a flying start and collected an enormous sum of money in cash, in kind, and in services.

At the end of a year our Fund was wound up and I believe that Lord Lloyd was not unappreciative of my services, for when I last saw him he offered to help me with anything I might desire. 'Just name it,' he said, 'and I will get it for you.' I told him that all I wanted was to get into the RAF. He looked astonished and asked me why. I said that it was the most go-ahead and therefore the most attractive of the three fighting arms and that because my father was Austrian born, and therefore an alien, it was proving difficult for me to get in. He made good his promise, all barriers fell before this powerful Cabinet Minister. Within a week I was accepted for the Intelligence branch of the RAF.

Only a week after that Lloyd succumbed to an attack of influenza followed by double pneumonia. I have an affectionate memory of the last of our great Proconsuls who would have fared better in an earlier age.

In the RAF a very different colleague was awaiting me: Squadron Leader, later Professor, S. K. R. Glanville, destined to be Provost of King's College, Cambridge, a man of talent and magnetism, perhaps the most lovable I have ever met. Glanville, or Stephen as I shall call him, had long been a friend of mine – ever since about 1925 when he joined the staff of the Department of Egyptian Antiquities in the British Museum.

Stephen now held the rank of Squadron Leader in a branch of the Air Ministry which became known as the Directorate of Allied and Foreign Liaison. As an old friend he knew that I would be a congenial colleague and thought that with my experience overseas I might be helpful to him in the difficult task of dealing with the allied Air Forces. There were many barriers to overcome, for the Royal Air Force was desperately short of equipment, and many of the regular officers had a strong prejudice against distributing any to foreigners who, as they thought, neither understood nor appreciated our methods of flying discipline and were therefore recalcitrant. Early on, however, the Czechs agreed that their squadron should be part of the RAF proper and were directly integrated within it. But even then we had difficulty in equipping. Fortunately, we discovered a laconic minute written by the Prime Minister. It said: 'Give the Czechs what they want.' This we used to invoke in case of dire need and the effect was instantaneous.

One of my tasks was to represent the Air Ministry on Lord Hankey's Committee which was concerned with co-ordinating the supply of equipment for our allies from all three of our fighting forces. To these meetings the Army and the Navy sent high-ranking officers, either some kind of general or admiral, but the aloof Air Force was content to be represented by a man of more lowly rank and Glanville, then only a Squadron Leader, should have undertaken that duty. The moment I joined the Air Ministry he delegated that task to me and I was truly terrified at having to serve in that high-ranking company. Lord Hankey sat at the top of a long table attended by every kind of civil as well as military expert and down at the bottom was I, an RAF officer with the lowest rank in the force.

I well remember my first experience and hearing Lord Hankey say: 'And what has the Air Force to say on the subject?' All eyes were riveted to the bottom of the table astonished to see that one with so few badges of rank was the only expert available. The question was the equipment of a squadron of Tomahawks, American fighter aircraft passed on by us to the Russians, and the nature of the armament to go with them. My briefing had not been thorough and although I had mugged up the subject as best I could, I felt woefully at sea and was helped out by some kindly general. I could give no very good account of myself to Stephen Glanville on my return, and was therefore not a little surprised when the kindly Lord Hankey, overladen with work, none the less wrote a letter to my branch to say that the RAF had been very adequately represented by its officer. Such generous consideration both touched and astonished me.

My first year at the Air Ministry, 1942, was eventful, exciting and often amusing. Agatha and I lived at Lawn Road Flats in Hampstead at the time and I often had to get home as best I could through the early bombing of London. I remember walking down the Strand during a severe air raid when bombs were raining down and many buildings were on fire. It was astonishing to see a complacent policeman sheltering in the porch of a shop between two plate-glass windows. No one was taking the raids seriously yet, and the following morning as I returned to work, the road was littered with debris including large quantities of paper from a wrecked bank, but I noticed that they were mostly concerned with income tax returns – never a sign of a banknote. There was some astonishment when I reached my office, for a pessimistic colleague had reported that I had walked straight into a rain of bombs and must have been killed. This was not my first experience of being reported dead and turning up alive.

At the end of twelve months our Directorate was asked for two officers to go to the Middle East in order to set up a corresponding branch of the Directorate of Allied and Foreign Liaison in Cairo. Two of us approached by Glanville immediately volunteered to do so, for we were anxious to get nearer to the scene of war and to see our allies in action in North Africa. I was then promoted to the rank of Squadron Leader and posted to Cairo where I was to join the Headquarters of the RAF in the Middle East. However before taking leave for service elsewhere, I must salute the man whom I was leaving, Stephen Glanville.

His career was typical of the man, for although he never gave himself the time to achieve any profound scholarship and had at the University a poor record of academic achievement he was without question awarded the Petrie Chair of Egyptology at University College, London and held the post with distinction. His interests were too wide to allow him to make a reputation as a specialist in any branch of his subject and in truth he was far more interested in humanity and the humanities than in Egyptology. When he saw a friend, Miss Pugh, writing a book on optics he had to rewrite it for her. He was the only man ever to have persuaded Agatha to alter the end of a book, against – as she maintains – her better judgement. Her own ending would have been more dramatic. It was the one that was concerned with Ancient

Egypt, *Death Comes as the End*. He savoured life to the full and was ready for any new experience whether at a séance with a medium, or digging in Egypt.

He was not without his enemies, and had little use for those that would not go along with him but, from beginning to end, he put his life to the service of his friends. He never recoiled from immersing himself in other people's difficulties; in his readiness to interfere in matrimonial troubles he frequently found himself wholly in sympathy with two antagonistic parties, each of which had placed the utmost confidence in him.

After only four or five years of office as a Fellow at King's College, Cambridge, in spite of his unsatisfactory career as an undergraduate, he was the unanimous choice for the office of Provost and when he died, the whole College from Senior Fellows down to the humblest bed-makers went into mourning.

My new assignment in Cairo was to maintain effective liaison with the Free French, Czech and Polish Air Force contingents. Among these it was the Polish Air Force that commanded my unstinted admiration. The efficiency and valiance of their squadron was second to none in the RAF. In the Battle of Britain their presence had been crucial and it was indeed for us a crowning mercy that trained Polish airmen had fought their way from their homeland to this country in the belief that we were at that time the last hope for a free Europe. If Britain had lost in 1940 that vital battle of the skies then Britain itself would have succumbed to Hitler's régime. Let it never be forgotten that one in twelve of the pilots in that epic battle was Polish.

Many of these men were the salt of the earth and their discipline was formidable. One of my friends, a Polish Flight-Lieutenant, one day said to me: 'I want you to take twenty-four hours' leave tomorrow in order to come to dinner with me.' On asking why I could not come to dinner without taking leave, he explained that every member of the party would be dead drunk at the end of the dinner and that a partici-pant who reported for duty not yet fully sober would be liable to court-martial and execution. Indeed at Dartmouth where a drunken posse of Polish seamen surrounded the Police Station it was said that on the morrow there was more than one funeral at sea. I have, it is true, drunk nothing better than the home-made vodka which the Poles used to provide for these occasions; and I soon learned never to go out to a Polish dinner without having a substantial meal first. The same Polish officer who invited me to these entertainments on taking leave of me said: 'You have been a good friend to me and I wish to reward you with some advice. When you go to prison, be sure to see that it is in Manchester Gaol. The food there is better than at any other prison in England.' My remarks about the Poles are in jest and illustrate only the merry side of them. But I repeat that many were the salt of the earth. Sensitive, one had to be very careful not to give offence intentional or unintentional; hard-working and tough, one could not have wished for more merry and delightful friends. I heard of a Polish tram-driver from Warsaw who, although 60, contrived to have himself accepted as a Ferry Pilot across North Africa, and never a minute was wasted on the turn round. These were dedicated men: I believe that after the war between half a million and a million of them were given British nationality for their services to the Crown. Never has there been a better leaven in the bread of this country. Whenever I meet a Pole my heart goes out towards him.

One is bound to ask the question, how much did our allies the Poles, the Czechs, the Free French and the Greeks contribute to the scale of our war effort and whether this aid was equal to their sacrifices and ours. It is obvious that measured against the size of our Air Force their squadrons were few and but a small fraction of the whole, but their support was invaluable beyond measure. They came to our aid, one and all, in our darkest hour when most people except ourselves believed that we, totally unprepared for war, would succumb to the threatened tyranny of Nazism and Germany under Hitler. These friends therefore came to us as a beacon of light and the stimulus to our morale was incalculable. Moreover to other countries they were proof that the struggle against the enemy continued from many directions, and that the occupied countries were not altogether vanquished. We owe a great debt of gratitude to all these men who for various reasons, some patriotic, some personal, made their momentous decisions in time of dire stress for them and for us.

Operationally, although it may be invidious to say so, the Poles played the greatest part, for not only were they numerically considerable but their skill and courage made them the right arm of our

Air Force, and both in Europe and in the Middle East they gave themselves unremittingly to our cause.

In Cairo I first lived at the Continental Hotel and later I shared a house with my brother Cecil. We finally rented a house directly overlooking the Nile, opposite the Gazirah Sporting Club, where we could watch Walter Hammond playing cricket.

Meeting my brother was indeed a coincidence, for on my first day in Cairo I found him at the Continental Hotel, sitting on the terrace and sipping a cup of coffee. He had volunteered in 1940 to fight in Finland against the Russian invasion, and when that gallant country surrendered and shortly afterwards perforce became allied to Germany, he was taken prisoner by the Finns who, however, through Field-Marshal Mannerheim behaved impeccably to the foreign volunteers. After a short spell of work for the British Council he was evacuated to Sweden and set to work as a lumberjack in the forests. After some months our Minister in Helsinki, Gordon Vereker, succeeded in negotiating an exchange agreement with the Finns who were repatriated, while the British volunteers then in Sweden were sent home to England. Incidentally it was said that Vereker received an official reprimand from the Finns because he was overheard singing the 'Volga Boat Song' while rowing on a Finnish lake. He was asked if the singing during the war of 'Deutschland über Alles' by a foreigner on the river Thames would not have caused a corresponding feeling of resentment.

Cecil was repatriated together with the rest of the volunteers after an eventful journey by train through France and Germany, travelling for two days and two nights. He had the experience, unusual for an Englishman, of witnessing a night raid by the RAF on Hamburg and after a further six months of sojourn in neutral Portugal reached England, whence he was dispatched by the British Council to Egypt as a director of its Institutes in Mansurah, Mahallah and Minya. Meeting him in this way was a fortunate encounter. Cecil was always the most amiable of men; naturally sociable he settled down happily wherever he served. After the war he married Dolores Kavaleff, a Finnish girl, who had befriended him in Helsinki. He had two sons by her, John, now a 'pollution scientist' and Peter, a solicitor, both of them married and faring well.

In Cairo I had two amusing experiences of the way 'Intelligence' works. In the Continental Hotel I learned from a waiter of the disastrous fall of Tobruk within a few hours of the event before the news had officially reached HQ, RAFME. On another occasion I was informed while standing in a tram next to the driver that Winston Churchill had been seen smoking a cigar in Cairo. At luncheon I met my friend Eiddon Edwards the Egyptologist who was then serving in the British Embassy and asked him whether there was any truth in this rumour. He looked at me with astonishment and suggested that I should disbelieve it. Later I discovered that on that very morning the staff of the Embassy had been called together and pledged to the strictest secrecy on a matter already known to the Cairo tramways.

I have come to the conclusion that during the war not a single secret was ever kept for long, but as so much false and misleading intelligence was in circulation, the enemy usually failed to recognize the truth when it filtered through to him. Nowhere was this better exemplified than by the invasion of Normandy, for the Germans, though aware of the proposed, timing could never believe that we would make the effective strike on such improbable beach-heads.

In 1943, after a year's service in HQ, RAFME, I volunteered as a civil affairs officer in Tripolitania where they were short of persons with a knowledge of the Arab world. I was glad to leave the hot and dusty city of Cairo though life there had been interesting.

After an interview with OETA (Occupied Enemy Territory Administration) I left Cairo in the early summer for Tripoli, Tripolitania, and was told to make my way there as best I could, first by train to Daba which was then the railroad terminus, and then by air where a Transport officer told me I should find an aeroplane awaiting me. He had, like many such officers, kissed the Blarney Stone. As usual, I had been sent off at a moment's notice without mess-kit or rations, but I ate the most delicious stews which had been cooked by Italian prisoners of war at desert railway stations, and kind travelling companions were ever ready to lend me feeding receptacles. How fussy one becomes in one's old age and how pleasant to recall that there was a time when one heeded the adage – 'take neither scrip nor staff and take no heed for the morrow'.

My journey into Tripolitania proved easy enough. Somewhere off

Daba I found a ship carrying war equipment into Tripoli. It was an old ship which had served in peace-time as a carrier for frozen meat from Vancouver and, as I found myself the senior officer on it I had to persuade the captain to feed all the military personnel thereon, for the crew would not part with their rations. German submarines were active in the Mediterranean at the time and a part of the convoy was sunk; perhaps this was the source of the rumour that I had been drowned in a submarine, as a colleague informed me after the war when to his astonishment I appeared in the flesh.

CHAPTER II

Tripolitania

Arrived in Tripoli, I was sent to comfortable quarters in the Waddan Hotel which Rommel had evacuated a day or two earlier. On the first night I had the pleasure of eating a tolerable dinner to the accompaniment in the gallery of a small civilian orchestra which had played for the Germans a few nights before. Hardly had I finished dinner before a heavy German bombardment attacked our shipping on the sea front and began hitting buildings. Some of my companions expressed alarm and sought the air-raid shelter in the basement, but I, accustomed to air raids over London, assured them that this was nothing and that I proposed to keep to my bed above ground. My confidence was misplaced, for a bomb made a direct hit on the mosque next door and we had to work half the night trying to excavate the men who had been trapped there. This task was not made easier by the assistance of some drunken sailors with whom we had a difficult tug-of-war.

From Tripoli my first assignment was to serve as assistant to Colonel H. C. E. Routh, the senior civil affairs officer in 'Western Province' which extended from Zavia to Zuara near the Tunisian frontier.

The headquarters of the Province were at Sabratha, an ancient Phoenician foundation overlooking the sea, rich in Roman ruins, temples, baths, houses and endowed with a superb theatre which had been restored by the Italians and used for performing classical plays. Some kindly guardian angel must have directed me to this heavenly spot where in the cool of the evening I perused the memorial inscriptions or visited the little Museum with its beautiful peacock mosaic and browsed in the library well stocked with the classics and books on history and archaeology.

This city had been the birthplace of the Emperor Septimius Severus; called to command the Empire when on campaign in Hungary, he died in York. I could hardly have imagined a spot more romantic or replete with memories affecting one who had come from England. As always the Italians had laid out the Museum and its precincts with delicate aesthetic taste; one was greeted by a carpet of mesembryanthemum which allayed the sand and when in bloom was transformed into a brilliant blue lawn.

We lived in the Italian villa with a tiled courtyard and patio over-looking the sea which washed its walls. In peace-time this had been the residence of a Sicilian prince named Paterno who owned the Tunny Fish factory hard by. On occasions we went out to sea with the great tunny fish nets and watched the poor victims entrapped in their death chamber; but the tunny together with local olives made a welcome change after our eternal ration of bully beef.

Our most interesting task was the allocation of grain rations to the inhabitants of our needy province and this distribution Routh managed skilfully. He sent me out on the first grain survey of the hinterland named the Gefara behind Zuara and I have rarely been given a more interesting assignment, although it was one for which I had no previous experience. But with the advice of a charming and intelli-gent little man, Miftah El Argheib, the Mudir of Sorman, I believe I made a satisfactory job of it.

Our plan was to drive out in a motor car as far south as we could go before getting stuck in the sand. We then mounted horses which had been sent out in advance and were ready to meet us together with two camels bearing great demijohns of Italian Chianti and a tent for cover against the scorching mid-day heat. We also had with us a commission of four men, assessors for the barley, a taxation expert and some local officials: this was harvest time and our task was to estimate for the British Military Administration the expected yield. The owners of all the plots, some hundreds of them, had been warned to be present in person or to send a representative to collect the tax assessment ticket.

As we approached each plot the owner was asked to make his assess-ment, invariably too low, the assessors to make theirs which tended to be too high. The Mudir of Sorman and myself then had to decide on what we deemed to be a fair figure. Among the party was an old man of long experience who, as I soon discovered, was head and shoulders above anyone else in judging the true yield. His figures were invariably near the mark, for he was both expert and honest. How did I discover this? By arranging for a party of reapers to cut the barley at any plot which I selected for a snap check. We reaped, threshed and weighed the corn and over a period of the day assessed in this way a large number of fields and gave estimates for hundreds of others in the Gefara.

My old man, the wizard of the party, could also assess losses due to rust with incredible skill. He would walk round and through a field running his fingers through the ears of corn in the course of his tests and would then make the necessary allowances. I soon found out that the crop owners were apt to distribute their plots far and wide, both as an insurance against local failures, and to make assessment more difficult. But through the methods I have described we minimized the opportunities for bribery and falsification of assessments, for no one on the commission knew when or where we would make the next snap check. In this way our motley cavalcade did a good job for the administration at its first harvest.

I noticed at the time an interesting phenomenon, namely that the sanding up of the big agricultural plain known as the Gefara was making headway and discovered that the Italians some years back had substituted the steel ploughshare for the old wooden ones which being less efficient cutting instruments saved from destruction much of the natural scrub which had allayed and arrested the encroachment of the sand.

My six months of happy initiation into Tripolitania at Sabratha was terminated on the instructions of the Chief Military Administrator, Brigadier Maurice Lush who wished me to take charge of an outpost in the Eastern Province at a lonely oasis named Hon, more properly spelled Hun, on the edge of the Fezzan, which backed on the Sahara and had been administered by the Italians from a 'beau geste' fort with an enormous garrison consisting of some thousands of men. Our administration took pride in the fact that the presence of one British officer was all that was required to keep order.

My transfer from the Western to the Eastern Province required a pleasant journey through Tripoli and Hon when I paid one of many visits to the wonderful Antonine city of Leptis or Lepcis Magna. A straight paved road runs from the north end of the site to the sea over a distance of nearly a mile, flanked by imposing columned buildings and inscriptions dedicated to the city by its Berber benefactors. In one of the shops there was a Roman tailor's measure; elsewhere there was an imposing fish-market; another amusing relic was an open-air clubman's lavatory, matching the one at Sabratha, where the citizens enjoyed their morning's gossip while performing their motions. In March as we passed the remains of two architraves adorned with a pair of winged angels we saw a superb vista running down the main street, a cascade of white broom pouring down into it like a waterfall from either side. At the far end was the mole of a majestic harbour, and on the quays some of the bollards were still intact.

Not far from Lepcis was Zliten, a beautiful Roman town shaded by trellised vines, where the Italians discovered a mosaic pavement illustrating the trapping of wild beasts and a gladiator fight, in which a man with a net, the *retiarius*, was in combat with an opposing swordsman.

In Misurata, the headquarters of the Province, I called on the officer in charge and then turned south in my truck through a desert and rock-laden country for the oasis of Hon.

The two-hundred-and-fifty-mile journey was tricky because one had to thread one's way through a minefield the sides of which were indicated by a stretch of rusty barbed wire on the ground. But I came to know the route well and on one occasion volunteered to lead a convoy through it at night.

Hon itself was riddled with mines by the Italians before their evacuation and living there was something of a hazard which on one occasion I turned to advantage. Headquarters in Tripoli sent me a signal enquiring about the state of the airfield as some high-ranking officer wished to pay me a visit, doubtless suitably accompanied by his staff, but I was not at all anxious to be disturbed in my abode which I ran with a minimum of interference. I therefore cabled in reply: 'Hon airfield mined on three sides, cemetery on fourth' – a statement not far from the truth. I heard no more of the would-be intruder.

The town had been prettily arranged; it was a small and compact oasis and my house and headquarters stood at the Fezzan end of a long avenue flanked by oleanders. I lived solitary and happily there, unguarded, until some officer in Tripoli without consulting me decided that I needed a posse of police for protection. On the first night a young Tripolitanian policeman was posted in the avenue not far from my office and enjoined to exercise the utmost vigilance. When I unexpectedly appeared from my office he fired point-blank at me at a distance of twenty yards but fortunately was a poor marksman and the bullet whistled harmlessly over my shoulder.

Hon was situated in the middle of two oases, Socna, fourteen miles to the west, and Waddan the same distance to the east. Waddan was an ancient Berber fortress, and had a fine upstanding castle where many years previously some heavy Tuareg gold jewellery had been excavated.

The inhabitants of Hon and Waddan were pleasant enough to deal with and caused me little trouble, but it was the men of Socna whom I found most endearing. Oddly enough though Waddan and Socna were as I have said no more than twenty-eight miles apart the inhabitants had not exchanged visits for ten years. This extraordinary lack of contact between two places that were the first inhabited spots 250 miles from the coast was due to a long standing blood feud. It appears that under the Italian régime a dozen men of Hon had been tried and executed for conspiracy, and rightly or wrongly the men of Socna had been blamed as informers. Ever since that time communication between the two oases had ceased.

During the whole of my stay in Hon there was one dramatic event that took precedence over all else. This was the result of a dispute over wells between two tribes with adjacent grazing grounds, the Megarha, about eight-thousand strong further to the west and the Awlad Sulaiman, a much smaller tribe, kinsfolk of the men of Socna. This dispute over water rights had lasted for at least two decades before we entered Tripolitania and was after many reversals of judgement due to be referred to the High Court in Rome. I was rash and inexperienced enough to believe that I could settle the matter with the collaboration of the French authorities who administered an adjacent territory over which the Megarha ranged, while the Awlad Sulaiman ranged over ground administered by the British. It seemed to me that if the two tribes were to be made to see that British and French were in full accord over a matter which concerned both administrations and the tribes, then these two warring factions would accept our judgement over the precious well-water which had in so far as possible to be fairly shared.

I therefore spent many weeks planning to assemble in Hon a conclave of the responsible tribal sheikhs of all the tribes and inducing them to come to a court presided over by myself and the French officer in

an oasis frequented by the Megarha. My French colleague was a young
and rather demoralized lieutenant who had been to his mind living in
exile in a god-forsaken and remote spot where life was only made
tolerable by cohabitation with a native woman. But I had impressed
on him the importance of getting this long-standing feud settled once
and for all and he was appointed as the responsible agent by his Colonel,
an admirable and co-operative man whose name I have forgotten.

Over the course of several days the tribesmen trickled into Hon, and
they brought with them about a hundred camels. When all the
responsible parties had arrived I called them together and gave them
two or three days in which to debate the matter between themselves
and come to an acceptable conclusion. I said that when this had been
done they were to come to me and that the French officer and myself
would put our seals to the treaty which would then be officially ratified.
Finally I added that if they failed to agree, the French officer and myself
would dictate the terms and arrange the allocation of the wells and
access to them, but I warned them that our solution, an imposed
solution from outside authority although less congenial, would be final.

For three days they debated in the hot assembly-room but came
nowhere near a solution. Towards the end of the third day rumour
reached me that the larger tribe, the Megarha, were about to flee from
Hon in order to escape my judgement. I therefore impounded all their
camels and in this way their escape was cut off, for they were tied to
their valuable beasts.

At this stage my anxiety over the proceedings was increased by the
fact that my French colleague had not arrived and this seemed to me
to be a grievous setback, for the success of the operation depended on a
demonstration of Anglo-French harmony.

But after I had given up hope, at the twelfth hour, my lackadaisical
colleague turned up and I immediately showed him my plan for the
distribution of the precious water and access to the wells, some to the
Megarha, some to the Awlad Sulaiman, some to be shared jointly. The
young Frenchman was intelligent and had a good grasp of the situation,
but his attitude was thoroughly cynical, and might have been summed
up by the expression *je m'en fiche* – I don't care a damn. He said that he
was prepared to sign jointly with me in the presence of the assembled
tribes on the next day.

The court house was full, and after the two head sheikhs of both parties had expressed their inability to agree, I called on my interpreter to read out the Anglo-French resolution. When that had been done the head man of the Megarha immediately resigned his office, because he maintained that he could not go back to his tribe as a party to this verdict. 'Resignation not accepted,' I said; 'you will be held responsible for observing and enforcing the prescription of this edict.'

I gave it out, again with the assent of the Frenchman, that the Megarha who objected to the judgement would have the right of lodging an appeal to the Chief Administrator in Tripoli, Brigadier Lush, and that his yea or nay would be final. In arriving at what was deemed a fair solution I had consulted three or four independent grey-beards between Hon and Misurata, and when my predecessor, Pickard Cambridge, who by that time had moved to Megarha territory, objected to my decision as biased, I was able to sustain my conclusion by evidence of this independent support.

The head sheikh of the Awlad Sulaiman, the smaller tribe, always liable to be bullied by the numerically stronger Megarha, when he had grasped the terms, declared me a friend for all time and was saddened when I explained that I could accept no present, not even the offering of a sheep. Oddly enough the dialect spoken by his tribe was one that I had no difficulty in understanding although the mixed Arabic of Tripolitania was strange to me, and I wondered why I was so easily able to converse with his tribesmen. After enquiring, I discovered that his tribe had, two or three hundred years previously, migrated from the Najd and spoke a brand of Arabic to which I had been well accustomed at Ur where many of our men were closely related to the Najdis. The tribesmen's Arabic is conserved by the womenfolk who bring up the young in the harem for the first four or five years and inject them with their traditional way of speech. In this way tribal dialects are preserved against later contamination.

Within thirty days of the trial our joint Anglo-French verdict was confirmed by Brigadier Lush in Tripoli and I received official congratulations, but whether they were justified or not I would not like to say, for I have no idea how long the edict was followed or what the position is today. The fact is that Arab tribesmen detest any official settlement of land and water disputes and much prefer such quarrels to remain in a state of flux.

But in the end I became friends even with the sheikh of the Megarha to whom I had caused so much grievous offence, for several months later when I had been promoted to the office of Adviser on Arab Affairs in Tripoli he paid me a visit and asked me to change a large amount of obsolete Italian currency into the new denominations issued by the British Military régime. Although long past the date-line I persuaded our finance officer to change the money, and took my Megarha sheikh to the top of a long queue in order to so do. He was duly impressed and never again made trouble for us.

During his visit I took a lift in an aeroplane to inspect the disputed wells and after detaining him for a morning in Tripoli was able to declare that I was satisfied and had noticed no breach of the water rights. Those were the latter days of the old British *imperium* when our writ was still respected.

After about a year I was posted away from Hon and left it with regret, for I had made many friends there but the life was solitary and one felt cut off from communication in one's own language. But I had the satisfaction of handing over my command to a friend, Captain Franklin Gardner, a man most sympathetic to the Arabs. No doubt owing to Franklin's persuasion the principal square in Hon was named after me – Maidan Milwan – soon to be obliterated under a less sympathetic régime.

Since my time Hon has been endangered by the threat of finding oil, but fortunately perhaps, trials revealed that drilling would not be profitable and the only source worthwhile exploiting was in the neighbourhood of Sebha within the Fezzan, from which arrangements were made for pumping the oil to the coast. But inevitably the enrichment of Libya which has come after intensive drilling has had its effect on the once unsophisticated denizens of Hon, Socna and Waddan who have been caught up in the drift of population to the larger cities on the coast, and are now I am told relatively deserted. *Aurum irrepertum sic melius situm* (oil unpumped so better placed) is what Horace would have said today.

After leaving Hon in 1943, I was temporarily posted to the coastal town of Misurata to take the place of Colonel C. C. Oulton then on leave. The comparative urbanity of Misurata made a refreshing change after the austerities of Hon, but I found that the paperwork involved in a larger and more complex administration hard to bear. I remember particularly one poignant incident. Lord Gowrie, one-time Governor-General of Australia, had lost his son in action and the boy was buried in the military cemetery on the coast a mile or two from Misurata overlooking the sea. The father had expressed a wish to have a photograph of his son's grave, and a corporal was dispatched from Tripoli to do this. Unfortunately he discovered that many of the wooden crosses which marked the graves had been removed and reported to Tripoli that the graves had been desecrated and the matter reached the ears of Field-Marshal Jumbo Wilson, then C-in-C in Cairo who ordered that instant and punitive action be taken and asked for a report within forty-eight hours. Brigadier Travers Blackley was then in command in Tripoli and I was summarily told to investigate at once and to demonstrate that I had taken effective and proper action.

On visiting the cemetery I discovered that some wooden crosses had indeed been removed, but I could not detect signs of anything amounting to desecration. The fact was that the tribes who roamed the district were desperately short of firewood, every stick of which had been removed by the various army divisions that had camped in the district on their way to join battle or returning from it, including the Fifth Indian Division. This was not surprising for they had been in action in the bitter cold and were often short of fuel for the night. But to make good their deficiencies they even removed every wooden door of the abandoned houses and had cut down every tree. The unfortunate tribesmen had therefore been left destitute of combustible material and I believe that in removing the crosses they were unaware of what they were doing, for they had no reason to be familiar with the practice of Christian burial.

However, it was clear to me that the crime such as it was must be expurgated by the local tribesmen, and I ascertained that this part of Misurata district had been a grazing ground for two particular camel-owning tribes, whose sheikhs I summoned to my office.

We held a solemn conclave of the sheikhs attended by six British officers – all that I could muster at the time – and in the presence of a distinguished Libyan, Sadiq Muntasser, who was our adviser and incidentally many years later served as Libyan Ambassador in Washington, I delivered a solemn address. 'You must learn,' I said, 'that the brave son of one of England's distinguished men has fallen in battle and is buried in a military cemetery by the sea on the edge of Misurata. The dead man's cross and other crosses have been removed, certainly by your camel drivers, and you will be aware that the Koran, under the edict of your own Prophet condemns the desecration of all tombs.' This brought a loud murmur of assent. 'I therefore declare solemnly in the presence of all these officers, that you yourselves will be surety against anything of the kind happening in this district again, and that your two tribes will pay into my hands a collective fine of one million liras within seven days, otherwise I shall take severe punitive action.' They left my office ceremoniously chastened.

While I sat back to await events the authorities in Tripoli telephoned to discover what action I had taken and on hearing of it were inclined to panic. 'What will you do if they don't bring in the money?' 'I have thought of that,' I said, 'and nothing could be simpler. Meat is now so rare and expensive in the district that a single camel is worth half a million liras, and I will drive out to the tribes and impound two of them.' That action was not called for. Within four days, a million liras mostly in filthy notes was brought into the office and we spent several more days in counting them. I built a safe in the wall and sealed up the lot. After six months had elapsed and no further incidents had occurred I gave the money back. I discovered later that the tribal chiefs who had never heard of a collective fine came to the conclusion that this was a most practical method of raising money and with some difficulty I had to restrain them from doing the same thing on their own behalf.

After some months in Misurata I was promoted to be Adviser on Arab Affairs in Tripolitania, in order to succeed Major Kennedy Shaw, formerly of the Long Range Desert Group, who after some five years' service overseas was at last being posted home. I thus spent a year among the higher echelons of the administration and was eventually appointed Deputy Chief Secretary with the rank of Wing Commander.

Although the work which I did in Tripoli gave me an overall view of the country as a whole I found it less agreeable than administering the provinces in a humbler capacity because I was no longer in touch with the nomads, small landowners, peasants, and the unsophisticated characters of the countryside. At first, when the British were new-comers there was a honeymoon period during which we were hailed as liberators after the expulsion of the hated Italian 'imperialists' who, since 1911, after they had driven out the Ottoman Turks had been in charge of the country.

In judging our predecessors it is not easy to come to a fair verdict. The Italians had done much for the country in establishing an orderly régime, in the development of Tripoli and other smaller cities, in pro-moting trade in this relatively unprofitable part of Africa where oil had not yet been discovered and the economy showed little prospect of radical improvement. With this in mind they had devoted their energies to the encouragement of farming and had sunk artesian wells. They had multiplied orchards and had increased the production of olive oil, had attended to the palmeries and prevented the decimation of the trees by regulating the control of leghbi, an alcoholic drink which em-anated from the fermentation of palm sap the collection of which was apt to kill the trees.

In the coastal areas they had organized two kinds of farms, one under the ownership of capable Italian private farmers, the other State developed, by name *ente*, which were much less successful. Among the *ente* farms there were smallholdings which Mussolini had made over to the riff-raff whom he wished to get out of the Motherland. Many of these allocations failed and were soon abandoned, the empty houses and waste land was a memorial to the failure of the scheme.

To the credit of the Italian Administration was the establishment of a legal system based on the Italian code of law, administered by Italian judges. The courts were fairly run, but there appears to have been little or no attempt to amalgamate a code ultimately based on Roman law with any tribal or African system appropriate to the country or to attempt a compromise between the two. On the other hand the most serious criticism of the thirty-year period of Italian régime is that virtually no attempt was made to establish any kind of native authority.

One notable achievement of the Italian régime was the care and maintenance of the ancient cities and monuments, notably Lepcis Magna, Tripoli and Sabratha as well as some useful excavations which have led the way to further intensive research. But above all the credit must be given to them for their artistic sense in the display of Lepcis and Sabratha where they took full advantage of the natural setting.

The last and not least onerous task which I was given before my term of office in Tripoli came to an end, was the revision of the entire pay structure of the Arab and Berber officials including the courts and the kadis. This I completed in the space of less than three months aided by a young finance officer whose name I recall as Puddefoot. He was a man of sound judgement and good at figures: my part was to see that invidious awards were avoided, that the senior officers in each province were consulted, that a proper respect for the dignity of office was maintained and that all wage-changes were based on a fair and reasoned calculation. A rise in wages had long been overdue and there would have been trouble, indeed serious trouble, if the Administration had not perceived that remedies had to be applied quickly. Threatened riots were thus avoided and the knowledge that reforms were in hand kept would-be troublemakers quiet. We toured some of the provinces in the course of our fact-finding mission and my previous service in many places outside Tripoli was helpful.

In revising the pay scales for the country, while we took account of local and public opinion, all officials were assessed according to grade, wherever they served, regardless of the higher cost of living in the more populous centres. There was much to be weighed in the balance, but our task was happily concluded at the cost of a modest increase which today would have been greeted with howls of indignation; by and large the Arab employees were highly gratified by the awards.

While serving for a short period as Chief Civil Affairs Officer in Suq el Juma'a I had the satisfaction of helping the break-up of what had been intended as a massive march on Tripoli. Before the instigators had time to organize themselves, and through judicious application of some mild police pressure the mob was prevented from assembling and this we achieved without making a single arrest.

During my time of service at Suq el Juma'a I was also instrumental in saving Tripoli from a much more serious threat when a case of the plague was reported in a particular house which I immediately went to investigate. This was a spacious and indescribably filthy mud-brick dwelling near the centre of the city: to scotch the trouble the entire house including bedding and furniture had to be burnt, and the inmates isolated for a time. These immediate steps were drastic, but no further case of the plague occurred as might well have otherwise happened in a big market-town where thousands congregated in the centre every Friday.

At last the time came for my return home after three years' service overseas. I was tired and could hardly wait for the day.

I flew out of the airport of Castel Benito, a delicious exit in contrast to my bitter entry through the vast Cyrenaican transit camp at El Adem where the water was undrinkable. We touched down in Sicily at the then devastated, decrepit and shabby city of Palermo where inaccurate American bombing had damaged many a church. In RAF uniform we were not greeted with enthusiasm. Landfall in England was at Swindon. It was in the merry month of May and the first sight that greeted me was that of the lofty horsechestnuts with their upright, sprightly candles of flower welcoming the home-comer, and at last a clouded sky; how I had longed for a cloud after the eternal blue of the Libyan heavens. It was a home-coming never to be forgotten and I was reminded of Heine's poem to which I regularly turn at this time of year:

> Im wunderschönen Monat Mai,
> Als alle Knospen sprangen,
> Da ist in meinem Herzen
> Die Liebe aufgegangen.

Staggering under the weight of my kit and helped by a kindly wayfarer, I arrived at our war-time lodgings in Lawn Road Flats, Hampstead, where miraculously Agatha, who was not expecting me, had returned from a visit to Rosalind in Wales, only a few minutes earlier. There we were reunited after our long and hard separation. Agatha, chased by flying-bombs and working as a dispenser in University College Hospital, London, had, it seemed to me, seen harder war service than I. God had been kind to us both and we experienced the matchless joy of being reunited again.

There is little enough to say about the last six months of my war service until I was demobilized in 1945. I served out my time with the Air Ministry under the command of an Air Commodore, a man whom I did not find 'sympathique'; his brains and his address did not, as it seemed to me, match his courage. There were some charming Waafs in that establishment, a Flight-Officer Alison Walters with whom unfortunately I have lost touch and a little administrative officer who when ordered by the Air Commodore to cough up some hundreds of clothing coupons to a distinguished foreign visiting officer flatly refused – to her eternal credit; she was of the lowest rank possible, unmoved by the wrath of her mighty superior.

On demobilization I was presented at Uxbridge with a civilian suit of excellent quality, a reward which I received with gratitude.

PART III

Agatha
1930 - 1975

CHAPTER 12

Agatha: The Person

After I had been demobilized I set to work once more on my book about Brak and Chagar Bazar which I had only half-completed on the outbreak of war. As before I did much of the writing at Greenway, in Devon.

The white house stands on a little plateau overlooking the river, against a foreground of steep, grassy banks and a backcloth of dark conifers. The mild climate has made it a haven for magnolias and rhododendrons; great oak trees mask the house from the river, not far from it is a walled camellia garden with one cork oak, the *quercus suber* and the drive is flanked by beech trees 150 years old on the one side, by eucryphias, magnolias, rhododendrons and azaleas on the other. Not more than about thirty-five acres in all, few visitors have failed to be moved by this little paradise.

Agatha, with her genius for decorating houses, had made it a thing of beauty. In recalling the happy days we spent there I must say something about our family life and devote a few chapters to Agatha as a person and to her career as a writer.

As a person she had a quality of elusiveness which stemmed from her earliest days – a defensive resistance to inquisitive probing, an inbuilt armour off which any questionnaire was liable to glance like a spent arrow. And yet she has been more generous than most writers in self-revelation; for she has written extensive memoirs, still unpublished and a novel under the name of Mary Westmacott, entitled *Unfinished Portrait* (1934), where we see many intimate flashes from earliest childhood till the beginnings of middle age. The book is not one of her best because, exceptionally, it is a blend of real people and events with imagination. Only the initiated can know how much actual history is contained therein, but in Celia we have more nearly than anywhere else a portrait of Agatha.

From the beginning Agatha was wrapped in the love of two devoted parents and nurtured by a mother of exceptional imagination which acted on her as a catalyst. Her home was a cosy nest which included an old nannie who expounded the most regal standards of morality and conventional beliefs which were sometimes difficult to reconcile with the ways of the world.

In *Unfinished Portrait* the child is named as Celia and we have a rare opportunity of taking peeps into her early happiness – the canvas of her youth which was a mixture of reality and dreamland. Part of reality was the huge, monumental cook who produced delicious treacle tit-bits, interspersed with her self-taught spelling lessons. Her mother had a prejudice against children being taught to read too early, not before the age of six, but Agatha had found the way on her own by the age of five and learned reading by sight rather than by spelling out the words. 'Please Nannie, is this word "greedy" or "selfish", I can't remember.' Spelling never came easily but Agatha broke into a new world of fairies, hobgoblins, trolls – real life was of a lesser interest. Very soon she was living in a world of fantasy peopled by her own creation, and there was a secretive element which greatly stimulated and elated her in this quest. It is revealing that on one occasion she divulged to her nannie the existence of a circle in which the principal characters were a Mrs Benson and the Kittens, and Nannie gave the secret away. Agatha overheard this exposure of her privacy with horror and never again divulged her esoteric world of invention. Her father taught her elementary mathematics and soon discovered that she had a natural mathematical brain. I think that this capacity appears in her books and in the neat solution of the most complex tangles, an ability in analysis as well as synthesis. I suppose that Agatha was no exception in that like many girls of her time, of good family, she was home-taught, except for a brief excursion to an arithmetic class. She was exceptional in that she never had any formal schooling at all until she went to a finishing school in Paris. It seems probable that had she been to school and forced into the deadly Procrustean bed of education the effect could only have been harmful, hampering her natural élan for production and creation, and above all constricting to her wonderful natural imagination.

Unfinished Portrait brings out two characteristic traits which Agatha shared with her mother, an inner sensitivity together with an intuitive understanding of situations hidden from more normal mortals. It is difficult to say how far the vivid imagination that went with these things was cause or effect.

Her mother revealed that in her youth, in true Victorian fashion, she enjoyed imagining herself as lying on a sofa and dying of hopeless love. 'All very silly but I don't know, somehow, it helped! – all that imagining . . .' No less revealing is an incident that occurred in Agatha's childhood on an excursion to the mountains behind Cauterets. When mounted on a mule, and about to start the homeward journey, the muleteer pinned a live butterfly, flapping its wings, on her hat. Great tears rolled down her face all the way home and no one was able to understand why: Agatha was spellbound in an agonized silence unable to divulge the reason for her sorrow, partly through fear of offending the guide. She was led weeping to the presence of her mother who immediately perceived the cause and unpinned the butterfly from her hat. Oh, the exquisite joy and relief at not having to explain her hidden sorrow. I doubt if this inner shyness ever left her, and with it went a capacity for understanding others similarly situated, an ability which coincided with a vivid working of the imagination.

Agatha's education in Paris brought out, more than anything else, her love of music. Her natural ability and technique in playing the piano was capable of development to professional standards: she was willing to practise for six hours a day and played Brahms, Beethoven and Mozart exceptionally well. But although in the solitude of privacy she was an executant of high calibre, when it came to performance in public she was liable to break down with nervousness. A perceptive music master therefore reluctantly explained to her that she had better abandon all thoughts of becoming professional, for an artist must be more than an executant, he must have the temperament to carry an audience with him as part of his artistic world.

It is interesting that this self-consciousness as a piano player was altogether absent when she sang. In this avocation she could perform without a trace of nervousness, and was wholly confident. Gifted with a high, soprano voice, she could probably have sung as a professional in concerts, and the entrée would have been made the more easy because she was extraordinarily beautiful, fair, blue-eyed, a Scandinavian type of blonde, with a lovely and winning countenance. Her voice she believed was not a part of herself but a presence outside her, impersonal, and this was why no trace of self-consciousness went with it. Her real ambition was to become an opera singer, but here she was made to realize by her teachers that she was not possessed of the volume of voice needed for opera. Yet another ambition in the arts therefore had to be abandoned. But with all her artistic imaginings, Agatha was also a realist, and wasted no time in recognizing her limitations. This practical sense was to serve her well when she finally adopted the career for which she was truly fitted.

Agatha combined a musical training in Paris with many visits to picture galleries and instruction in painting. Enforced visits to the Louvre resulted in an aversion from the Old Masters which took many years to overcome, in spite of a love of form and colour, and is yet another indicator of the damage which might have been done by a formal education. She had no gift for painting and was unable to see the shadow behind the flower and could not understand the desire for its botanical dissection and analysis.

After Paris, she returned to her beloved home in Devon, Ashfield, a peaceful paradise, with its great beech trees, green lawns and little copse. Her mother, now impoverished by her father's death, lived on a shoe-string, but still in comparative comfort, and Agatha never enjoyed more happiness or harmony than in her company. Somehow the money was found for a season in Egypt, and this helped to decrease though not to overcome her abnormal measure of natural diffidence. Also at Ashfield for her last years was her Victorian grandmother, aged 99, masterful, lover of her possessions, entirely certain of her values, of the criteria of right and wrong conduct, imperious, firm and kindly, devoted to her family though often disapproving. Agatha has left us a living portrait of this striking and typical mid-Victorian character, humorously and affectionately portrayed.

Life at Ashfield went happily for Agatha in her twenties and we have an account of a succession of suitors, rich, comfortably off, poor as church mice, who sought her hand, for she had a radiant beauty combined with a natural charm, kindliness and humour. At last she became engaged to a faithful dobbin, a gentle, leisurely, kindly soul, with whom she would have found a secure and placid happiness. Named in the book as Peter Maitland we see him portrayed as a gentle modest character, unable to believe that he was a worthy metal for his fiancée as he made plain to Agatha's mother. 'Don't be too humble, women don't appreciate it.' A serving soldier, he was due to return to India for two years and thought it fair that during that time Agatha should have the chance of finding a more worthy man if she fancied one. Agatha wanted him to take her at once. 'If you really loved me, you would want me to marry you at once and come with you.' 'Oh my love, my little love, don't you understand that it's because I love you so much?' Fifteen months later she was married to another.

The 1914 war had broken out and Agatha was wooed, a whirlwind courtship by a masterful airman of great charm and determination, a man who never failed to get his way. Expectation of life in that war was brief and they were soon married. Peter took the news with sorrow but without resentment, he pathetically recognized his failure. Agatha had lost the opportunity of steadfast happiness and surrendered it for the overweening attraction of high adventure. Archie's charm, good looks, ability and decisiveness impressed all who met him, but Agatha's mother at once recognized and feared a certain ruthlessness of character which gave her forebodings for the future, well aware as she was of Agatha's vulnerable, sensitive temperament not shaped for stoicism or the bearing of unhappiness. Archie (named Dermot in the book) was overwhelmed by her beauty. 'Celia – you're so beautiful – so beautiful. Promise me you'll always be beautiful.' 'You'd love me just the same if I weren't?' 'No, not quite. It wouldn't be quite the same. Promise me, say you'll always be beautiful . . .'

Unfinished Portrait vividly portrays the happy years of this marriage, the enjoyment of planning, stage by stage, and the gradual growth of prosperity. Agatha's modesty and extraordinary diffidence in confronting domestic help, the birth of a daughter, in practical realism so like her father, not at all endowed with the fanciful imagination of the mother. After a time an absurd barrier appeared – it was the game of golf which caused a separation of interests. This weekend amusement brought about the end of the early happy companionship on Saturdays, and even on Sundays – perhaps something about golf ought to be written into the Social Contract, in the faint hope that some reformation of this pleasure, or modification of it might be observed. In those days it used to be said that men expected their wives to be no more than housekeepers and bedfellows; now with Women's Lib the boot is on the other leg. However that may be, golf was the beginning of the end and until I read Agatha's book I was unable to understand the vehemence with which she extracted from me a promise not to play the game.

To Agatha, as to most wives, companionship in marriage was an essential component of happiness, the sharing of experiences and of feelings, and the joyful expression of them. To her husband, Archie, enjoyment of what one did was sufficient in itself; there was something both embarrassing and silly in harping on them. There was foolishness in friendly talk and showing off at a dinner party although he himself had a keen sense of fun. But it was the loss of companionship that led to a parting of the ways. Agatha began to try her hand at writing – early on, ill-shaped imaginative stories about Wales which were pure figments of her imagination. Why not try writing on some subject that you know about was her husband's advice, or try to find out about it – you know nothing of Wales. A more perceptive would-be publisher advised the opposite. You are a born story-teller and can make anyone believe that what you say is real; write about the world you don't know rather than the world you know. This encouragement was on the right lines and before long Agatha was making a respectable income from the writing of detective fiction. Writing was in the beginning a release from boredom, a yearning to get away which at times she felt as keenly as her desire to travel – to Persia, to Isfahan and to Shiraz, even to Baluchistan; but such distant ventures, she thought, would never be within her reach. Still, these were but the normal frustrations, common enough in most marriages, and she could not conceive of life without a husband to whom she had been married for eleven years, and by whom she had conceived a beloved daughter, nine years previously.

Suddenly the blow fell. Her much loved mother on whom she had depended so much, died when Agatha was away. She was advised by her sister to return urgently but arrived too late to say farewell. On the way, in the train, the certainty came upon her that her mother was dead; a desolate feeling of utter cold, and on checking her watch she discovered afterwards that this was indeed the hour at which her mother's end came. Not only did she feel a terrible sense of desolation, but she was burdened with the melancholy and wearing task of clearing the house in Devon of a generation's accumulated paraphernalia.

This was the time at which Archie became infatuated by the love of another woman.

It is a grim and melancholy phenomenon of life that misfortunes come, not singly, but together, and Agatha was no exception to it. In the midst of her loss Archie broke the news to her that he had fallen in love with another woman and that he had reached the point of no return. The news came as an unexpected and shattering blow, never remotely suspected. This was a human and social tragedy, a setting reminiscent of a drama by Ibsen. The divorce laws of the time look to us now as well-nigh incredible, and I believe that the late A. P. Herbert played a major part in instituting their reform, an improvement, but one that still remains deleterious to the stability of marriage.

The shock proved too much for Agatha's hyper-sensitive temperament and she gave way to blank despair, to a loss of memory, and to acts which came near to *auto-da-fé*. There is no need to recapitulate what has been told in *Unfinished Portrait*; an account which still moves the reader to a feeling of deepest sympathy. Suffice it to say that sorrow cannot endure for ever, a few staunch friends and a natural interest in life slowly applied themselves as a healing balm, although deep scars left marks that never wholly disappeared. Four years later Agatha married again and we have experienced together the joys of a companionship which has grown and matured over the forty-five years of our union.

To the tragic ending of her first marriage there is a curious epilogue. Archie it must be said, was a born soldier, a man of exceptional ability who became Colonel in the Royal Flying Corps, and was awarded the CMG and DSO. He could have risen to the highest rank had he wished to remain in the services, but he was bent on making money, and preferred life in the City where he did sufficiently well. Sixteen years after his second marriage, his wife died and Agatha, then settled to a new and happy way of life, wrote and expressed her sympathy, and wrote kindly. He replied saying that he was much touched that she did not grudge him his sixteen years apart from her and so ended a heart-rending separation on a kindly note.

Agatha and Archie had one daughter, Rosalind, who married Hubert Prichard in 1940. A born soldier, with a bent for poetry, he was tragically killed in action shortly after D-Day, in the invasion of Normandy.

In 1949, however, Rosalind happily married Anthony Hicks who became kindly step-father and counsellor to her son Mathew, a natural sportsman, who as captain of cricket at Eton failed only by a few runs to make a century at Lord's in a classic match against Harrow under the admiring eyes of a famous headmaster, Robert Birley. Mathew, now in his thirties with three children, was the youngest ever High Sheriff of Glamorgan. Incidentally he will also be its last one, for that county has now been sub-divided into three different components. Mathew has inherited the sense of hospitality and merry temperament of his mother Rosalind, whose charm, natural affection and social graces combined with her artistic gifts and capacity for running a full house efficiently and without fuss has made Greenway a happy house for many.

But I must return to Anthony Hicks, a character who reminds me of Davey, a charming hypochondriac, who figures in two of Nancy Mitford's novels – *Love in a Cold Climate* and *The Pursuit of Love*, the only man who could contradict Uncle Matthew with impunity and was treated by that old Bull as the oracle. Davey was teeming with recondite information of an unexpected kind, especially on antiquarian subjects, ever ready to detect decay in things as much as in himself and by his original conversation, a perpetual delight to those with whom he was associated. In all this I have recognized Anthony.

Anthony had courted Rosalind at Greenway and spent much of his time reading an enormous Tibetan dictionary, a book which lost me some money, for my friend Rodney Kannreuther who was staying there at the time bet me five pounds that such a vast volume must contain the Tibetan for Butler's Pantry. He was right and I have never ceased to wonder at it. However that may be, Anthony was at the time reading Tibetan as well as Sanskrit at the School of Oriental and African Studies, and had he desired it, a post in those subjects would have awaited him, for he had a deep interest in Oriental religion, stimulated by a sojourn in India during the war. Trained as a barrister and called to the Bar, the thought of practising was distasteful, and though he had the capacity, I do not think he had the right personality for that profession, for he lacked the rapid mental agility so useful in

Court. He was a born scholar and a man with profound and wide interests capable of outstripping many a professional in a variety of subjects, but his natural brilliance was unaccompanied by a particle of personal ambition. I think he is the kindest man I have ever known and literally would not hurt a fly, for he has Buddhist sympathies. In the end he turned his attention to horticulture and has benefited Greenway not only by his knowledge of plants but through a natural flair for the economics of the business.

Greenway presented us, at first, with many a headache for neither Agatha nor I had the experience of managing a rare garden which had been abandoned for two years and was partly a jungle when we moved in. The solitary gardener, Hannaford, a born and bred Devonian, was not the most hard-working of men, but he went with the place, for John of the Ford is mentioned in Domesday Book and by rights, like his mongrel terrier whom he closely resembled, he should have died in the grounds.

At Greenway every prospect pleases and it is an added satisfaction that we know when many of the rarities were planted. 1921 was the year in which the magnificent *Magnolia Delavayi* went into the ground; the finest specimen has grown nearly a foot a year since that time. In front of the house is a glorious white *M. Conspicua*, a still older tree, and against the drawing-room window the scented *M. Grandiflora* with its mahogany leaves now spans a century. We ourselves in about 1950, had the satisfaction of planting the glorious *M. Veitchii*, a feast for the eyes as one looks out of the front porch, and finest of all, on the tennis court, a *Magnolia Campbellii*, which, if February is mild, yields a thousand crimson blooms; it flowered as we expected in precisely its twenty-fifth year – when we planted it in about 1945, it was aged about seven. But all the rare shrubs and trees yield pride of place to the green banks covered in due season with primroses and bluebells, a sight for the gods indeed. How long Greenway can survive the grim economy that we live in remains to be seen, but perhaps as Keats said, a thing of beauty is a joy for ever.

A description of Greenway has been given by Agatha under another name in her novel, *Dead Man's Folly*, where familiar landmarks in the garden can be identified. And it is to Agatha's books that I will now turn.

CHAPTER 13

Agatha's Books

At the time of writing these lines, Agatha has written 85 books, one for each year of her age, a miraculous record of productivity rarely exceeded. How to account for this phenomenon? It arises I think from a permanent condition of fantasy. From her earliest childhood Agatha has lived in a dream world of her own, and lived constantly with creatures of her imagination. Almost from infancy she saw in her dreams a terrifying gunman against whose appearance her devoted nanny and her mother had to reassure her. But fortunately she also lived with a much wider circle of imaginary and kindly friends who were engaged in fascinating pursuits. And her mother too, was a wonderful story-teller, constantly inventing and relating absorbing tales which she could never repeat. 'Tell me the story of the Candle Mother.' 'I can't remember it, dear,' and would invent another one no less weird. Agatha, when her time came, was equally inventive for her grandson, Mathew – 'Tell me just one more bunny's dream, please!'

After Agatha became well known it was not unusual for her fans to write and offer a plot, either free or from mercenary motives and the reply was invariably: the greatest satisfaction enjoyed by an author is the invention of plots, the rest is hard work. If you have a good plot, keep it for yourself. And indeed there were in Agatha's notebooks, brief sketches of half a dozen plots abandoned, unfinished, because she had become diverted by other ideas. Hers has been a life of boundless invention. It is not surprising therefore, that sometimes she has been drawn to the writing of poetry, and that her first poems were entitled *Road of Dreams*; her last ones, *Poems*, were published in 1973.

Perhaps her most charming and among the most original of her works was a little series of religious stories written for Christmastide, entitled *Star Over Bethlehem* (1965). These sweet tales have given unalloyed pleasure to many. They may fairly be styled 'Holy Detective

Stories'. Very successful also was an excursion into archaeological life entitled *Come Tell Me How You Live*. This was an account of daily life on an archaeological expedition to North Syria between about 1935–1938 – scenes which every Oriental archaeologist will recognize, and highly comic at that. Here, Agatha's gift for narrative and for relating humorous exchanges of conversation between all manner of men and women in unusual situations, is rewardingly displayed. There have been many calls for the republishing of this exceptionally entertaining book and it has been done again in 1975. Many have been called to Oriental archaeology, but few have been able to leave so happy a record of it.

Among the other genres on which Agatha has tried her hand are the stories which go under the title of *The Mysterious Mr Quin*, first published as a collection in March 1930. This is detection written in a fanciful vein, touching on the fairy story, a natural product of Agatha's peculiar imagination. The mysterious Mr Quin, an invisible presence acting as a catalyst at critical times, emerges from nowhere and without giving any overt help, inspires Mr Satterthwaite to think out the solution to any mystery which happens to be preoccupying him at the time. Mr S, a born snob, who moves preferably in the highest aristocratic circles, appreciative of the arts, arrives on the scene, usually of murder, at critical times. He is preoccupied with 'pushing aside the shutter and looking through the window into the truth of people's lives' (p. 128).

My two favourite stories are, 'The Soul of the Croupier', concerned with pride and humiliation, and 'The Man from the Sea', which gives a profound reason for deterring any would-be suicide: a similar theme occurs in *Towards Zero* (1944). Most charming is 'Harlequin's Lane', which brings this collection to a close. These stories bear witness to Agatha's concern with music and incipient interest in modern art. The last story in this series, 'The Harlequin Tea Set', was published separately in *Winter's Crimes 3* (Macmillan 1971).

Yet another successful form of imaginative tale by Agatha is a series of stories collected under the title *Parker Pyne Investigates* (1934).

Mr Parker Pyne is a consultant of a unique kind, possessed of scientific skill in dealing with affairs of the heart. One of my favourite stories is 'The Case of the Middle-Aged Wife', in which the successful intervention on Mr Pyne's part saves the lady from losing her husband when all the cards are stacked against her.

Two stories are topical. The first is 'The House at Shiraz', an imaginative reminiscence based on a visit which we paid to this lonely abode in about 1933. It had an altogether unexpected painted ceiling which included a series of panels illustrating the owner's visit to England in the 1880s – among them was a panel illustrating Holborn Viaduct. I believe that this house is now used as a summer palace by the Shah. Agatha's story about it is a particularly original one and a masterpiece of psychology. Another topical tale is 'The Pearl of Price', which records a visit that we made about the same time to Petra. This collection of stories again illustrates the extraordinary range of Agatha's imagination.

It is hardly becoming for a husband to set himself up as a critic of his wife's books and this I shall not attempt, neither am I competent to do so, in spite of having read the lot, with no less enjoyment than the average reader. When it comes to criticism it seems to me that the literary critic of detective fiction labours under a heavy disadvantage, for he is under an obligation not to reveal the resolution of the story. The essence of good detection is the setting of a problem and the skilful stage by stage unravelling of the skein – which is often a tangled one. Literary analysis can therefore ruin a book for the reader. I have the feeling, unfair perhaps, that the analytical critic of detective fiction is either a knave or a fool. This opinion absolves me from attempting more than a few comments on the personal impact that the stories made on me and my relationship to a few of them.

Fans often write to Agatha and, after revealing their own preferences, ask which stories are her favourites. Her reply is that her opinions change from time to time, but as a rule she mentions *The Murder of Roger Ackroyd* (1926), *The Pale Horse* (1961), *Moving Finger* (1943) and *Endless Night* (1967). The last-named book is also a favourite of mine, partly because of its construction; the penetrating understanding of a twisted character who had a chance of turning to the good and chose the course of evil. The latent study of good and evil is never far absent in most of Agatha's books together with an original and intuitive understanding of the associated psychology. In *Endless Night* the perspective is dramatized by the setting of the accursed field named

Gypsy's Acre, one that was pointed out to Agatha on a Welsh moorland and made a deep impression. The book lent itself to a film and much beautiful photography, but the production appeared to me to be difficult, the characters lost their depth and for Agatha and many of her readers all was ruined by the introduction at the end of an erotic scene altogether alien to Agatha's ideas.

In another favourite, *The Pale Horse*, a title which refers to the Book of the Revelation of St John the Divine, Agatha derived a peculiar satisfaction from the use of a poison, which had been suggested to her by a doctor in America. This poison could result in many different kinds of death, but there was one symptom which was diagnostic of the way in which the victim had been killed. To understand what that was you have to read the book which is based on scientifically grounded technical knowledge. The book had a rare and unusual sequel in real life which was communicated to Agatha in a fan letter from a Latin-American country dated 15 June 1975. The authoress of the letter, who shall remain anonymous, recognized that she was being confronted with a case of attempted murder in the course of which a young wife was attempting to take her husband's life by repeatedly administering poison over a longish period in small doses. The letter concluded as follows: 'But of this I am quite, quite certain – had I not read *The Pale Horse* and thus learned of the effects of thallium poisoning, X would not have survived; it was only the prompt medication which saved him; and the doctors, even if he had gone to hospital, would not have known in time what his trouble was. With my sincere regards and admiration.'

In *The Mirror Crack'd from Side to Side* there is again an unusual application of medical lore, the deliberate and wicked transversion of German Measles under peculiar circumstances.

The Moving Finger is set in a remote English village and relates to a small closed society engaged in simple worthy avocations; gossip is of course the breath of life. Into this milieu we are plunged to discover that a poison pen has been at work and brought tragedy in its train. A series of baffling murders is resolved with the help of 'someone who knows a great deal about wickedness', alias the analytical Miss Marple. A romance unusual in character adds gilt to the gingerbread. The complex story of crime is unravelled with the aid of one of Agatha's original and wholly unexpected twists. This is deservedly a favourite with many.

To *The Murder of Roger Ackroyd* I have referred again in another chapter. It is perhaps the most famous of all Agatha's books, because of the element of surprise and the difficulty of detecting the murderer. Oddly enough the basic idea of the book was suggested in a letter written by no less a person than Lord Mountbatten in early middle age, who had been preceded by Agatha's brother-in-law James Watts, another devotee.

Two novels were set in Egypt, partly because we travelled together there, but they have no particular reference to archaeology, though some of the places in which we stayed, for instance, the Winter Palace, and one of our travelling companions, old Lady Vernon, an amusing character figure, bring back personal memories. She figures in *Death on the Nile* (1937), a Poirot novel which in 1946 was turned into a play *Murder on the Nile*. The second Egyptian-based novel is *Death Comes as the End* (1945).

More closely related to our work is *Murder in Mesopotamia* (1963), which would not have been written without a knowledge of Ur of the Chaldees and the parts of director played by the late Leonard Woolley and his masterful wife Katharine. Here perhaps Agatha touched rather near the bone and for once was apprehensive about what this *dramatis persona* might say. Fortunately, and perhaps not unexpectedly, Katharine did not recognize certain traits which might have been taken as applicable to herself, and took no umbrage. In this book I figured as Emmott, a minor but decent character.

If we look at her long succession of detective stories, we find common to all of them an exciting narrative that holds the addicts spellbound. Many there are for whom detection holds no appeal, but the addicts have run to millions. The stories are written in a plain everyday conversational English, excellent in its simplicity, direct, unpretentious, sometimes ungrammatical as conversation often is, to the point. There is humour, drama, tense excitement, and the reader is held entranced to the end. The character drawing is firm and deft, some critics say lacking in depth, but as a Frenchman has well put it, '*Ce ne sont pas des caractères, ce sont des traits de caractères.*' They are not characters but character sketches, and the more interesting because the reader is frequently left to make his own effort to penetrate the surface. Above all there is incredible ingenuity, the element of surprise which so often leaves the reader disillusioned, deceived and finally confronted with an unexpected and wholly plausible solution. Agatha takes endless trouble over her technology and gets her facts right on medical matters, poisons and their antidotes; from her experience as a trained dispenser, who practised in hospitals, she has the expertise of a professional. She has been no less careful to consult professional authority on police practice, on the law, on procedure in the courts. That is why her books are read by the scientifically trained. Agatha has in the course of her life received thousands of fan letters, a few critical, the overwhelming majority grateful. It gave her some satisfaction when a solicitor wrote complaining of her ignorance about the law of inheritance, for on such matters she takes the greatest care. On this occasion she was able to demonstrate that the lawyer himself was outdated, that the law had been changed and that her statement was correct. We shall return in a moment to her code of ethics, but since we have touched on her character sketches we must look at her again in another guise, as Mary Westmacott.

Agatha's success as a writer of detective fiction had one disadvantage, in that her publishers discouraged her if ever she expressed a desire to work in some other literary medium. No other writer of detection has written in that form for so long. Dorothy L. Sayers, perhaps the best known of her contemporaries, gave up after seven or eight highly successful books and turned to religion, to Dante, and to other forms of literature.

Nevertheless the time came when Agatha insisted on release and began writing under the name of Mary Westmacott. Her gift for narrative is such that these books at once took on as readable and commanded a wide public. It was many years before the anonymity was breached. As Mary Westmacott, Agatha was able to embark on many themes in which she was interested. Music, the drama, the psychology of ambition, the problems of artists. *Giant's Bread* ranged over such themes. But I think that in this form of writing the true release came in that it gave her freedom to range over characters in depth, freed from the constriction of the detective plot to which every personality had to be subordinated. In a detective story in which the reader is chal-

lenged to unmask the murderer, it is difficult to arrange for a continuous study of one character – still more of several characters: under
a new name she was released from a strait-jacket.

Beginning with *Giant's Bread* (1930), dedicated to the memory of her
mother, she wrote a story about a musical composer, a genius who had
to liberate himself from the love of human ties in order to achieve his
end and create his masterpieces . . . Was the price too great to pay? The
reader is left to make the decision. This tragic story, was I think, in part,
the result of being in touch with a musician whose parents were well-
known to Agatha's sister – Roger Coke, long dead. Next in the series
came *Unfinished Portrait* (1934), an autobiography mixed with imagination about which I have written in detail in the preceeding chapter.

After this comes *Absent in the Spring* (1944). This again had a familiar
background for it was the story of a woman returning from a visit to
her daughter in Iraq, immobilized on a train through the flooding of
the railway track. The story is introspective, a re-evaluation of character, reflection on the danger of always knowing best. It received high
praise in the *New York Times* from Dorothy Hughes who wrote: 'I've
not been so emotionally moved by a story since the memorable *Brief
Encounter* . . . *Absent in the Spring* is a *tour de force* which will be recognized as a classic.'

A Daughter's a Daughter (1952) has as its theme, a familiar one in
life, the potential love-hate relationship between a mother and her
only child, and, fortunately, recognition of the links which make for
the final reconciliation.

The Burden (1956) is about the burden of loving and of being loved
and the easy rejection of wise counsel, once again an introspective
study, and the realization that total escape is in the end impossible.

The Rose and the Yew Tree (1947), in my opinion the most powerful
and dramatic of all, described as a novel of romance and suspense,
centring around the person of one Gabriel, a brave and intensely
ambitious man, capable of great good and evil, a holder of the Victoria
Cross who has in him the capacity for suffering and supreme re-
nunciation. In this book I enjoyed the portrait of the aristocratic Lady
Tressilian, and the effectively-drawn contrast between her and the
aristocratic Isabella with her plebeian wooer. For me this one is in the
classical vein and will not be destined for oblivion.

The Mary Westmacott novels are of uneven quality, but every one of them is readable and has studies of character easily absorbed thanks to Agatha's extraordinary gift for telling a story. At best these books are dramatic and concentrate an interest on the solution to situations which arise out of the high tensions in life. It will be a pity if they are forgotten against the popular achievement of the detective fiction. I do not think that they will be.

We return to detection. What is it that has made for this overwhelming success, one that has led to their reading by something like 2000 million persons?* First the supreme art of telling a story, held by a continuous thread so that when you have read one chapter you cannot resist going on to the next; and it is a positive pain to put the book down. The only other author that I know who has this gift in equal measure is Graham Greene. The style is conversational, a part of real life, and of that I became vividly aware when I used to hear her dictating through the dictaphone. 'Who has come to visit us today?' I used to say to myself as I overheard a vivid conversation going on in our little morning-room at the foot of the stairs in Wallingford.

That experience I had when she was at work on her last straight novel, *Postern of Fate* (1973). Tommy and Tuppence who were the detectives, had worked as a pair in the First World War, now appeared as septuagenarians and gave many readers renewed pleasure. The chronology of this book was imperfectly worked out, but one of the delights of Agatha's works is that occasionally and rarely the sharp know-all, incapable of writing an imaginative work himself, is able to detect a flaw.

An added delight are the detectives, now heroes of this form of fiction. Poirot has his man, Hastings, his foil, as was Watson to Sherlock Holmes: Poirot's own words well-described the relationship. (*Poirot's Early Cases* (1974) p. 211.) 'Sometimes, Hastings, I regret that I am of such a moral disposition. To work against the law, it would be pleasing for a change.' (p. 294) 'How I miss my friend Hastings. He had such an imagination. Such a romantic mind! It is true that he always imagined wrong – but that in itself was a guide.' Irritating as Poirot became to

* In 1975 it was reliably estimated that her sales had reached 400 million and if we reckon on the basis of lending libraries that there were 5 readers to a copy, this would give a grand total of 2000 million.

Agatha, with his little grey cells, his clowning, his eccentricities, his antics and his vanity, he had so far endeared himself to her readers and publishers that she was not allowed to abandon him; though Poirot's last case, *Curtain*, long ago written, has at last been published in 1975; a brilliant little masterpiece of exquisite craftsmanship, with a dramatic and superb ending.

The favourite by general acclaim, however, is Miss Marple, the sage old lady who sits in her parlour quietly observing all that goes on, an implacably shrewd observer with a genius for deduction and prognostication, deceptively mild, a realist with an acid taste, and an experience of human nature which has left her with a disguised cynicism. This gentle but determined character has found a permanent place in the hearts of her readers. There is one more Miss Marple story, *Sleeping Murder*, published posthumously and, if this has the success of *Curtain*, it will establish yet another record.

Last of the imaginative detectives was Mrs Oliver, lightly sketched, but a portrayal of Agatha herself, for example in *Elephants Can Remember* (1972) and in *Cards on the Table* (1936), a clever story. A pretended scattiness was one of Mrs Oliver's assets. In *Cards on the Table* there is a very good description of the pain and toil of writing and I think the passage on this subject must have been written with a view to debunking some of her fans who so often wrote and said what a wonderful thing and a pleasure writing must be.

There is no doubt, however, that Agatha's most widely known detective is Hercule Poirot. As hero of the film *Murder on the Orient Express* his fame reached into every corner of the world.

CHAPTER 14

Orient Express

I can remember few things more exhilarating than travelling on the Simplon Orient Express, sweeping through country after country, leaving Europe behind, then speeding across the great plains and through the mountains of Asia Minor into Syria. This was a journey of sheer delight, watching the ever-changing scene from a cosy bunk in the Wagon-Lit, or better still through the great plate-glass window of the dining car. One incident from that vantage point I shall never forget.

I was sitting with three companions at the luncheon table, one of them the celebrated French archaeologist, Claude Schaeffer, on his way to excavate at Ugarit while I was on my way to Chagar Bazar. Suddenly his assistant Georges Chenet leant across the table and said to me: 'Have you ever read a detective story called *The Murder of Roger Ackroyd* by Agatha Christie?' 'Yes indeed,' I said, 'a truly original piece of work, not easily forgotten.' 'Ah,' he went on, 'and what about *The Man in the Brown Suit* and *Murder on the Orient Express* – have you read them?' 'Yes I have, and in addition all the rest of the novels by the same author for I happen to be her husband.' For a little while this remark was greeted with disbelief, partly because two of my companions were aware of the situation and treated the questionnaire as a jest.

Murder on the Orient Express, however, was no laughing matter and I take some special pride in the book, which I see from the fly leaf was dedicated to me in 1933. I had as it happens, suggested to Agatha a new form of involvement in murder, which I do not propose to divulge for fear of spoiling the readers' fun, but it was Agatha who as usual chose the unexpected and highly successful setting, a particular railway train alas long vanished. It was lucky that she lived to write the book, for not long before penning it, while standing on the railway station at Calais, she slipped on the icy platform and fell underneath the train.

213

Luckily a porter was at hand to fish her up before the Orient Express started moving.

The book was a good one; and countless readers have enjoyed it, and so helped towards the achievement of a unique record, namely that when made into a film in 1974, it was the most successful adaptation to the cinema ever attempted. Not only was there the delight of seeing the long-defunct Simplon Orient Express come to life again, but the cast composed exclusively of stars blended unexpectedly well. Albert Finney, though unlike Poirot, gave a masterly performance. Technically the handling of the characters within the narrow confines of a corridor in a railway train was brilliant, and visually the complicated dénouement of the plot was more easily unravelled than in the book. Agatha herself has always been allergic to the adaptation of her books by the cinema, but was persuaded to give rather a grudging appreciation to this one – which was described in *The Times* as 'touchingly loyal' to Mrs Christie, and the same critic (David Robinson) added, 'It stays precisely at the level of Agatha Christie, demands the same adjustments, the same precarious suspension of disbelief.'

This is not an unfair criticism if we recognize that for most of Agatha's readers there is nothing precarious for she has, through persuasion, the magical art of transporting us bodily into the world of her dreams, no matter how fantastic. Plots which may rank high in the order of improbability can never be declared impossible and for the moment become fact. It is this traumatic transfer to reality that the writer who has lived in the fantasy can effect for one. And contrary to expressed opinion the little actualities are treated with a meticulous care and realism. The pen of the same *Times'* critic slipped, a *lapsus calami*, when it wrote that the director of the film (Sidney Lumet) 'doesn't even trouble to hide the oddity that one notices in the novel that the Express should on this occasion be such a short and unpatronized train'. But Agatha knew from long experience that there was often only one through carriage, and that was precisely why every berth had to be booked far in advance. Correct handling of unexpected details, such as this, adds enchantment to the discerning reader's enjoyment.

In other films, however, there have been some disgraceful travesties, notably by that splendid character-actress, Margaret Rutherford, grossly miscast as Miss Marple – and ridiculously associated with a livery stable. Misrepresentations of this kind are galling enough to an author, but they are made harder to bear when fans write to say how much they have enjoyed the show, never giving a moment's thought to whether or not the picture is a true reflection of the original composition on which it has been based.

None of these distortions appeared in *the Orient Express* however, thanks to the brilliant vision and imagination of Lord Brabourne its producer who deserves full credit for visualizing the book as adaptable to the cinema. Indeed, this was Great Britain's biggest export for the year 1974, an unchallenged winner which has been a world-wide success. The film was given a tremendous send-off at the ABC cinema in Shaftesbury Avenue, and was graciously launched by Her Majesty the Queen, here seen in the photograph greeting Agatha. Nearly all the cast was present and I have a vivid personal impression of the charm and high intelligence of Ingrid Bergman who schooled herself to learn Swedish English for the performance. The film itself won three out of seven of the British Film Awards for 1975: it was acclaimed as the Best Picture of the Year; Albert Finney was nominated as the Best Film Actor; and Wendy Hiller as the Best Actress of the Year.

The first night was celebrated by a gala banquet at Claridges, the last public performance in London which Agatha was well enough to attend, at the age of nearly 85. She enjoyed it greatly and I retain the picture of Lord Mountbatten, Brabourne's father-in-law, escorting her out of the dining-room at midnight and raising her arm in farewell. Shy as always, she enjoyed this occasion to the full.

There have also been a number of other successful movie pictures based either on Agatha's books or on her plays. The first was *Alibi* based on *The Murder of Roger Ackroyd*, another success, with Francis Sullivan playing the principal part. Most successful of all was *Witness for the Prosecution* taken from the play and produced very well in America by Billy Wilder. In these productions two of the great actors of the time took an outstanding part, Charles Laughton and that mountain of a man and charming character, Francis Sullivan.

Some of Agatha's plays have earned as much fame and popularity as her books and I think that most critics would name *Witness for the*

Prosecution as the tops: the Old Bailey as the theatrical *mise en scène* held a magnetic attraction for the audience, which felt itself in dock; no one who has seen the play will be able to forget it – the highest tribute one can pay to a work of art. Patricia Jessel gave a brilliant performance, and the play was destined to a good run, but the size of the cast, the amplitude and the inconvenient location of the theatre, the Winter Garden, prevented it from enjoying the long run that it deserved. When the play went to New York it was hard to persuade the principals not to transfer the scene from the Old Bailey to the House of Lords. In London this is the only occasion on which I have known Agatha enjoy the agony of a First Night: from the opening it was clear that this was a winner, and at the end the cast bowed in unison to the authoress. Peter Saunders who produced a wonderful scenario and has never stinted any production said that he had never seen the like of this finale in which one and all displayed their sincere admiration.

In my opinion, if *Witness for the Prosecution* was Agatha's best play, the next was a much less known one, *The Hollow*, which I have only once seen produced in a manner worthy of its construction. This was at the Princess Theatre, Torquay, in 1973, under the sensitive presentation and direction of Charles Vance, who made it come alive as a coherent whole in which the plot held the audience's sustained interest throughout – no mean feat when detection is on the stage, for concentrated attention is required without intellectual strain. In this production there was no star, but the cast pulled its weight as a team, and very effective it was. The contrary was the case in other productions of the same play – when it was done at the opening in London by that celebrated comédienne, Jeanne de Cassalis, who acted throughout as the Queen Bee, to the detriment of the hive.

Years later I saw it done in Guildford by that endearing and winning character, Cecily Courtneidge whose fooling the audience loved, but her performance, in my opinion, ruined the play. Here they came to see Cecily, not Agatha. The audience, of course, enjoyed Cecily's acting, but my acclaim went to Jack Hulbert, who played a small part – that of the butler – a most distinguished performance which impressed me as that of an outstanding actor. But seeing Cecily reminded me how often a production is a battle between the playwright and the

Agatha at the time of her marriage to Max, 1930.

Agatha and Max on the battlements at Greenway,
overlooking the river Dart.

Greenway.

Agatha cutting her 75th birthday cake
watched by Sir William (Billy) Collins.

Agatha is presented to Her Majesty the Queen at the film
première of *Murder on the Orient Express*, 1974.

Agatha and Max, 1970.

actor, and how difficult it is for the producer to reconcile the two. When he succeeds he deserves an artistic triumph.

The Hollow was brilliantly adapted from the book by Agatha herself in a manner that shows her flair for the theatre and it is interesting to compare the book published in 1946 with the play, which was presented by Peter Saunders at the Fortune Theatre in 1951. Here Agatha exploited the dramatic potential of the novel to the full, with the utmost economy in assembling the plot, incidentally with the omission of Poirot who figures in the book. The book itself is in my opinion not one of her best, for it is disjointed and tends to ramble, but exceptionally it features a number of romances, and the portrayal of the women is penetrating, the result of a perceptive feminine outlook. There is a biographical touch which I like to remember; a slight travesty of the facts but very near the mark. 'Do you remember, my dear,' says Sir Henry (p. 53 paperback), recalling a nasty incident on the Bosphorus, 'those thugs that set upon us that day on the Asian side of the Bosphorus? I was rolling about with two of them feeling for my throat. And what did Lucy do? Fired two shots in the mêlée. I didn't even know she had the pistol with her. Got one bad man through the leg and the other in the shoulder. Nearest escape in the world I've ever had. I can't think how she didn't hit me.' This episode is a true one and the only difference is that Agatha, unlike Lady Angkatell, had armed herself not with a pistol but with a boulder which she was prepared to drop on my opponent's head. Rarely have I felt in greater danger of death by stoning. Fortunately in those days I had a strong pair of hands and my enemies took fright and ran away. I was particularly glad because I had shortly before been to the bank and my pockets were bulging with Turkish liras. There is also one remark about Poirot which I particularly like (p. 62): 'He did not care for trees at any time – they had that untidy habit of shedding their leaves. He could endure poplars and he approved of a monkey puzzle – but this riot of beech and oak left him unmoved. Such a landscape was enjoyed from a car on a fine afternoon.' One more remark in the book appeals to me (p. 186): 'To the sculptor's mind truth comes first. Truth, however bitter, can be accepted, and woven into a design for living.'

We come at last to *The Mousetrap*, the play with the world's longest continuous run, so successful that it has inevitably attracted the attention of the green-eyed monster – jealousy. To jaundiced critics it has been an unpardonable offence that any one play should monopolize a theatre for so long. I have little fancy for such bitter lemons.

Agatha herself predicted a three months' run for the play when it came to that diminutive and charming theatre, the Ambassadors, and few, except perhaps Peter Saunders, would have thought differently. In fact it celebrated its 23rd birthday on 24 November 1975. Many things combined to contribute to its phenomenal success over and above the natural genius of the author, which it is all too easy to forget in the analysis. First there was the comparatively exiguous size of the theatre which housed an audience of no more than 500, 490 to be precise. The capacity of the St Martin's Theatre next door, to which it has moved, is 550. Once the play caught on there was competition to see it; indeed a frenzied desire to get a seat; of this Peter Saunders who presented the play took full advantage and perhaps no other man could have done so well in his crafty organization, sense of publicity, and courage in seeing the play through bad periods – for bad periods there inevitably were. The play was fortunate too in having two theatrical stars of high magnitude to send it off – Richard Attenborough and his beautiful wife Sheila Sim – both of them lovable and great artists with a faultless sense of timing. They started the long line of different casts who have spanned the 25 years' run that has now elapsed since the opening in 1952; no less than 132 persons have played a part in it so far.

Once the play was entrenched it was hard to move, and seeing *The Mousetrap* became part of the American Tour, as important as a glimpse of Buckingham Palace and a visit to the Tower of London. I have a friend, Dr Werner, for long Director of the British Museum Research Laboratories, who took his wife to see it shortly after his marriage in the first year of the run – seven years later he took his daughter and, after 21 years, his granddaughter. Thus has the play spanned the generations.

The setting of the play is part of the English scene, a country-house, Monkswell Manor, a rather inefficiently run country hotel, at which the guests are caught in midwinter, and we feel in our chilled bones the despairing attempt to keep warm. Suspense, surprise, a sense of bafflement, and the nervous wait for the dénouement of the murder grip us to the end. But added to all these there is something more. It is a feeling of cosiness and of being part of the English scene. We become one of the family, embraced in it as we are when we attend a play by Gilbert and Sullivan when the audience expects and awaits the jokes with a happy sense of anticipation. The atmosphere at *The Mousetrap* is charged in this way, and all foreigners who come to see it fall under its spell. I remember my happy surprise when I saw the French presentation in Paris under the title *La Souricière* at the Théatre Hebertot. The French audience which I should have expected to be all at sea and baffled by the English scene and police procedure, was captivated: the play had a surprisingly long run of over two years between 1971 and 1973. All said and done, *The Mousetrap* clicked: all went right for it from the day of its birth under a favourable star.

Not so favourable was the star which presided over the birth of Agatha's most beautiful and profound play, *Akhnaton*, brilliant in its delineation of character, tense with drama. The play moves around the person of the idealist king, a religious fanatic. obsessed with the love of truth and beauty, hopelessly impractical, doomed to suffering and martyrdom, but intense in faith and never disillusioned in spite of the shattering of all his dreams.

Akhnaton the poet, hater of the concrete and lover of the abstract, wished Egypt to abandon the old religion of the trumpery god Amon introduced by his forebears, and to substitute the worship of the heat of the sun disc, the Aton, instead of the monstrous statues of Amon. He was bent on pulling down the old temples, on iconoclasm of the old gods, and would have encouraged the abolition of the little scarabs piously dedicated to Osiris by the simple faith of the people; such offerings were comparable to those of the humble Roman Catholic who lights a candle and makes his vows to the Virgin Mary. Like all profound thinkers he was in advance of his time, out of step both with the orthodox and with the common people, a hater of the old priesthood, man of peace opposed to all men of war, lover of artists, of his court sculptor Bek, and of his effeminate satellites. Most effective is the young king's touching affection for his soldier general, Horemheb, who is seen as if on his way out of an Ancient Egyptian Sandhurst, inevitably destined to be a general. The soldier vowed to the service of king and country finds himself before long torn in a conflict of loyalties, and this is the focus of the play. Is the suffering imposed by the Establishment any worse than that of a disordered state beset with another kind of corruption, and are the old gods, easy to comprehend, less valid than the concept of a single abstract divinity; is the new art, are the new temples and the luxuriously designed Palace of the Horizon (still surviving as a wreck at Tell El Amarna) to be preferred to the ancient architectural and sculptural forms? The problems of Ancient Egypt are eternally with us; the sacrifice of the old inevitably involves a different kind of suffering and the jettisoning of good and loyal men doomed to death instead of the king's enemies.

In no other play by Agatha has there been, in my opinion, so sharp a delineation of the characters; every one of whom is portrayed in depth and set off as a foil, one against another. We have a captivating portrait of the shrewd and experienced old Queen Mother Tiy, adept at managing men, her vain attempt to advise the foolish and beautiful Nefertiti, so much beloved of the Pharaoh that with his own hands perhaps, he was inspired to carve the most lovely head in the world. We see the old priest Ay instructing the king in the new theology, but nevertheless advising him at the same time against the folly of persecuting the old state religion.

Undermining the king by a network of intrigue is the ambitious and scintillating Nezzemot, the queen's sister, admirer of Horemheb, determined to captivate him, judging the Pharaoh as a humourless, impractical fanatic engaged in the ruin of Egypt.

The play moves to its finale like an Aeschylean drama; it is Horemheb who is driven to confess that every man has his breaking point while the king, though all is in ruins about him, still puts the love of the world before the love of his country. Here is an earlier image of Christ, forsaken and abandoned, but unrepentant in despair.

Egypt between 1375 and 1358 BC is but an ancient reflection of the world today, a recurrent and eternal tragedy. Perhaps one day this lovely play, first published by Collins in 1973, will be performed on the stage. Good judges of the theatre have deemed it beautiful, but would-be promoters are daunted by the frightening thought of an expensive setting and a large cast. Nevertheless I can see no reason why this should not be simply performed without paraphernalia in front of a plain backcloth in the manner in which the Chinese play *Lady Precious Stream* was so successfully enacted many years ago. The public in this country, as indeed in many countries elsewhere, are attuned to an appreciation of the subject following a world-wide enjoyment of the exhibition of the treasures of Tutankhamun's tomb. A play about the father, Akhnaton, should thus present no difficult intellectual exercise.

Before the writing of the play Agatha herself had a long preparation. As long ago as 1931, we visited the Tomb at Luxor and became friends with Howard Carter, a sardonic and entertaining character with whom we used to play bridge in the Winter Palace Hotel. Subsequently Stephen Glanville, a lifelong friend, and one of the renowned Egyptologists of the day, Provost of King's College, Cambridge, put Agatha on the track of the literature. A dynamo for setting the engines of his friends into action, he discreetly fed Agatha with the ancient literature – with the Amarna letters and other records until she became deeply versed in the subject. The treatment comes as near to historical plausibility as any play about the past can be. The Egyptian court life and the vagaries of Egyptian religion come alive. This is the way to learn painlessly about Ancient Egypt and to become imbued with an interest in it. It seems to me that the characters themselves are here submitted to exceptionally penetrating analytical treatment, because they are not merely subservient to the dénouement of a murder plot, but each one is a prime agent in the development of a real historical drama. The play is studded with some lovely passages of Ancient Egyptian poetry and the portrait on the dust cover, that of a little-known statue of the king, is an impressive image of sensitive and delicate feeling.

CHAPTER 15

Agatha's Craft

In the end, to addicts of Agatha's works, it is I think the psychology, the insight into human nature, the verdict on it, never overstated, and lightly sketched, that provides an enduring and reflective interest. *Towards Zero* (1944) is a good example of the deft treatment of human character, in a story that is beautifully constructed on the estuary at Salcombe – the Yealme in which all the landmarks are discernible. Here is a place of pilgrimage for those who are disposed to identify the setting of a most ingeniously planned crime.

One of my own favourites is *Cards on the Table* (1936), because of the ingenious technique which makes use of no more than four characters; only one of whom has committed the murder, and the difficulty in spite of the apparent simplicity of the circumstances, in determining which is the guilty party. For a personal reason I like *Ten Little Niggers* (1939), one of the few novels in which I have guessed the culprit with a feeling of certainty for purely psychological reasons. This novel was read . . . and tried out at a house-party in Devon and great was Agatha's indignation when I won the prize for spotting the murderer – for the wrong reason.

Many have been deterred from pursuing this type of literature because of an innate distaste for the subject of murder and its attendant cruelty. Perhaps this does not make congenial reading for the squeamish, but Agatha has always scrupulously, though perhaps unconsciously, observed Horace's instruction – '*Ne coram publico Medea pueros trucidet*' – Medea should refrain from murdering her children on the stage – an admirable precept. Murder is always brutal, but it is one of the facts of life. Agatha never gloats over it, or describes it beyond the necessary minimum of detail – there are no obscenities. And how often have clergymen and the parents of growing children applauded the cleanliness of her books, the absence of any immoral or degrading features? Those who disapprove of murder stories usually do so for frivolous reasons and fail to realize that Agatha's books are the modern version of the medieval morality plays, concerned with the exposure of evil and calling the wicked to account for his criminal actions by paying the appropriate penalty. The task of Hercule Poirot, of Miss Marple and all others in her books engaged in the detection of crime is the relentless and fearless pursuit of the wicked. Here there is no room for any relaxation of moral standards. Evil must be pursued to the end.

The enunciation of these standards in a period of moral decline has won praise from many, but none more gratifying than the words of Geoffrey Jackson in his book, *People's Prison*. Sir Geoffrey was HBM's Ambassador to Uruguay and in 1971 suffered the cruel experience of being kidnapped by the Tupamaros, a band of guerrilla terrorists dedicated to defiance of the government and persons decreed members of the Establishment. Their purpose seems to have been to draw attention to what they regarded as a society constituted on an evil structure, by committing acts of urban violence – a Spanish S. American form of IRA. After the kidnapping our Ambassador was concealed underground in two successive dungeons, no more than a few feet square, couched on a plank bed, at best illuminated by a dim electric light. As time went on the harsh oppression of solitude was at last relieved by the copious provision of reading matter, in various languages, all of which were familiar to the well-stored mind of this polyglot. The heroic bearing of the captive was due in part to a natural philosophic disposition, combined with a special sense of humour and an ability to enter into a tolerable relationship with his captors through a deep understanding of his fellow creatures and a genuine interest in their motives. These talents enabled him to bear his confinement with a rare fortitude, and a dignity, which never compromised his standing as a representative of the Queen. Most of all his mental survival depended on a deep religious faith which carried the victim through his darkest hours.

The chapter in *People's Prison* (Faber and Faber, 1973), describing the wide reading which sustained and nurtured him in the ordeal, is therefore of peculiar interest. Most gratifying is this passage: 'But my truest escapism was achieved the day when one of my gaolers enquired if I could tell him anything of a compatriot of mine of whom they had received some books – her name was "Agata Creestee". From that moment I never lacked an escape – visits back to my native land, an escape-route of far greater and more instant efficacity than the "space-warp" beloved of science-fiction writers. With the help of Dame Agatha, and a small effort of will, the infinite separation of the galaxies were instantly bridged, the opposed dimensions of captivity and freedom were brought together at their time-gate, the propositions of Einstein and the Laws of Thermo-dynamics – with all but a few spatial and temporal formalities – effectively bypassed. To the subjective joy of so improbable a time-journeying could be added a particular intellectual bonus – the spectacle of young revolutionaries, drenched in a relativist view of society, drawn towards two such implacable defenders of moral absolutes as Miss Marple and Monsieur Poirot. In intellectual discussion my hosts unfailingly revealed themselves as total pragmatists; politically and tactically their yardstick was unvaryingly "Does it work?" Yet here they were, betraying an ardent nostalgia for the more intransigent criteria of "Is it right?" and "Is it wrong?" Miss Marple – as too, Monsieur Poirot in his perhaps subtler way – possesses a quality of candour, even of innocence, but combined with a nose for evil which would impel either of them to pursue the scent of murder to the end of its trail with all the tenacity of the bloodhounds of Heaven itself. Yet these characters, symbols of a whole ethic, attracted the unqualified admiration of young terrorists who, nevertheless, could rationalize even murder to their total satisfaction. I did not know whether to weep for their lost innocence, or to pin my hopes on these disarming evidences of its vestigial survival.'

Many fan letters are both charming and perceptive as well as being grateful. 'We overheard that you could be tough – it's to be hoped that you will put your foot down in future if any of your novels are featured or put on the stage.'

'Young and old are great admirers of your books, and I know many invalids who bless your name . . . God bless you for the happiness you have given millions of people.'

From a lady who had lost father, son and husband: 'Maybe you'll be surprised but my form of escapism is your quality of who-dun-its – by quality I mean . . . not dealing with trigger-happy and bed-happy heroes – but of the kind you write. Recently too, I came across *Cat Among the Pigeons* [1959] and was deeply impressed with the way you put over deep moral social teaching so cleverly disguised.'

Some missives are comic, and occasionally from abroad they have to cope with the difficulty of writing in a foreign tongue; one from W. Germany is in this style. 'Dear Mrs Christie, I know millions of persons – I mean people write you to say you are a wonderful woman. I want to say exactly that. For me there is a woman, who is THE WOMAN: is a woman in two parts, one and first you Agatha Christie and the second part Golda Maier, you made me happy – always. You have a reguard in this world – fame and perhaps money. I wish there are more for you afterwards. Your smile is a sun – "and" your "ideas" . . . your "ideas" . . .!!! Love you got from me too.'

From Mexico. 'In spite of the million letters you must receive from unknown admirers, I appeal to your benevolence to read one more from someone who carries in the blood a great admiration for your work and personality. I must have inherited this from my grandfather, the Spanish Republican General Miaja, the famous "Defender of Madrid" during the Spanish Civil War. He loved to read your novels as a mental relief to his many preoccupations.'

'I make use of this letter to congratulate you very deeply for your absolute success as a novelist. I had to thank you for the great happiness I have experience every time I took the challenge of guessing a murderer's identity in the web of any of your plots. In fact I must tell you that, with Dickens, you are one of the two authors whose books I enjoy most. How can I ever forget experiences such as *The Mysterious Mr Quin, The Labours of Hercules* or *Endless Night*? I have even enjoyed publications such as *The Mousetrap Man* (by Peter Saunders) which I bought at the Ambassador's Theatre last year, and others where I can learn more about your personality . . . I beg you to excuse my English, but I am only learning it when my studies in Chemical Engineering and Criminology (my hobby) let me.'

Sometimes there were unexpected coincidences, for example, one from Mary Ann Zerkowski, the Principal of the Amanda E. Stout Elementary School in Reading, PA., USA. 'I have just finished reading your novel *Passenger to Frankfurt* [1970], and was astounded to find myself playing the part of an undercover agent. I was really thrilled to be cast in such a role, but I am just a little bit curious as to how you came to christen your fictitious spy with my name. Your book has created quite a stir in my home community in Reading, Pennsylvania. I am receiving many telephone calls and letters from friends addressing me as Countess Zerkowski.'

Agatha replied with amusement that the name Zerkowski was picked by pure chance, probably out of a telephone directory or from a birth, death or marriage column in a newspaper and congratulated this good-natured lady on becoming a Countess.

From Morsang-sur-Orge, a letter written in French. 'Madame, I am an artist, a painter aged 36. I lack M. Poirot's subtlety and wit and I am not enamoured of Miss Marple. But reading in the French newspapers that you are the richest author in the world arouses my (envious) admiration and to learn that your father never did a stroke of work in his life overwhelms me with admiration! What a family! To come to the point, why do I write this letter to you. A mystery that you would perhaps be at great pains to solve. With my respectful admiration.' The author might have been interested to learn that Agatha had long parted with her money, mostly in charitable trusts, not to mention tax!

Perhaps this minute selection of fan mail may be appropriately closed by a writer from Columbus, Ohio. 'I've been a fan of yours since I was 12 years old and read *And then There were None* [American title of *Ten Little Niggers*]. I love the book and have reread it many times. You have a great sense of wit and fun mixed with a flair for suspense and goosebumps. Never stop writing!'

Such fan letters have found their way from all over the globe, including from behind the Iron Curtain, for example Czechoslovakia, where there are many admirers. Many of the envelopes are comically addressed, but eventually find their way to the author – such styles as Mrs Agatha Christie, The First Lady of Crime, Great Britain, are not uncommon, and reflect knowledge as well as discernment on the part of the Post Office.

Agatha has rightly been described as the most modest person in the world – vanity she has none in spite of the fact that her books have been translated into more languages than Shakespeare's plays, and that up to 1973, she is believed to have entertained about 2000 million readers scattered over the world. *The Mousetrap* has been translated into 22 languages and played in 41 countries. 'I regard my work as of no importance – I've simply been out to entertain.'

Herself of high intelligence and integrity, but never claiming to be an intellectual, a woman without ambition who could have shone in many avocations, it was unnecessary for her ever to have been interested in Women's Lib. Agatha has always had a genuine respect for her readers, for their intelligence, and has fairly claimed that she never cheats – 'the one invariable rule in writing I have never broken'. The solutions to her problems have the hallmark of a logical and mathematical mind as well as a creative one. Not the least remarkable of her activities has been her flair for the telling of a story which coincides with some new turn in the behaviour of society. *Passenger to Frankfurt* (1970) coincided with one of the early cases of hijacking. She herself has said that a detective novel should be subtle and interesting like a good crossword puzzle, and indeed this is the secret of her success. Her books are problems, as wholly absorbing as a game of cards; they require just that degree of concentration which is enough to compel complete detachment from the surrounding world. The most worried reader becomes carefree as if by magic and can instantaneously switch off his troubles. For those who can take the medicine this is an anodyne indeed.

To the letters of appreciation I must add my own 'Birthday Ode' written for Agatha on her 80th birthday, 15 September 1970. This contains allusions to our beloved dog, Bingo, who in his time has caused some trouble as well as joy. He figures as a portrait in Agatha's novel, *Postern of Fate* (1973), and is portrayed on the back cover of it:

ODE TO AGATHA ON HER EIGHTIETH BIRTHDAY

15 September 1970

Oh Agatha this is your Birthday Ode
Presented to you in your Greenway abode
Where family, friends and the doggies unite
To wish you all joy in the World's fierce despite.
This task is for me most especially weighty,
Because you are now at the grand age of eighty,
Gay and companionable, full of your think,
And all this achieved without ever a drink

Oh would that we had but one half of your wit
Or could have achieved but one tenth of your writ
The shelves of our houses are filled with your books
They fill every cranny and are crammed in our nooks
Eighty titles are yours and what man doesn't know 'em?
I wish I could weave the whole lot in one poem.
Not Murder is hard, but 'Murder is Easy'
Even Miss Marple and Poirot feel queasy
Clues thick and fast fall into the lap
Of that poor fellow Hastings and Inspector Jap.
We admire in your books the masterly craft
The puzzles that baffle us till we are daft
What mystery is there could ever be bigger
Than that which emerged with your tenth little nigger?
In your books you condemn all that *is* foul and mean
Many's the party, but always kept clean.
Yours is the role of Morality Play
Wherein all the wicked find crime doesn't pay
Blackmailer, killer, scoundrel and crook
Sooner or later are brought down to book.
Let justice be done and triumph the right
The wicked enshrouded in dark 'Endless Night'
And that's *why* Queen Mary gave her command
And when *she* was eighty you met her demand
'The Mousetrap' you wrote to honour her name
A play that has brought you an immortal fame.
Fan mail pours in with its flattering snorters
The telephone rings all the day with reporters.
Our Bingo has bitten the Mail and Express
For those two reporters there is no redress
But to bite Peter Grosvenor and nip Godfrey Winn
Shall not be accounted to him as a sin
Tis better than when he indulges in passes
At Cocoa's and Golly's protruding arses.
But today all our dogs are joined in full amity
To spare you the shame of such a calamity
Such conduct they say would now be atrocious
For this day at least we will not be ferocious.
On the contrary now we do nothing but smile
There is nothing but sweetness from Ros'lind this while

Agatha's Craft

And Anthony ceases to talk about wine
His conduct is perfect his demeanour is fine
That young farmer Mathew is home from the plow
He's abandoned his children to be with you now
And so has his Angela, who has lost even more
For they cut out her tonsils and her throat is still sore
And here is Dolores who one day will strive
To cook Fesinjan upon which you may thrive
While Cecil may join her to help with the pan
For he after all is her servant and man
And who knows if Peter will do something rare?
He may go to the barber and shorten his hair
While John fresh from resit and back as mechanic
Will collect all the glasses in haste and in panic
Patricia will press *on* at the stove for our dinner
We're all counting upon her to cook us a winner
So blessings upon you our Agatha dear
And remember this birthday with never a tear
Throughout the wide World, in East and in West
You are loved for your kindness your craft and your zest.

PART IV

Nimrud and its Remains
1945 - 1975

CHAPTER 16

The Institute of Archaeology

In writing of my family life with Agatha and of her books and plays, I have digressed from my archaeological work and in particular from the preparation of my book on the excavations at Brak and Chagar Bazar. Its completion took me two years from 1945 till 1947.

My good friend Professor Sidney Smith, on a visit to Greenway, saw the manuscript and was, I think, suitably impressed, for he set about, together with Stephen Glanville, finding me an academic post. In due course, with the backing of Professor Gordon Childe, I was appointed to be the first occupant of the Chair of Western Asiatic Archaeology at the Institute of Archaeology in the University of London.

The Institute was then lodged at Bute House, in the Inner Circle, Regent's Park, where Agatha had taken tea with the family in her youth. Never before had I realized the advantages of living under a rotunda: the great dome over the central hall held together the society living under it and as most of us taught with open doors, everyone knew what was going on. I suppose that the architectural merits of a Mohammedan mosque express themselves in the same way and unify worshippers; and in this they have an advantage over the Christian Church which is trisected by a nave and two aisles. Certain it is that our old Institute was preferable to the new box into which we moved in 1957, at the cost of about half a million pounds, probably more. There everyone had his little compartment, every door unlabelled, and we became, as it seemed to me, an impersonal institution, out of touch with one another. It should now be the function of every Director to restore the feeling of a closely knit society and to weld its multifarious activities together.

The old original Institute was an exciting place to live in, for it was still possessed of the happy amateur pioneering spirit and had not yet been touched by the heavy hand of professionalism, which eventually must take charge of established societies. A reluctant University was, in the end, forced to integrate us with it and to carry archaeological millstones which ultimately turned to gold.

Members of our Institute in its early days participated in three Oriental ventures which became famed throughout the world: the excavations at Jericho, Mohenjo Daro and Nimrud, directed respectively by Kathleen Kenyon, Mortimer Wheeler and myself, who then represented the British effort in Palestine, in India and Pakistan and in Iraq. These activities, as well as those conducted at home, brought prestige to the Institute and attracted to it a host of Oriental archaeologists. Nor should we forget the presence of Professor K. de B. Codrington, an eccentric character not easy to comprehend, who held a Chair of Indian Archaeology shared between ourselves and the School of Oriental and African Studies. One more Oriental activity should be remembered here, namely the devoted work of Olga Tufnell, who spent years completing the publication of Lachish.

Over all was our first Director, Professor V. Gordon Childe, a man of brilliant intellectual capacity, whose writings were admired far beyond the archaeological circle. Gordon was a professed Marxist and intellectually dedicated to the cause, but the Party was too clever ever to admit him officially: outside it he was an invaluable ally, from within he would have been a menace. Good at languages, ancient and modern – he could read Sanskrit and was familiar with Pindar – he none the less termed himself a 'Pots and Pans man', for this label fitted with Marxist materialism. This impractical man, an innocent abroad, clumsy with his hands and an indifferent digger, through his imaginative mental powers shed lustre on any activity in which he was engaged and was a personal magnet in the circle of archaeology. A good companion and the kindliest of men, he was the ideal choice for a newly-founded Institute. He entertained well and enjoyed good living: when royalty came to visit us, his good manners got the better of him and he was impeccably polite. Few of us took his political ideas seriously, and no one could have been more welcoming to a Pole exiled from Cracow, Professor T. Sulimirski, a lovely man who had been obliged to flee from the Communist régime.

Childe was at first an ardent follower of Stalin, but towards the end of his days was gradually becoming disillusioned. He was no administrator and retired from the Institute at least two years before his time;

he felt that life, for all his interests, held but a bleak prospect. He returned to the land of his birth, Australia, for a last visit and in due course hired a taxi to drive him to the cliffs on the outskirts of Sydney. Blind as a bat, he left his glasses on the cliff top, stumbled on the way down and was found dead at the bottom. There is little doubt in my mind that he committed suicide, and like Ibsen's Master Builder, he deliberately chose this dramatic way of casting himself down from a height. Not long before his death he wrote affectionate letters to most of his friends, including one to Agatha; and a last article, which was published in the Bulletin of the Institute of Archaeology, was capable of being interpreted in this way. Thus ended the life of this extraordinary man – the ugliest I have ever met, indeed painful to look at: his blue nose, like that of Cyrano de Bergerac, conditioned his nature, and had he not been the victim of polio which disfigured him in his youth he might well have conformed normally to the society in which he lived; but archaeology would have been the poorer without him. His Marxist concepts, his economic outlook, were a stimulus to archaeological thinking, and all prehistorians with proper concepts of food gathering and food production owe a debt to his work.

Childe played his part in attempting from time to time to integrate the teaching of the Institute, and encouraged us to take part in public lectures within the building, in order that each of us might make known our activities; many were also invited from the outside world and everyone who was engaged in distinguished archaeological work was asked to make himself heard. Childe himself, though always interesting, had a poor delivery and his sentences often ended in a falsetto squeak. He was as painful to hear as to see: the impact was always forceful.

My Chair at the Institute introduced me to the business of teaching which I greatly enjoyed, for I had the desire to share knowledge with others and to see how far I could persuade them to absorb it. Above all I found teaching a two-way traffic, for the pupil, although the receiving instrument, is a sounding board that must reverberate on the master. Personal instruction is a method of interlocking the minds of two human beings and must depend on some measure of chemical sympathy. It thus follows that master and pupil must establish a *rapport* and attempt to become congenial. For my own part, although I found that the instruction of clever pupils inevitably gave satisfaction, I know nothing to compare with the pleasure of watching a pupil, who at the beginning appeared to be a dullard, responding to stimulus. I have a notion that some University dons are mentally too lazy to take trouble over these dullards, whom they naturally tend to neglect by comparison with the more gifted.

My first pupil was Margaret Munn-Rankin, whom I encouraged to leave the Civil Service for archaeology. A natural academic, she has become well established as a lecturer in Oriental history and archaeology at Cambridge, and is a recognized authority who might have written more, but whatever has come from her pen has the mark of distinguished thoroughness. For a season Margaret joined me at Nimrud, but she was of a retiring disposition and the rough and tumble of life overseas was not suited to her withdrawn and modest temperament. A conscientious and exceptionally well-informed teacher, many pupils at Cambridge have benefited from her instruction.

Seminars, and time devoted to a single pupil, are obviously a better way of exchanging knowledge than lectures. In classes that were not too large, I invited listeners to interrupt whenever they wished, but I sometimes found that this permissive attitude was mistaken, because some bore other than oneself was then liable to take charge and irritate everyone. On one occasion I had to ask a voluble commentator whether he was giving the lecture or I, and said that I was ready to step down from the rostrum. Such sallies made for lively entertainment and were in accord with my belief that dull instruction is an unforgiveable sin. Sometimes it was important to ascertain whether one was intelligible, for occasionally Oriental students were either too timid or too polite to intimate that the teacher's words were not clear to them. I once read in a novel called *Sagittarius Rising*, that in the old days many Chinese learner-pilots were killed because they had been too polite to explain that they had not understood their teacher's instructions. In the same way I discovered that one Iraqi student had for long been under the impression that when I talked about the Water Table I was referring to some kind of aquatic furniture. The fault was mine, not his. In these days of prohibition against discrimination between the sexes it may seem reprehensible to say so, but I used to reckon that often enough I was only beginning to make headway with a female pupil when I had reduced her to tears – a *reductio ad absurdum* distressing to both of us but thoroughly wholesome. However that may be, I have never thought that time spent on a pupil was wasted. I have always been the wiser for coming to grips with their difficulties and the merrier for their camaraderie. Up to my seventieth year, so long as I was in good health, I regarded it as part of my duties never to fail to reply to a letter seeking enlightenment on some aspect of archaeological knowledge, and again, have never resented the amount of time spent on that exercise.

My closest associate at the Institute was Rachel Maxwell-Hyslop, who assisted me in my Department, and proved to be an admirable liaison with the laboratories, with which she was always in close touch and thus sucked up scientific information. Rachel has become a recognized authority on archaeological metallurgy and the economics of metal distribution in the ancient world. Author of many invaluable articles, her book on Ancient Oriental Jewellery has won acclaim and she is a mine of information on ancient methods of metallurgical production.

Two more of my associates in the Institute of Archaeology loom large in my memory. Sir Mortimer Wheeler was one, whose first wife, Tessa, through her energy and drive, deserves much of the credit for the foundation. Mortimer Wheeler or Rik, as he was familiarly known to his many friends, was a monument and always looked like one. This megalith of a man, an over-engined dynamo, strode through life breathing fire, a fire which either burned opposition or was miraculously cleansing, a process of cauterization which healed and reanimated. He was possessed of the kind of genius with which my old master, Leonard Woolley, was endowed: namely that whatever he touched came to life, whether it was the Institute of Archaeology, the British Academy or Mohenjo Daro.

No man was more effective in Committee and it was as Secretary of the British Academy, an institution that he reorganized and transformed, that he could be seen playing his most forceful role. Always histrionic, he was born to hold the stage and in the Presidential Chair at the Antiquities Society he looked like King Lear: his presence was overwhelming. At the British Academy, where he exercised plenary powers, he was seen at his best because he knew exactly what he wanted, had a quick and alert mind which was rapid in action and gave little thought to diplomacy: he never wore kid gloves. When an assembly was locked in debate his authority was ever ready to cut the Gordian knot. He was a rare combination of artist and practical man of affairs. As an artist he was a leading figure of his time in the world of television and no one will forget him as a *tour de force* on the programme entitled *Animal, Vegetable, Mineral,* ably sponsored by Glyn Daniel, who was the impresario. From all this it follows that he was not everybody's cup of tea and that there were persons who could not abide him: he was merciless on the inefficient and although prepared to gamble on human nature he was rarely wrong in his judgement, in spite of a readiness to be hoodwinked by flattery.

As an archaeologist his outstanding achievement was the pioneering of a method of digging which appreciated the fact that no excavation could be successfully conducted unless there was a proper understanding of stratigraphy and an ability to expose and illustrate its sequences. Here he owed much to Pitt Rivers, but Wheeler's instructions on this score have been observed the world over, and archaeology has thus internationally acknowledged him. A master of organization, his spell in India as Director-General of Archaeology, re-established the services and revived an efficient and effective Department. In Delhi he formed a School of Archaeology which has perpetuated his method. His magnetic and often endearing personality soon won him the allegiance of his Indian subordinates, in spite of a high-handed authority which brooked no opposition. He quickly gained the confidence of Nehru. He dug at many places, but perhaps the hill fort at Maiden Castle and his little dig at Arikamedu, where he put back the Romans into India, will be most closely associated with his name. He was a man who above all things had flair, that was one side of the medal; the other earned him the occasional title of 'the old mountebank' and 'Flash Alf', for he could not resist self-advertisement. No one has done more for young men striving to establish themselves. By nature a philanderer, he could command the utmost loyalty from women, for although at times insufferable they found him good fun and could give him their devotion, despite his lack of consideration and sometimes brutal manner. He was a man of achievement inclined to intolerance and always impatient of human shortcomings; he could publicly blast his best friend intemperately for failing to conform to some standard that he had set himself. I recall an insensitive letter that he wrote to *The Times* after the death of his dear friend, Ian Richmond. Ian had fallen short of publishing all his excavations during his lifetime, and for this Wheeler publicly blamed him, partly because so much of his time had been devoted to the small man and to lecturing to humble societies *gratis* – something that Wheeler never would have done, and much to Ian's credit. I speak as a dwarf in criticizing the giant Rik, but dwarfs must be allowed their say and it is something to have served at the Institute of Archaeology beside this colossus.

The second dominant figure at the Institute of Archaeology was Kathleen Kenyon, now Dame Kathleen, whose achievements are not less well known, though she was never a television personality. Woe betide those who opposed her, or were not of the same mind. I was often asked how we got on together at the University and I always replied, 'Perfectly, because I always gave way.' Indeed I have long forgiven her for any intransigence, because though often offensive in confrontation she spoke good behind one's back, and belied an occasional rough manner by great kindliness of heart, for which an inclination to bossiness is readily overlooked. I could wish that my own autocratic tendencies might be forgiven in the same way.

While at the Institute Kathleen was a dragon in promoting its welfare, and lent lustre to it through her excavations at Jericho and subsequently at Jerusalem. The riddles of Jericho, a complex site, were solved by Kathleen's impeccable method of digging, and her discoveries were dramatic. It became clear that the site was somewhere about 8000 BC, a unique oasis whose fortunes depended on a natural spring. Its fortifications and great stone tower were a revelation of human achievement at the time of the mesolithic to the neolithic revolution. Nothing was more startling than her discovery of the Jericho skulls decapitated and remodelled with an overlay of plaster, the eyes in-filled with shells. These skulls were then reburied under the floors of houses, a unique mortuary cult of the dead strangely paralleled, according to Herodotus, by an account of a partly similar practice in Ethiopia.

Kathleen seemed destined to become Director of the Institute of Archaeology, which she might have controlled with an excess of single-mindedness. Instead she was appointed to be Principal of St Hugh's

College, Oxford, and presided over its fortunes with distinction and, through her natural kindliness and humanity, as well as authority and shrewdness in the conducting of its affairs, was a success; she was also a powerful fund-raiser for the College. The ultimate cause of this appointment was a strange one.

Kathleen was devoted to dogs, for the most part stray mongrels rescued from the Battersea homes, but unfortunately these animals were not acceptable to all at the Institute, where they were considered to be a public nuisance, noisy and insanitary. Neither the Secretary of that time nor the Director, W. F. Grimes, was at all canine in outlook, and this intolerance resulted in a direct confrontation between Kathleen and the dogs on the one hand and the Director on the other. When I was in the middle of a season at Nimrud I received a letter from Grimes explaining the *impasse* and hopefully implying that I might agree with his views. I replied in a contrary sense, to the effect that I had always preferred dogs to human beings and that not so long before my time, a predecessor at New College, Oxford, had kept a bear in his rooms without demur from the authorities: I am not particularly against the alleged insanitary practices of animals and believe that excessive attention to sanitation weakens our natural resistance. The situation was, in the nick of time, resolved by an offer to Kathleen to take charge of St Hugh's, and it is my opinion that but for the dogs Kathleen would have elected to remain at the Institute which we both left at the same time, I to take up a Fellowship at All Souls.

My years at the Institute, 1947–60, gave me a sense of fulfilment and made for a stimulating distribution of my energies. I was at the time of my appointment aged 43, strong and active, and, looking back as a septuagenarian, I envy my health and strength at the time, for my powers of concentrated work, allied to a fair modicum of relaxation and enjoyment, extracted the maximum out of a 24-hour day and night. My work was equally divided between home and abroad and each year brought with it several months of travel or field work at Nimrud in Iraq, to be followed by exposition of the results at home. Public lectures were stimulating to the ego and I believe to the audience, which at Annual General Meetings of the Iraq School at the Royal Geographical Society could command a full house of over five hundred persons.

There were four ancient Assyrian capitals which I might have chosen to excavate in Iraq – Nineveh, Nimrud, Ashur and Khorsabad. The first three were strategically placed on sites chosen for the cohesion of the Empire. Nineveh, and Nimrud (Calah) about twenty miles south were both on the east bank of the river Tigris, the latter city a day's march, and Assur on the opposite, west bank, was 40 miles below it.

The fourth Assyrian capital that invited consideration was Khorsabad a dozen miles to the N.E. of Nineveh, in closer touch with the mountains; but this was an Assyrian flash in the pan, the unfinished home of an old boy made good – the usurper monarch Sargon, 722–705 BC – in which his successor showed but little interest. This attractive site had, however, been extensively dug by the French at the hands of Botta and Place, later by an American expedition from Chicago and in my opinion there was little more of historical importance to add to its annals, though I do not doubt that more remains to be found there and I know where to go in order to do it.

Not unnaturally I considered a resumption of work at Nineveh where many British pioneers, Rich, Layard, George Smith, Chaldaean Rassam, Budge, King and Campbell Thompson had made many rewarding discoveries. But my experience of working with Thompson (1930-31) had convinced me that any large-scale work at Nineveh required finances far beyond our means. The whole of the top twenty feet of the citadel is a churned mass of debris which has been intensively plundered and vandalized ever since Assyrian times. Several generations of workers would be needed to sort out this gigantic confusion. Below the top hamper, however, lies a wonderful succession of prehistoric remains which span a period of at least four thousand years. I like to think that one day some brave team of men will set to work on this venture and cast a flood of light on the whole of Mesopotamian prehistory. Ever since working there I have remained impressed by the vast area, 1800 acres in all, embraced by the site and the intriguing layout of the outer town beyond the acropolis, as well as by the massive defences; the hydrography and marvellous remains of Assyrian irrigation. Alas, this wonderful spot is now heavily ringed with modern buildings, but in my time Nineveh was much as Layard saw it, unspoiled in its pristine beauty, and even Sennacherib's great stone dam stood free. But for me there was never a hope of excavating the great

Assyrian arsenal known as the Nebi Yunus because of the sacrosanct mosque which by tradition concealed the bones of the prophet Jonah. None the less Fuad Safar, and later Tariq el Madhlum, ventured to do some excavation on one of the gates where the statuary of the Egyptian Pharaoh Taharqa *c.* 650 BC has been startlingly revealed, while Tariq has conducted rewarding work on the Ninevite Gates and discovered sculptured reliefs left behind by Layard in the palace of Sennacherib.

Ashur, the old religious capital where the Assyrian kings went for burial, had been thoroughly excavated by the Germans, 1903–12, and brilliantly worked out by a man of supreme ability, the late Walter Andrae whom I had had the privilege of meeting when he went to visit Leonard Woolley at Ur. A rift between the two men had appeared because of some critical remarks of unbelief expressed by the German authorities about the date of the Sumerian houses which Woolley had correctly solved, but was healed by a handsome apology and the ceremonial presentation of a large bunch of bananas on the top of the ziggurat at Ur. Andrae was then nearing the end of his career, and he had crowned his assistance to Koldewey at Babylon with a no less distinguished achievement at Ashur. We now know that this holy site was also an important trade entrepôt for the exchange of metals, particularly round about 2000 BC, when tin imported from Iran and clothes were exchanged for great quantities of copper through the Assyrian merchant colony of Kül Tepe in Cappadocia. The story of Ashur's great part in the history of western Asia had now been sufficiently unfolded.

It was therefore clear to me that the potentiality of Nimrud was greater than that of any other site in Assyria, though many significant pointers might have attracted other diggers elsewhere.

To many travellers there is no more romantic spot than Nimrud, where forty years ago the bearded heads of protective stone *lamassu*, half man, half beast, stuck out of the ground outside the gates of the ancient palaces, the last of the faithful servants that guarded the warrior priest kings of Assyria. This is my memory of it as I first saw the place in 1926 after my first season's work with Leonard Woolley at Ur of the Chaldees on the barren steppe of southern Babylonia. Here I realized was an archaeological paradise where one day after I had done my apprenticeship, I might be privileged to enter. And from this intention

I never faltered as I drove up over the years along the old royal road which ran in Achaemenian times from Susa to Sardis – a road studded with ancient *Tells* all the way from Kirkuk to Erbil and Mosul.

The opportunity for undertaking a major excavation came at last, for my post at the Institute of Archaeology allowed me to take up work overseas for a period of three months or more annually. Consequently when I decided to return to Baghdad in 1947 I had ample time to consider what might be done with war savings accumulated by the British School of Archaeology in Iraq, amounting to £2000.

Two years later, in 1949, I was sitting in the office of the Director-General of Antiquities, Dr Naji el Asil, who was then sponsoring the great prehistoric excavations at Eridu conducted by Fuad Safar and Seton Lloyd – a rewarding task brilliantly achieved. Naji el Asil said to me: 'I have just granted permission to the University of Chicago to renew the excavations at Nippur – you may be interested to hear this news.' 'Yes, indeed,' I said on the spur of the moment, 'for I was about to ask for your Department's permission to dig Nimrud, a happy hunting ground for archaeologists from my country.' This was an appropriate time for making the request because exactly a century had lapsed since the beginning of Layard's excavations on the same spot.

The Iraq Department of Antiquities under the benign influence of its Director soon acceded to my request and neither of us ever had any reason to regret this happy accord.

CHAPTER 17

Nimrud: The Acropolis

There is no more beautiful mound in all Assyria than Nimrud, a lonely spot still untouched by modern development. Its great acropolis which embraces about sixty-five acres is a greensward, a favourite grazing ground for sheep. The *Tell* and its ziggurat tower over the surrounding plains and dominate the cruel waters of the rushing Tigris which flows between steep banks nearly two miles to the west. From the top of the ziggurat the eye scans the northern landscape of rolling downland and the old Islamic city of Selamiyah, four miles away, near to which there is a ford which has always made for easy access. To the south we have a seven-mile view of the fertile plain as far as the upper Zab where the high-standing Tell Kashaf represents the remains of a once-powerful fortress, an ancient bastion of Nimrud itself. To the east lie the Jebel Maqlub and the distant Zagros mountains of Iran whose high peaks may be discerned in the soft purple light which is so often associated with them.

In favourable years this is good grazing ground, indeed in Layard's time the backs of the sheep were in the spring dyed scarlet with ranunculus, a rare sight in our time. But in the stark summer the landscape though barren is still rewarding enough to admit herds of gazelle which, in the early days before near extermination by unlicensed shooting from the motor car, were a regular and beautiful spectacle across the plain on the way from Mosul.

In the early spring of 1949, a member of the Iraq Antiquities Department, Dr Mahmud el Amin accompanied me to Mosul in order to make the first arrangements and to find lodgings for us in the village of Nimrud itself. After torrential rains our car became firmly bogged down in the mud as we reached the ziggurat. But the undaunted and ever-smiling Mahmud said he was game for the rest of the journey, and like a pair of slow-moving hippopotamuses, but waist deep in mud, we made our glutinous way to the Sheikh's house, Abdullah Najeifi, not the brightest member of that once wealthy and intelligent family of landowners, but a thoroughly decent and honourable man though never free from debt. We were lucky to find him as our Sheikh, for although he justifiably had the natural suspicions of the peasant, was both hospitable and friendly and, to the best of his ability co-operative, as he immediately demonstrated by laying out one dozen bottles of whisky, obtained on credit in the bazaar at Mosul, for our entertainment.

When at last Mahmud and I reached his house after an hour and a half of wading he ordered an attendant to bathe our legs and feet in warm water, to be followed by towelling and delicious massage worthy of the one-time Turkish baths in Jermyn Street.

This was in every way a satisfactory visit, for we fixed both our own accommodation and that of some twenty Sherqatis, skilled workmen from the district of Ashur who were to be lodged in two big rooms off the courtyard of the Sheikh's khan. Most important of all I discovered on that visit through the Sheikh's uncle, Mohammed Najeifi, what was the proper wage for the humblest and most numerous body of workmen – the basketmen. The old man had a wanted job done for the day and in front of my eyes cast two lots of 150 fils at the two peasants. This was the equivalent of three shillings or fifteen new pence and was exactly three times what we had paid at Nineveh about two decades earlier. The course of inflation can be measured when we recall that a century earlier, in 1849, Layard paid his workmen one piastre or two and a half (old) pence a day: since his time therefore the wages of a daily labourer had multiplied over fourteen times.

For the first season the supervisory staff amounted to no more than four persons: Agatha, Mahmud, Robert Hamilton and myself. To Agatha I have already devoted four chapters: she was a wonderful helpmate, an ever-smiling hostess, a brave and happy companion on all my digs and in addition was photographer and helped with the cleaning and registration of the small finds.

Mahmud, as the representative of the Iraq Antiquities Department, kept the record in Arabic and was an endless source of good cheer and amusement. During the war he had obtained a doctorate in Oriental languages in Berlin in the nick of time before the Germans walked in.

Eventually he found his *métier* as a teacher in the University of Baghdad. By nature he was as happy-go-lucky as he was indolent.

In Robert Hamilton a greater contrast could hardly be imagined, but the two men were congenial companions with a natural tolerance for one another. Robert, a Wykehamist and a classicist by training, spoke Arabic beautifully: I have rarely met a more modest, talented and self-effacing man. He was gifted for drawing, a surveyor, and kept the architectural record, had preceded me at Nineveh and loved the country. I was fortunate to have his services – a regular little spitfire with the workmen as Campbell Thompson styled him – possessed of a keen wit and a sense of humour.

After Nineveh, although under thirty years of age he had, on the recommendation of Thompson, been appointed Director of the Palestine Antiquities Department and resided in Jerusalem. His tenure of office ranked as a high water mark in the annals of that Department and of the Museum, for he was an artist as well as a craftsman and organizer. His detached impersonal approach induced both Arab and Jewish members of his staff to work in harmony and the break-up of the original Department was a tragedy both for them and for him. Though impartial in his dealings he was a staunch upholder of the justice and rights of the Arab cause.

His principal achievement in the field was the excavation of the Ummayad palace at Khirbet Mafjar: his masterly and incredibly skilful reconstruction of the architectural record earned the applause of the late (Professor) Sir Archibald Creswell – high praise indeed.

After he left Palestine he found employment in Oxford and was appointed Keeper of the Oriental Antiquities Department in the Ashmolean Museum. But oddly enough in that office his brand of formalism was not suited to the stickiness of University administration which he found a trial. A natural recluse, he was by nature a philosopher and I think would have been equally happy as a metaphysician and a gardener. Although ready to be sociable his friendship had to be excavated and he was possessed as it seemed of a deep inner melancholy.

The four of us who composed the first season at Nimrud in 1949 were lodged in a wing of the Sheikh's mud-brick house. Agatha and I shared a bedroom on the top floor; Robert and Mahmud another opposite it. Down below was the living-room, dining-room, Antiquities Room and dark room all in one, and opposite it the kitchen and servants' quarters. We lived in near-slum conditions but were perfectly happy, and as it rained continuously for the first month were rarely dry.

Our Indian servant, Ibrahim, cooked us delicious curries of saffron rice and made excellent cakes, but after the season was over made me promise never to take him up to Nimrud again. Few visitors other than the Dominican Fathers made their way through the appalling Nimrud quagmire to visit us, except Philip Bradburne, the young British Vice-Consul whose second in command was a Nestorian named Aprim, the 'Proconsul' as he was grandly called. The third man at the Consulate was a beaky-looking fellow nicknamed the 'Snipe-Shoot'. Philip's wife, Esme, devoted her life to the upkeep of the English Cemetery and was famed for her good works. In addition there was the enthusiastic Director of the British Institute, John Springford and his wife Phyllis who were most anxious to see us 'turn the first sod'. The highlight of our own hospitality was to entertain to tea in our small living-room the entire Dominican order in Mosul, on that visit amounting to no less than fourteen monks most of whom sat on the floor, with the possible exception of Father Tunmer, the charming and able head of the Order and the archaeologist, Father John, who subsequently under the name of Le Père Fiey wrote valuable books on recondite subjects concerning the history of Iraq, of Mosul and of Assyria. It is sad that for the time being the work of these good men has been suspended, for they were never politically minded, were men of learning, contemplative and worthy representatives of Christianity.

In our small house we were now and again banished from the living-room which Agatha had perforce to use as a dark room for developing negatives, an easy transition, for there was never much light in it! We were then forbidden to walk about upstairs, otherwise mud fell into the photographic dishes with a resounding plop.

That first season was indeed a baptism of mud the like of which fortunately we did not see again. The feat of negotiating the morass between the mound and the village was achieved only because we had purchased in Baghdad for the sum of £150 a four-wheel-drive Dodge station-wagon of immense horsepower which was virtually am-phibious. Every evening it ploughed its way through the mud filled

with ancient pots and pans, foremen and workmen clinging to the
sides like the one-time population of a Cairo tram. The further struggle
to negotiate the 22-mile journey to Mosul for the purchase of supplies
was on those comparatively trackless ways, an arduous undertaking:
that wonderful vehicle deserved to end its days in a Museum.

After the first 30 days of downpour the sun suddenly came out and
the heavens were dry: the ground turned into a hard rutted crust and
was riddled with our fossilized tracks, some of which for all I know
may have remained as a memento, for I remember seeing in the
steppes of Libya tracks that were reputed to be fourteen years old.

The acropolis was situated at the S.W. end of the great walled city
which comprised in all nearly nine hundred acres of ground. All our
predecessors had, however, concentrated their efforts on the palaces
and temples of the inner citadel. Eight years were to elapse before
we deemed ourselves in a position to excavate outside it.

When we began to use our knowledge of what was a fair wage for
our work force, the application of it required firmness and obstinacy
on our part. On the first day when we made our offer of 3/- to anyone
ready to move dirt in a basket we were accompanied from the village
to the mound by a booing crowd which, doubtless encouraged by
Sheikh Abdullah, proclaimed that ten, not three, shillings was the
proper wage. As we marched on, however, we were joined by some
blacklegs from across the river who were anxious to work for whatever was offered: the addition of these new arrivals was the signal for
a series of free-fights with maces and knives which resulted in a number
of bruised and wounded heads. I thought it prudent to dispatch my
two companions, Robert Hamilton and Mahmud, to Mosul in order
to bring out a small posse of police and did not expect to see them for
some time. But after further scuffles on the mound I sorted out a body
of some seventy men who were happily at work by the time the
official representatives of law and order arrived. Some of my recruits
had been among my workers at Nineveh and Arpachiyah and referred
to Agatha as their aunt. From that time onwards we had very little
trouble with the men though the presence of the Sherqatis was at first
resented. Indeed when these skilled men had set to work on the
previous afternoon, a few shots were fired over their heads by a rude
member of the Najeifi family who thought he would try a little

intimidation. He did not succeed in his aim.

This achievement of starting the work on a fair and reasonable wage level was of fundamental importance for it made the financial operation of the dig a practical proposition and allowed for the inevitable rises and increments which have to be faced in the course of continuous employment. Nor was the apparently low wage unfair, for in the season immediately before the harvest there was no other employment in the countryside. The cash enabled the peasant to buy tea, sugar and cloth as well as a little jewellery for the wives and made life tolerable after the merchants had given him a minimum of ready money to buy his seed and had perhaps advanced him something in the expectation of a part of his harvest.

As the excavations progressed there were always at the beginning of a new week men fighting to obtain work and our modest wage enabled us to support more of these needy fellows. The villagers from the district were, like peasants the world over, good companions and responded well to a firm hand and fair treatment.

In these pages there is no need to expound the progress of the dig in detail, but it is worth recalling our aspirations and expectations as we set to work on the 65-acre acropolis to which we confined our efforts.

The primary function of Nimrud was to serve as a main base for the army on its annual military campaigns particularly in the ninth century BC, in the course of the acquisition of the empire which became the greatest hitherto known in ancient western Asia.

The two kings who were the principal architects of its expansion were Ashurnasirpal II, 883–859 BC and his son Shalmaneser III, 859–824 BC. Assyria was fortunate in that these two great men of the same family spanned a continuous run of 60 years in which the highly complex administration of the empire was founded on a firm basis and the army became more efficient than any other of the time, not only through its organization but because of the superiority of its weapons, many of which were made of steel.

Nimrud, or ancient Calah, continued to be used as a predominantly military centre in the eighth century, particularly during the reign of the forceful Sargon II, 722–705 BC. His successor, however, Sennacherib, 705–681 BC, abandoned this city in favour of Nineveh, but his

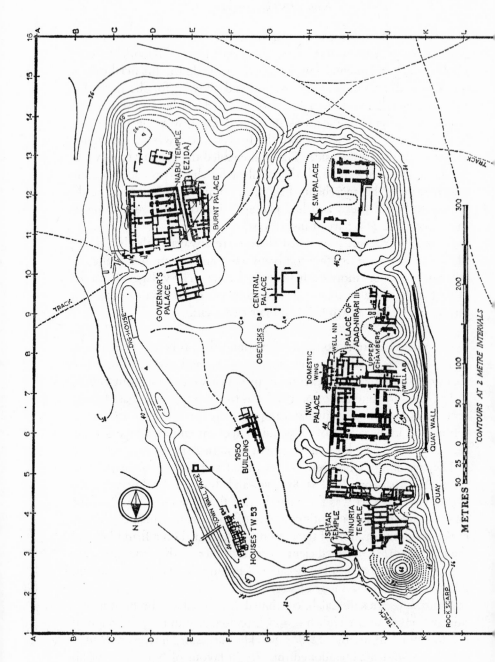

Contour map of the acropolis showing the
position of excavated buildings (1957).

son, Esarhaddon, 681–669 BC, began to return to it at the end of his reign and aspired to make it once more into the capital of Assyria.

In essence, however, Nimrud served primarily as a military base and was big enough to accommodate a large army for which a substantial part of the food supplies had to be imported from Syria. The extraordinary wealth which that country accumulated during the time of this expansion was nowhere better illustrated than by the massive finds of carved ivories discovered in the great palace known as Fort Shalmaneser at the S.E. end of the outer town.

Our immediate objective was to make contact with Layard's tracks on the western flanks of the mound and then to attack the eastern sector, comparatively unknown ground which he had barely probed for a good reason.

In selecting the acropolis, and indeed Nimrud itself for excavation, we kept before us two primary objectives. First to discover more ivories, for I was convinced that many more remained to be found. Second and much more important, to discover cuneiform records, for apart from the royal standard inscriptions which accompanied the Assyrian bas-reliefs, no clay tablets in the cuneiform script had ever been recorded by Layard and it seemed incredible to me that so large a city could have been devoid of economic, business, historical and literary texts. I would have staked my life that in the end we would find all these things, and find them we did.

Our first efforts were therefore directed towards the chambers in the N.W. Palace of Ashurnasirpal, where Layard had discovered his finest ivories. They were labelled by him V and W and without troubling to bring up his map we precisely located chamber V in our very first afternoon in the month of March and set our Sherqatis to work there. What we wanted to know was not only how many fragments he had overlooked, but how the ivories had originally been situated. In both chambers we found a piteous mass of splinters, but there remained one ivory of rare delicacy, a model of a cow in the round, about half a hand's length in dimensions, originally represented as giving suck to a calf. It was lying on a raised patch of mud in one corner of the room and later I understood the meaning of its position: it had fallen from an upper chamber which had overlaid the ground floor of V, and indeed many chambers in the palace had been two-storeyed.

In a doorway of one of the chambers leading to Layard's ivories there was an inscription of Sargon II (722–705 BC), recording that here was the treasure which he had captured from Pisiris, King of Carchemish, but it is probable that while some may have been contemporary with him, others should be ascribed to the period of Shalmaneser III (859–824 BC), who had campaigned in Phoenicia: some of his trophies were therefore of Phoenician origin made under the influence of Egyptian art and he himself may well have imported Phoenician workmen into Assyria.

Our lovely ivory cow was a trophy inevitably claimed by the Iraq Antiquities Department which in those days allocated a representative share of the finds to the digger, who could only raise funds from a sponsoring institution on the understanding that he might have something to offer for their money. Fortunately, during that same season, we found an equally beautiful cylinder seal of amethystine quartz with a design of mythological creatures carrying the sun across the sky: its date was about 800 BC and it must at one time have belonged to the governor of Calah. When it came to the division of the spoils I said that I must be able to take back to the British Museum either the cow or the cylinder seal, otherwise I could not return for another season. The matter was hotly debated in the Department and generosity prevailed, by only one vote – so narrow was the margin which enabled us to continue at Nimrud for another ten years.

That first season gave us an understanding of what needed to be done on the acropolis and of why relatively little had been excavated on its eastern sector to which we now turned our attention, for its buildings proved to be exclusively composed of mud-brick that Layard's untrained diggers were incapable of freeing from the surrounding soil unless confronted with the hard guidance of stone bas-reliefs. Day after day, driven on by the wet from one trench to another, we gained an understanding of the less spectacular but important historical potential of the Assyrian buildings. Our first solid achievement here was the excavation of a big administrative building which we called the Governor's Palace, mainly the work of Adad-nerari III and the powerful Queen Mother Sammuramat, famous as Queen Semiramis in Greek historical memory. Over the years we were to enlarge considerably on the plans of our predecessors, Layard, Loftus and George Smith and in succession made rich architectural and archaeological discoveries in the Burnt Palace, in the Temple of Nabu and at the N.E. end of the mound, where we excavated a series of private houses, hitherto undiscovered, which commanded a magnificent view of the outer town from their massive base in the eastern wall of the acropolis.

In the beginning when excavating the Governor's Palace and the Burnt Palace we found bands of ash which were clear indications of a widespread sack. Because at first the associated cuneiform tablets could be dated to the last few years of Sargon's reign, 722–705 BC, I erroneously concluded that Nimrud had been sacked in a revolution that had occurred directly after his death. But prolonged excavation revealed over the years that this terrible holocaust should be attributed to the final sack of Assyria by the Medes and Babylonians, 614–612 BC. The surprising preservation of Sargon's deeds and documents was due not to any sack or revolution, but to the deliberate neglect and abandonment of Calah by his successor Sennacherib who was bent on rehabilitating Nineveh and was so far careless of Nimrud that many buildings fell into disrepair. This situation was changed by Sennacherib's son, Esarhaddon, who reversed his father's policy and determined to rehabilitate Nimrud-Calah: towards the end of his reign he was engaged in the construction of formidable masonry walls at Fort Shalmaneser in the outer town.

The record of history and archaeology goes hand in hand. When we look on the royal succession we find that a new monarch either wished greatly to improve his predecessor's house or else to neglect it altogether and move elsewhere. The history of Assyrian buildings is one of megalomaniac vanity whereby every monarch had to be seen to be possessed of more power than his predecessor. This was a psychopathic state of mind which stemmed from a fear of not being able to retain the servitude and vassalage of an over-extended empire, fraught with potentially disloyal foreign elements in the homeland itself: a pompous show of power was deemed to be the best form of propaganda and a deterrent against those who might be inclined to rebel and were looking for any sign of weakness.

The Burnt Palace, however, although a building of no mean dimensions was comparatively modest for a king's dwelling and was used either by his governor or by Sargon himself while he was designing his new abode at Khorsabad. Among Sargon's most interesting relics was a cuneiform text which recorded the difficulties which his governors were already having with a northern people called the Gimirrai, a foretaste of the power of the Cimmerians who a few decades later, probably in 694 BC, as stated by Eusebius, were to become dominant in Anatolia and brought to an end the mighty Phrygian city of Gordion: this date has been accepted by Rodney Young who excavated the remains of that city in the heart of Cappadocia.

Also found in the Burnt Palace was a beautiful set of small ivory heads, mostly female, which appear to delineate the features of the king's mixed harem. The importance of this distinctive group is that it can now confidently be dated to the last few decades before 800 BC because of its close resemblance to another dated group discovered by Robert Dyson at Hasanlu in N.W. Iran. Here we have a significant landmark in the development of the Nimrud ivories.

One more of the many important discoveries in this sector of the mound must be singled out for attention. It is the discovery of the remarkable set of 'Vassal Treaties' imposed by Esarhaddon on nine princes of the Medes at the climax of his reign in 672 BC. Each of these princes was forced to swear an oath of allegiance to the king of Assyria, and in the event of perjury or forswearing of the oath, was threatened with a series of curses abominable in character and prescribed in detail at a commination service in which some of the maledictions appear to have been dramatically illustrated, for example by the driving of a blood-bespattered chariot and the melting of a waxen image in the fire. Incidentally these tablets contained the last Will and Testament of the king of Assyria and the arrangements he made for his two sons to share the *imperium*, one in Nineveh, the other in Babylon. The tablets were found together with a big set of ninth-century ivories smashed and mutilated in the throne-room of the Nabu Temple. These accursed documents are an immortal witness to the fallibility of treaties once their practicability has expired and to the impermanence of human agreements: assent under duress has ever been in vain.

The master text, a treaty with a Median prince named Urakazabana, was 674 lines in length. D. J. Wiseman, now Professor, spent three years on the task of reconstituting the text from hundreds of fragments, a remarkable feat of stamina and methodical discipline as the world of learning will recognize, for he achieved his task by a masterly tabulation of the pieces, all of which had been generously loaned to the British Museum. He arrived at his office one hour before due time every day and left an hour after it. Such persistent discipline had its reward. Only a few lines are missing.

This brief commentary must suffice as an introduction to the numerous important discoveries on the eastern side of the acropolis. I would only tempt the reader to look in *Nimrud and its Remains* for an account of the private houses; one of their occupants, an old man named Shamash-resh-usur was in business for half a century, a wealthy merchant engaged in many kinds of business transactions such as advancing money against the harvest and supplying birds for the sanctuary at Erbil. This old man is a monument in the annals of gerontology and demonstrates that to survive for so long in Assyria, a man had to be well-nigh indestructible, and that in such conditions the expectation of life increases with advance in age.

We may now return to consider our discoveries on the western sector of the mound. Our main efforts from the first season onwards were devoted to revealing, in so far as we could, the extent and nature of the northern and southern wings of the North-West Palace of Ashurnasirpal, for it was immediately apparent from an examination of Layard's plans that he had concentrated his main efforts solely on the State Apartments whence he recovered the wonderful series of stone bas-reliefs which have for so long been proudly displayed in the British Museum.

We first set to work in the domestic wing on the southern side of the Palace and here found entrancing evidence in quarters occupied by the princesses. Not only was there a rich collection of ivories, among them an unusually large figure of a bull attributable to Sargon's reign, but also little feminine trinkets including a collection of shells which contained cosmetics in the form of malachite eye-paint, one of them engraved with a scorpion associated with the goddess Ishtar and favoured by Sennacherib's queen. In one room there remained a collection of spears probably abandoned by runaway guards. Nearby there was an inhumation grave capped by an inscribed stone tablet of Ashurnasirpal recording the foundation of the city wall and no doubt removed by Esarhaddon when he repaired it two centuries later. The grave contained the remains of a princess for whom there had been deposited the famous Nimrud jewel which is now in Baghdad. The centrepiece was an amethystine quartz seal amulet engraved with a scene depicting two standing figures playing the pipes on either side of a tree. The pendant was attached to a golden chain with beautifully forged links fastened to a swivel. The princess's tunic was held together by an 'elbow' fibula or safety pin of the seventh century BC. The privacy of these apartments was secured by a long stone paved passage, closed by heavy doors, through which the king passed day after day guarded by a great winged angel, an impressive bas-relief standing at the end of the passage.

The northern administrative wing provided other remarkable discoveries. Here were the royal filing cabinets, compartmented brick benches which had contained *inter alia* the records of provincial administration under the reign of Tiglath-pileser III 745–727 BC, and an account of a rebellious Babylonian chieftain named Ukin-zer. This fascinating story has been collated by one of our team, H. W. F. Saggs, (now Professor). The same king's records (Tiglath-pileser III) also included a number of documents relating to taxation and HM's Commissioner of Inland Revenue in the Phoenician cities of Tyre and Sidon where the Scythian police were obliged to bring defaulters to heel. Here also was a great stone prism describing the intrigues of a wily fox, a Chaldean Sheikh, who was a thorn in the side of no less than four Assyrian monarchs. Sargon had removed this seditious inscribed cylinder from the Babylonian city of Erech and supplied an 'improved' version of his own, the first known instance of blast and counterblast in propaganda. Suffice it to say that the layout of the chancellery was a new contribution to Assyrian architecture and that it was a stroke of fortune to find so many archives in their appropriate rooms lying deep in ash, attributable to the final sack: the last firing had of course saved them from destruction though here as elsewhere at Nimrud the salt in the soil had caused many clay tablets to disintegrate.

These discoveries were all made in parts of the N.W. Palace hardly touched by Layard, but the most remarkable of all was made in ground overlooked by him outside the main entrance to the throne-room.

In 1951, while examining the main entrance I could see that many layers of mud-brick had collapsed from the top of the wall and it seemed possible that beneath it something of interest might have been buried and that a great stone *lamassu* or winged guardian, half man, half lion may have been staring at something. Indeed he was. In a niche filled with the collapsed brick there was a wonderful sandstone stela, a monument just over four feet high erected by the founder, Ashurnasirpal, inscribed back and front with 154 lines of text and recording the completion of the city in the fifth year of his reign, 879 BC.

The account is an inventory of the city's principal buildings, of the construction of the palaces, the temples and the walls as well as the royal parks and botanical and zoological gardens. The king loved his flowers, was a keen horticulturalist who gathered many different kinds of trees on his campaigns abroad, collected wild animals on the march, and trapped elephants in pits for the sake of their precious ivory tusks. The Assyrians were intelligent conquerors and reaped the bounty of foreign lands. The stela concludes with an account of a sumptuous banquet served on the acropolis over a period of ten days to 69,574 persons, including a substantial proportion of distinguished visitors: the spacious acropolis of 65 acres could, it is clear, comfortably accommodate about 7000 persons a day, and one has a living vision of the feasts held in the spring of 879 BC, vast *al fresco* meals served no doubt mainly in the spacious courtyards, except perhaps to the privileged few who would have been entertained in the royal apartments. The account of the food, drink, meats, fruit and vegetables, wines and beer makes good reading and is a mine of colourful information.

The most remarkable feature of this text is that it provides a rare basis to attempting some account of a population census at this period, although the 70,000-odd persons here assembled were in Calah for a special purpose. David Oates, now Professor, who joined us in our fifth season, 1953 and in the last years of the dig became Field Director, has in his profoundly interesting book, *Studies in the History of Northern Iraq*, made a reasoned attempt to calculate the population which the district of Calah-Nimrud could out of its own resources, be expected to sustain, with the support of the elaborate canalization inducted by the second founder, Ashurnasirpal, who had reanimated the city about four centuries in the wake of Shalmaneser I. Oates argued from the premise that farmers with land directly dependent on Calah could not be expected to live more than seven or eight miles away from the city, as may be deduced from the limitations of our own workmen both at Nineveh and Nimrud who were prepared to tramp that distance, but rarely more to and fro in a single day. On this basis and reckoning also the area of cultivable land available in these precincts we reach the surprising but plausible conclusion that the native population that could be adequately fed from Calah's own resources amounts to no more than 25,000 persons.

On the other hand we must also reckon from the layout of the buildings, from the space available within the walls that enclosed the acropolis and the outer town, a perimeter of nearly five miles, as well as from the annals of the later Assyrian monarchs and from accounts of their armies, that at times the resident civilian and military population must have reached a far higher figure. We can in my opinion, reckon that there were periods when the population numbered no less than 100,000: indeed in Fort Shalmaneser we found a tablet which recorded the inspection of over 36,242 bows, and that implies an army strength of at least double, perhaps three times that number.

Such calculations are of fundamental importance to our understanding of the progress of Assyrian history. The bulk of the peoples living in Calah and doubtless in other Assyrian cities could be described as parasites in so far as they were living on the backs of the food producers, and they can only have been sustained by importing the surplus from abroad, mostly from the rich granaries of Syria, later fully exploited under the Roman Empire.

Moreover the megalopolitan centres of Assyria required a tremendous labour corps for the building and maintenance of their vast public works. We know that one of Sennacherib's numerous aqueducts leading to Nineveh contained over two million blocks of masonry.

Assyria thus became the prisoner of its own economy which obliged it, for reasons of necessity and security, to depend on a disproportionate number of immigrants for the maintenance of its cities: Syrians, neo-Hittites, even Iranians. The sequence of history at Nimrud well illustrates this state of affairs; the growth, rise and climax of conquest in the ninth century, the difficulties of holding together an enlarged empire in the eighth, the onset of adversity in the seventh and the impending doom which foreshadowed the inevitable fall as things began to go wrong under the last three monarchs from Ashurbanipal onwards. The Assyrian empire is the best illustration of the optimistic statement in the history of Polybius that knowledge of the past is the readiest means of correcting conduct, a view also held by Comte. No one should wish to emulate the Assyrian *imperium* though many have done so.

On the acropolis and particularly in the royal apartments we were rewarded by the discovery of the finest trophies of the Assyrian minor arts that have ever appeared. In our fourth season, 1952, our *annus mirabilis*, we decided to tackle the difficult and dangerous operation of clearing three wells in the Administrative wing.

In the first, AB, Layard himself had dug down to water level and there stopped precisely when he should have continued. Descending deeper we found the remains of sixteen ivory boards and a number of wooden ones. Fragments of cuneiform writing on wax, a form of inscription once very common, were the first ever to be recovered, a text beautifully written in a small cuneiform on its plastic yellow background, a compound of beeswax and orpiment which made it usable. The masterpiece of this discovery was the ivory binding de luxe, inscribed with the name of king Sargon (722–705 BC), telling us that this long astrological omen text, invoking the name of the sky-god Enlil, was made for use in his new palace at Dur-Sharrukin (Khorsabad). We know that Sargon spent a part of his last years preparing to move into his new and unfinished capital. We were lucky to escape from that well without loss of life, for directly after we had hauled up our old well-digger, an ancient from Assur who had worked for Andrae, the bottom of it collapsed with an almighty roar.

This deterred us from getting down to the bottom of another well, AJ, not far away, where 40 years later the Iraq Department of Antiquities, undeterred by such inhibitions, successfully extracted a dozen splendid ivories which seem mostly to be in very fair condition. There is a section of tusk worked at the narrow end into a female figure supporting the bust in her hands, with arm-bands and hair ribbons overlaid in gold leaf. There are two lion bowls, a piece of ajouré plaque and other smaller pieces. The main surprises are a shallow rectangular tray, at least thirty centimetres long, with a shallow circular depression in the centre, at each end a lotus flower attached by a mortise and tenon and other smaller attached pieces which are rams' heads. The other main piece is the head of a eunuch in the round, slightly smaller than the Mona Lisa, the largest of our ivory heads, with some surviving paint, and elements of the body as well, which was evidently composed of interlocking chunks of solid ivory. There are the feet, two pieces of the shoulder and chest with square drapery pattern over them, and some other pieces which probably belonged to the lower left part of the figure, also of course draped. The whole would come out at *c.* fifty centimetres in height.

Our main triumph, however, was achieved in a beautifully built brick-lined well – over three hundred courses in depth, with a corkscrew bend in the middle of it. Many of the bricks were inscribed with the name of Ashurnasirpal. When I consulted an American oil-well expert, he said that every well claimed a life. This one was merciful, for we continued to go down and at an approximate depth of between seventy and eighty feet we found a king's ransom in the sludge under water. Towards the bottom we had to dig day and night, for as fast as we dug the water oozed up. Nevertheless with the aid of hurricane lamps, and spread over two seasons, the job was safely completed. Again I shall mention only a few of the principal finds, all of which have been described and illustrated in *Nimrud and its Remains.*

The most wonderful find was a pair of chryselephantine plaques illustrating a cruel scene, a negro in his death agonies, seemingly the ecstasy of death, mauled by a lioness in a thicket of papyrus and lotus flowers which were disposed in alternate rows waving back and forth in the wind. The little cloisons of the coloured flowers were inset with lapis lazuli and carnelian domes; the features of the negro were perfectly delineated, and the crisp curly hair was rendered by fine ivory spikes capped with gold. These two miniature plaques designed for the back and front of Sargon's throne were a miracle of ivory carving and it is generally supposed may have been the work of Phoenician craftsmen, if so, perhaps imported from Tyre and Sidon to complete their task in Calah. The miraculous discovery of a pair enabled us to claim one of them for this country to which in the course of time, it will have drawn millions of viewers. A big coloured poster which advertises this ivory is displayed in the London tube-railway and attracts visitors to the British Museum from home and abroad, a mark of world-wide esteem.

How well I remember meeting this distinguished visitor at London airport, one Saturday in May 1952, and taking it straight to the British Museum Research Laboratories where Dr H. J. Plenderleith applied his skilled hands and wisely took an X-ray photograph of the back which revealed an internal crack right across. In this way it was possible without delay, to decide how best to conserve it. The other, well-nigh perfect specimen, is one of the most honoured objects in the Iraq Museum, Baghdad. The wise provisions of the Iraqi law at that time have allowed these two gems to be distributed between two far distant capitals: there could in this dangerous age be no better insurance against the total loss and destruction of both, and no better way of allowing the East and the West to enjoy them.

The same well yielded other incomparable ivories: the large head of a fair maiden with black tresses of hair and rubicund lips, dubbed by us, 'The Lady at the Well', and by Naji al Asil 'The Mona Lisa' – famed it will remain for all time. The soft features of this lovely head made a remarkable contrast against another head no less large which we rudely named 'The Ugly Sister', executed in a different technique and probably a century older – that is, made some time in the ninth century, perhaps for Shalmaneser III. This one which was allocated to the expedition was passed on by us to the Metropolitan Museum, New York, which had contributed most generously to the financing of our expedition from 1951 onwards. I have known no more understanding and enlightened supporter from overseas than Charles Wilkinson, then Curator of the Near Eastern Department in that Museum: artist, sensitive craftsman and man of learning, he backed us loyally and liberally and encouraged his successors to follow in his footsteps. Two more ivories out of this big collection found in the same well need an honourable mention: a pair of horses' cheek-pieces adorned with a winged female sphinx in relief; from under the skirt emerges a winged cobra and a quasi-Phoenician inscription adorns an otherwise empty space in front. Obviously Phoenician work, almost certainly of the eighth century it illustrates a strange deformation of Egyptian scenes, which were misunderstood by these craftsmen, a meretricious attraction for the Court of Assyria unfamiliar with the genuine masterpieces. However that may be, the main interest of this discovery is that it illustrates the elaborate equine adornment of the royal chariot teams.

For the preservation of the objects and their treatment in the field, Agatha's controlled imagination came to our aid. She instantly realized that objects which had lived under water for over 2600 years had to be nursed back into a new and relatively arid climate. The 'Lady at the Well' was therefore kept under damp towels for several weeks and we reduced the humidity day by day until she was accustomed to a drier atmosphere. Prognosis and treatment were perfectly adjusted to the patient and results have confirmed their correctness for they are alive and healthy today.

We must now take leave of the imperial treasures on the acropolis, for otherwise they might detain us for many chapters.

Wherever we dug on the N.W. Palace proved rewarding: in objects, alabaster vases and seals, in the understanding of its extended plan. A re-excavation of the Ninurta Temple on its northern side revealed much historical information about the course of events from the time of the foundation in the ninth century until the final sack in the seventh: there were valuable deposits and a series of impressive oil tanks which witnessed to its wealth. On reopening the Ninurta Temple, we exposed at the portal of one of its long halls a wonderfully carved, bearded human head of a stone colossus, one of a pair that had been reburied by Layard because it was too heavy for removal. In so doing we had the advantage of Layard for whom the camera was not available although while he was digging his friend Fox Talbot was making it so.

Of surpassing interest were the mighty acropolis walls still standing to a height of 43 feet and 120 feet wide with a carriage-way at their base on the eastern side, and the exposure of the great stone-quay wall on its western side. This stretched for a distance of about two miles and was composed of powerful masonry blocks originated by Ashurnasirpal and, as he records, dug deep beneath the raging waters of the Tigris. The last man before our time to record this tremendous quay was Xenophon, who in 401 BC, after the battle of Cunaxa marched dry-shod along the old bed of the river as he led his 10,000 Greeks on their heroic journey to the Black Sea and jotted down for posterity notes, substantially correct, to which we were able to add 2350 years later.

In conclusion let it be said that we were vividly aware of how much remained to be done in the excavation of the ziggurat alone, an enormous task that involves deep digging over a number of years and should settle the problem of its approach and staircases. Its wonderful stone and brick northern façade, if fully exposed, would be an impressive spectacle for the visitor approaching Nimrud. But every inch of the acropolis is worth re-excavation, including the great Centre Palace of Tiglath-pileser III whose stone bas-reliefs mark an important stage in the history of Assyrian sculpture.

A final word of praise is due to the Iraq Department of Antiquities and its energetic staff which over many years has been engaged in restoring and maintaining the N.W. Palace, its façade, throne-room, and State Apartments, and in this way have permanently commemorated the signal achievement of its founder.

CHAPTER 18

Nimrud: Fort Shalmaneser

For the best part of a decade we served our apprenticeship on the acropolis, but during that time I had been gaining the confidence of the landlords with the intention of persuading them to allow me to dig outside it.

One Sunday, a day of rest in March 1957, as I was walking round the outer town with our Danish epigraphist, Jorgen Laessoe, on rising ground we picked up a brick inscribed with the name of Shalmaneser III. From that time I labelled this area F.S. and my colleagues were curious to know why. It was not long before they discovered that these initials stood for Fort Shalmaneser and indeed Fort Shalmaneser it proved to be, though that king himself had described it as his Palace: a later renovator, Esarhaddon, called it, more precisely, an arsenal. This vast building when fully exposed covered some twelve acres of ground and comprised over two hundred rooms: it was about double the size of the N.W. Palace: the founder was determined not to be outdone by his father. The eastern flanks were protected by the great towers that ran along the town wall and are today represented by an impressive series of hummocks concealed by turf as they stretch along the skyline. The lofty southern defences are protected by the Patti Hegalli or 'Canal of Abundance' and by a steep approach to the powerful gateways.

The western flanks of the site are more than a mile distant from the acropolis but are easily visible alongside two high landmarks at the S.E. corner of the outer town. Here were two lofty mounds obviously composed of accumulated mud-brick, which gave the impression of being a small ziggurat. Situated 150 metres apart, they were named Tulul el 'Azar: the eastern one was the higher. The ubiquitous Rassam had tested them in 1873–4 and found, as it seems, a few broken ivories but fortunately not enough to encourage him and he soon retreated. The western one of these two high mounds remains to be probed, but we know that it overlies and is probably connected with Esarhaddon's extension and restoration of a Palace-fort already ancient in his time. One day some digger will reveal what is concealed here and if any of it represents the work of the founder.

We soon discovered how to account for the eastern and higher one of these two *tulul*. It represents the debris accumulated from the fall of the massive walls of king Shalmaneser's throne-room, which in size and in height had overtopped every other wall in his Palace and dominated the plain from afar. I have estimated in *Nimrud and its Remains*, that these walls had once stood to a height of not less than 12 metres (just under 40 feet), and were thus comparable with the masonry walls of Achaemenian Gordion (in Asia Minor) which stood at 13 metres (over 42 feet). David Oates, who was charged with the excavation of this sector of the Fort, was unable to embark on the expansive task of clearing the entire throne-room but judiciously excavated the east end of it where a line of plaster exposed by rain had indicated that there was a rebated niche capable of admitting the back of a great stone base for the king's throne, and so it proved to be. After many days of deep digging a huge stepped podium weighing over fifteen tons appeared in its pristine condition. Depressions at the top indicted that the throne, long removed, had changed its position three times in the course of its history.

Fortunately the throne-base itself was too heavy to be dislocated by the Medes who were in a hurry to move elsewhere in order to complete the extermination of Assyria which involved investing Ashur and Tarbisu before the final attack on Nineveh.

A long inscription on the throne-base records that it was set up in the thirteenth year of the reign of Shalmaneser III, in or about 845 BC, when the palace was virtually completed. The scenes on the sides and front illustrate in relief the triumphs over the king's enemies, particularly in Syria. and in Chaldaea as far south as the Persian Gulf where he obtained tribute which included great elephants' tusks here seen carried by porters. The Syrian tusks were supplied by Qalparunda, king of Unqi, that is the 'Amuq plain, a happy hunting ground for the Pharaohs five centuries earlier.

The long friezes which run round this throne dais are smaller than the father's bas-reliefs in the N.W. Palace, but skilfully executed and illustrate Shalmaneser's preference for miniature as on the Black Obelisk and on the bronze gates of Balawat. The place of honour, on the front, is devoted to a scene which shows the king of Assyria touching hands with Marduk-zakir-shumi whom he had reinstated on the throne of Babylon. The celebration of this event takes place under the awning of a royal canopy and vividly illustrates the two kings, their attendants and paraphernalia; the scene thus underlines the importance to Assyria of attracting to itself the religious prestige of the holy city of Babylon: political relations with that city could make for a state of peace or war between Assyria and Chaldaea in the south. Enough was exposed of the throne-room to demonstrate that the walls had been decorated with beautifully executed mural paintings which were a substitute for the stone reliefs preferred by the King's father. They have been reburied for conservation until such time as it may be possible to expose them safely.

It was also apparent from indentations on the dais that the throne had been shifted three times, once perhaps by Shamshi-Adad V (824–810 BC), for an ivory label found in one of the magazines can be taken to mean that he repaired it. Beneath the throne-base there were traces of fallen paintings which proved that it had been shifted at a time when the room was being redecorated and refitted. A pair of post-holes had been sunk deep into the floor in front of the base in order to support the sagging roof which had no doubt been partly dismantled by the enemy. The attempt to rehabilitate the room after the first collapse was, however, ineffective, for there is abundant evidence both here and elsewhere that the last and final sack occurred very soon after the first one. Thereafter a few more generations of men continued to eke out a miserable existence in this one-time military capital of Assyria.

Most important was the associative evidence which combined to suggest that a multitude of ivories, many of them Phoenician in style, had been carved expressly for Shalmaneser III.* On the throne-base occurred the name of Hazael, king of Damascus, and in another chamber, T.10, the name of Irhuleni, king of Hamath, both known to

---

* The date at which the Phoenician-style ivories appeared at Nimrud is controversial. Because they have never been found at Phoenician sites such as Tyre, Sidon and Byblos, in a ninth-century context, some archaeologists believe that they did not appear in Nimrud till well after 800 BC. But Tyre and Sidon have been comparatively

have been his contemporaries. Such evidence strongly reinforces that obtained from Samaria where Ahab's Phoenician queen from Tyre had doubtless encouraged him to build his 'ivory house'. Ahab again was a contemporary. However, the stratification of Samaria itself affords a strong indication, if not positive proof of the fact that Phoenician-style ivories were associated with the ninth century palace at that site. Finally there is also evidence that designs found on faience chalices from Egypt, made in the workshops at Hermopolis and not later than the tenth century must have influenced the Phoenician style. Other evidence from Egypt, notably metal from Tahis of the ninth century is also relevant.

Access to the throne-room was through two doors in its western wall as in the N.W. Palace, and there was another approach through chamber T.3 on its eastern side. Here overlapping the towered entrance from an easterly courtyard T, the approach had been made glorious by a magnificent polychrome glazed brick tableau done in five colours, white, black, green and yellow on a blue background. This striking panel which represented the king twice, standing under a winged disc beneath the tree of life with a surround of gazelle and foliage, was skilfully restored by Julian Reade. It stood to a height of just over four metres and was over three metres in width. This wonderful relic had been saved for posterity because when the portal above which it stood was fired in the sack of Calah, the entire panel detached itself from the mud-brick wall which it had lined and as it lay flat on the ground was protected by the fallen superstructure. Near to it was the great hall T.10 which as I have already indicated was fitted with Phoenician-style ivories which can now be confidently ascribed to the period of Shalmaneser III.

It is impossible in a confined space to do justice to the vast layout of over two hundred rooms which, by the time of Esarhaddon, had earned the official title of *Ekal masharti* or arsenal, a building intended for the ordinance of the camp, the maintenance of chariots, stallions, weapons of war, and spoil of the foe of every kind, a description which corre-

little excavated and the evidence is defective. I do not doubt that one day they will be found at these sites well-stratified and associated with some building that was erected before 850 BC. Their absence from Byblos which has been extensively dug, is more surprising; but it is Tyre and Sidon that need reinvestigating.

sponds very well with what we found in it. What Esarhaddon did, after a period of neglect by his father Sennacherib, was to repair and transform a part of the southern wing: his hand could be discerned in many places and more effectively by the ostentatious southern façade which had been grafted on to the old mud-brick wall of Shalmaneser. Esarhaddon's new entrance which superseded the original one was devised through a long ascending passage flanked by mural paintings. On either side of the entrance an inscription on the beautifully-drafted limestone masonry commemorated the work of this monarch who in his last years was evidently bent on re-establishing Calah as his capital instead of Nineveh as was also suggested by an unfinished palace at the S.W. end of the acropolis excavated by Layard. The show-piece façade at the south end of Fort Shalmaneser was continued along the eastern wall but this remained unfinished, for death intervened to prevent the completion of the grand design.

The southern wing of the building also contained a residency which included a relatively small room decorated with mural painting in the style which could be ascribed to Esarhaddon's reign. In this room there was a pair of stone 'tram-lines' leading up to a dais which has dis-appeared: it could have been made of wood or of mud-brick and the rebated niche which should normally have been situated behind it was absent. I am therefore tempted to make the bold suggestion that this apartment was used as a reception room by the queen, for such rooms must have been provided for the powerful queens of Assyria. More-over, in the vicinity of this apartment there were halls and store-rooms with which several female names were associated – the *shakintu* of the palace, perhaps the queen herself and a woman magistrate. In this wing we have indubitable evidence of a harem. Next to this throne-room was a pair of robing and ablution rooms. Much treasure includ-ing some superb ivories was recovered from these apartments, and one room, S.10, was crammed with ivories burnt black and grey in the avenging fire.

Found on the threshold of a hall near the queen's apartment was a superb ivory lunette illustrating a winged sphinx with leonine body and winged cobra, a *uraeus* pendant from a Phoenician-style skirt. This wonderfully sensitive piece, superbly modelled, I am inclined to associ-ate with Esarhaddon himself, for to the best of our knowledge no monarch before his time was interested by the sphinx, but there are several examples in stone associated with him; notably in the S.W. Palace though admittedly in the Assyrian style. It is true that this is the only Phoenician example, but the sensitive and deep modelling of the features is revealed in all the sphinxes associated with him. In *Nimrud and its Remains*, I suggested, without any strong evidence, that this ivory lunette might have been executed either for Tiglath-pileser III or for Sargon, that is in the latter half of the eighth century BC, but in the absence of positive proof this new ascription is no less possible if we bear in mind the fact that Esarhaddon set foot in Egypt, extended the Assyrian *imperium* to it, and was in close contact with Phoenicia. A sphinx lunette would therefore have been singularly appropriate to his, or his queen's throne.

It is difficult for those who have not seen Nimrud to visualize Shalmaneser's far-flung walls and the dramatic impression made by its long series of projecting mud-brick towers stretching for 300 yards along the eastern sky-line. The organization of these cleverly-articulated buildings has been recorded in plan and described in detail in *Nimrud and its Remains*, vol. II. A series of vast courtyards gave access to magazines, royal residences and soldiers' barracks which were amply furnished with bathrooms, for, to the Assyrians, cleanliness came next to godliness. In the course of time various monarchs added to or restored particular apartments and one mansion erected by Adad-nerari III, 808–782 BC, contained a unique set of free-standing open-work ivories which illustrated negro porters carrying monkeys.

The south-western wing incorporated the residency and here, as we have seen, remote of access was the harem, carefully designed for seclusion of the princesses. Some apartments, David Oates believed, were graded according to rank. Here too was dramatic evidence of the final sack and a mass burial of those who had been slaughtered by the Medes and Babylonians whose assault was well demonstrated in the massive western, towered entrance which had been breached by sappers. The elevation of the tower with its flight of steps, *chemin de ronde* and crenellations was vividly illustrated by a drawing on a potsherd. Striking evidence of the military presence was also provided by an extensive brick saluting base in the south-eastern courtyard.

In surveying this great building one has in the imagination to reconstruct an upper storey which was often approached by wooden steps long perished, although in some chambers the brickwork treads had survived. Most of the ivories had been kept on the upper floor which had invariably collapsed on to the ground. There was, however, one example of a big ground-floor chamber, S.W. 7 in which we discovered a series of throne- or chair-backs stacked for repair after the first sack in 614 BC. These had been made in about 730 BC and provided a unique illustration of the furniture of that period. After two years' respite the second and final sack occurred in 612 BC and this treasure chamber remained buried thereafter until the time of our discovery in AD 1957.

The excavation of Fort Shalmaneser was the last effort of the British School of Archaeology of Iraq at Nimrud and will remain as a glorious addition to the annals of Assyrian archaeology. Probably the collection of ivories in this building was greater than any other concentration of them. It would be impossible to summarize the variety and range of these carvings, but among the most beautiful are the animals, open work, in the round, of oryx, gazelle and other horned beasts. It is surprising that no rendering of the elephant was ever found, the source of the expensive luxuries with which the Assyrian Court was so well endowed. Up till now it has been generally believed that the majority of the ivories came from the tusks of Syrian elephants, an Asiatic species of the Indian elephant known as *Elephas Indicus var. Deranyagala* obtained from herds which had migrated to the 'Amuq plain, and had been hunted by the Pharaohs in the fifteenth century BC. These herds had probably been exterminated by an excess of Assyrian hunting shortly after 700 BC. There is a unique rendering of the Indian elephant on the black obelisk of Shalmaneser III, carved in 841 BC, on which are to be seen Jehoram (?) or Jehu, king of Judah kissing the feet of the Assyrian king.

The excavation of Fort Shalmaneser was no light task for a staff which never exceeded twelve persons. But large staffs distract a director who has to spend time organizing them instead of attending to his main preoccupation – the dig – however well he may delegate his authority. A more serious objection is the expense involved in maintaining, feeding and providing travel funds which may be crippling to an expedition. For so large a dig we managed on the ideal modicum: director and his wife, senior assistant, architect, surveyor, two or more epigraphists, at least one pottery expert, laboratory supervisor, two or more field assistants and, last but not least, a secretary. This last office was filled for most of the years by Barbara Parker who was expected to do everything, especially to take the blame when things went wrong: the catchword was 'sacked again' and what we would have done without this paragon I do not know. Barbara, a woman of dauntless courage, usually dressed in white, red or blue Kurdish trousers, florally adorned, took all crises in her stride and volunteered to go out before the beginning of every season, repair the roof and make the house habitable. Inclined to be forgetful, she was often driven to borrow money from the men in order to pay them. This they took in good part and were grateful to her as their medical officer ever ready to minister to ailments that ranged from bloody flux to stoppage. Barbara was no less of an asset to the staff for at table she kept us continually amused with entertaining conversation and was ever ready to take the part of Court Jester or Shakespearean clown. We owe her a debt also for her professional services as epigraphist; as a photographer she performed extraordinary balancing acts on packing cases in order to bring small objects in focus under the lens. Interested in ancient religion, Barbara related an incomparable knowledge of cylinder seals to the interpretation of their iconography.

> 'Is that a fog horn that I hear?
> Rising in the morning air.
> No, it comes from Barbara's tent;
> Up she gets on duty bent,
> Dons her Kurdish trousers gay
> Once again it's ladies' day!
> And once more the trumpet goes
> As our Miss Parker blows her nose!'

A second ode was also dedicated to her by Agatha: it runs as follows:

> In Blessed Nimrud there did live
> Saint Barbara the Martyr
> In generous gestures she would be
> Invariably a starter

271

Her trousers or her scrambled eggs
  She willingly would share
(Her breakfasts never would go down
  At tea time she was fair)

Accounts she did from morn till eve
  Photography as well
The stern Director, none the less,
  Would simply give her Hell.

'Whose fault is this?' he'd curtly ask
  And Barbara, standing by
Would murmur meekly 'it was me.
  At least – I mean – it's I.'

'My function here I understand
  It is to get the sack,
To say: "Of course it's me (or I)"
  And never answer back.

'But I'm the Nun of Nimrud still
  Miraculous my cures
And those who swallow Sodi Bic
  Will see my fame endures.

'Last night I dreamed when snuggled down
  Beneath my *Ferwa* packed
That once again I heard the words
  "B. Parker, you are sacked!"

'Good Lord,' I said. 'Good Gracious me.
  (And do not drink my gin!)
No more I'll bring a drink to you.
  I'm through. I'm quite done in.

'I'm going to a Ministry
  Accept my resignation.
What Ministry? How can you ask?
  Of course – misinformation!'

One of our important preoccupations was the search for food. Every day we scoured the countryside for eggs which we consumed in hundreds every week so that by the end of the season they were hard to come by. We also attempted to run a small turkey-farm, the most economical kind of meat, preferable to the tough mutton and inedible beef that could be bought in Mosul.

Journeys to the post office and the purchase of liquor were assigned to our stalwart Jacobite Christian driver Petros. Like many drivers he was a maddening fellow, pig-headed, and rich in impracticable suggestions but he had a marvellous memory which was no doubt due to the fact that he could neither read nor write. He could keep every item of our 100 purchases in his head and relate them to me when he returned to Nimrud after sunset. Once without orders he brought me an axe with which I threatened to split open his head, but he was honest after his own standards, though not averse to taking opportune advantage as on one occasion in the summer when he impounded our vehicle because he had persuaded himself that we would not return to collect it; but we soon got it back again. The expedition leaned affectionately on this endearing pillar: he had the one indispensable qualification, a strong sense of humour.

Among the many who took a picturesque place on the canvas of Nimrud, I must not forget my dear friend Donald Wiseman. Ever ready to turn his hand to anything and of imperturbable good humour he took in good part our gentle mockery of his fundamentalist inclinations and submitted bravely to Robert Hamilton's cross examination. He was not the crabbed type of scholar: no grammarian's funeral for him, but he was fearless in his readiness to risk committing errors of textual interpretation in preference to bottling up knowledge. Donald was the extreme opposite to the scholar who is so much afraid of making a mistake that he produces nothing. An indefatigable, rapid and therefore sometimes inaccurate epigraphist, the learned world must be grateful to him for his remarkably quick presentation of the text on the Ashurnasirpal Stele, published within six months of its discovery, and for the reconstruction of Esarhaddon's Vassal Treaties. No other scholar could have completed that formidable task so promptly and so well: the emendations and criticism of that rendering are relatively unimportant. Had he done no more he would have deserved well of us.

We enjoyed many a hard drive together over rough country though he was sometimes a maddening optimist in a black situation. He had a wonderful record of counter-intelligence in the interception of signals for the Royal Air Force during the war and was a youthful Group Captain. Thus he came as a breath of fresh air to the British Museum and to the School of Oriental and African Studies where he was awarded a professorship. In whatever station he has served he has been ready to shoulder administrative burdens and has never begrudged a quota of his time for that purpose. On behalf of the British School of Archaeology in Iraq, he has carried more than his fair share of duties. He has not always been very clear in oral explanation and when at Nimrud we asked him how the British Museum organized its catalogue it was hard to discover whether the like existed at all. Agatha's ode which I quote here alludes to this questionnaire:

> You are wise, Mr Wiseman, the Examiner said,
> And fluent no doubt in your speech
> Pray give me the answer to Question Sixteen
> And give what conclusions you reach.
>
> 'That depends,' he replied, 'if you mean . . . I should say
> Well, perhaps I had better suggest
> No, on second thoughts really it's hard to be sure
> If the answer can – well, for the rest
>
> 'It is certainly true that a – No, perhaps *not*
> One cannot, I find, be exact,
> But the general trend – though I could not assert
> That it follows – well, that is the fact.'
>
> Your reply, Mr Wiseman, the Examiner said
> Is one I cannot but applaud
> Evasion eight marks, volubility nine
> I may say I speak for the Board.
>
> In a masterly way, you have managed to yield
> No informative matter whatever
> We are pleased to award you herewith a D.M.*
> Mr Wiseman awoke and said: 'Never – '

* D.M. Doctor of Mystification

Many others there were who served at Nimrud and though I can only allude to a few I feel nothing but gratitude to one and all of our helpers. Peter Hulin, an epigraphist from Oxford University, has done valuable work notably on the inscription relating to Shalmaneser III and therefore particularly appropriate to Nimrud: he is a meticulous scholar for whom accuracy is of paramount importance. A practical man inclined at times to be overbearing if his 'rights' have not been respected. He was always kindly, ready to be good humoured and complaisant. We enjoyed sharing an equal measure of obstinacy and aggression and I hope he will take no offence at this affectionate record.

Peter's passion for buses and concern with their timetables was commemorated by Agatha who imagined his dream at Nimrud.

> A million buses coming in
> In standardized formation
> A million buses going out
> Of the suburb bus station.
>
> No more, a humble scribe, I toil
> Of contract tablets free,
> I'm Bus Controller No. 1
> To Shalmaneser Three.

Jorgen Laessoe, our colleague from Denmark, a professor, deserves honourable mention. He was assistant with us for three seasons and brought welcome financial support from the Carlsberg Foundation as well as cans of beer. This kindly and brave man had served with the Danish Resistance during the war: the hazardous life which he led during that period left its mark on him. A gifted scholar, after his experiences in the field at Nimrud, he moved on to conduct important excavations at Shemshara in the Dokan and was fortunate in his discoveries at that site, especially of cuneiform texts. But considering his ability, his published output has been disappointing, all the more so because whatever he has published bears the hall-mark of scholarly excellence. I was instrumental in assisting him to obtain a year's Fellowship at All Souls College, Oxford, but he has yet to bring the work which he accomplished there to fruition. He will long be remembered for an epic walk in the mud when his car broke down at the village of

Aqub late at night on a journey from Mosul. He was carrying a heavy suitcase under one arm and a Sumerian dictionary many kilos heavier under the other; he arrived in camp exhausted, in the small hours of the morning. A highly strung man, he was liked by all his colleagues who hope that he will get the better of the impediment which stands between him and the completion of his publication.

To J.L.

The erudite Laessoe
Omitted to say so
But Texts from the Town
Were getting him down.

At the close of the day
In a fever he lay
And muttered, much vext,
Sundry fragments of Text:

'If a dog bark too oft ... (?)
If a Guard spit too soft ...
If a cock loudly crows ...
(If I stay here – who knows? ... (?) (...))

'If there's ice in the river ...
(What's wrong with my liver?)
If an IPC chicken! ...! ... (?!)'
The plot starts to thicken.

His final vexation
Was this kind of equation:
$(.\,.\,.\,.\,.) = (.\,.\,.\,.\,.)$ (?)
E–pig–ra–(PH)–ist's (JAR)–gon
Relating (?) to (S) ar – (GON)?

(A kind of Inscription
That beggars description!)
He awoke with a cry
Of: 'My typist must (DIE)!'

To preserve him from Crime
There arrived, just in time,
His four hundredth Letter!
And soon, he felt BETTER.

Jorgen Laessoe brought with him a contingent of Danes who were, like him, training for the work at Shemshara; there were two architects, Mogens Friis and his attractive Norwegian wife Anne Tinne, who was an ornament to the expedition; they began the outline plan of Fort Shalmaneser in its early stages and were assisted in the field by another Dane named Fleming. Our most distinguished visitor was the famous Danish Palaeobotanist, Hans Helbaek, who has enriched my *Nimrud and its Remains* by presenting a comprehensive account of the cereal and vegetable matter discovered in Fort Shalmaneser. Helbaek married another member of our expedition, Diana Kirkbride, who went on to conduct rewarding excavations in northern Iraq at the early neolithic site of Umm Dabaghiyah as well as in neolithic Beidha in Jordan. For some years before retirement Diana was appointed Director of the British School of Archaeology in Iraq, but her natural bent was towards working on her own, an eighteenth-century explorer, with an aptitude for digging, without fear of embarking on difficult tasks in lonely places.

Jorgen Laessoe's three Danes were thus commemorated by Agatha:

There came three Danes a'sailing, a'sailing on the sea,
And they were bound for Nimrud, to survey and to see.
Their names were very odd indeed, unto our English ears!
Though 'Yawn' for Jorgen is easy. (That only took two years!)
Norwegian Anne Tinne we mastered without groans
But what defeats us utterly, is what *sounds* just like 'Moans'.
He's not so gloomy as he sounds – in fact he's very gay.
And now we've added Fleming – we'll know them all one day!

I now come to two more pillars of the expedition, Joan (Lines) as she was when she first joined us and David Oates. Joan, an American, served for several seasons and applied a skilled hand to the pottery – a formidable undertaking. A superb organizer and exceptionally competent, she has subsequently written learnedly on many subjects of

Oriental archaeology. At Nimrud she was the cynosure of every young archaeologist's eye and many gravitated towards her like flies round the honey-pot. Happily, during the second season, she became engaged to David Oates, whom she married shortly afterwards, and has lived with him at Cambridge happily ever after.

> With Catalogue before me I
>   Was busily inscribing
> And using all the classic terms
>   For pots I was describing.
>
> N.D. One nine five three. Complete.
>   The rounded shoulder pleases
> Grooved ribs, an ovoid body, yes.
>   (Loop handles merely teases)
>
> The body clay is pinkish buff
>   An off-white homewashed slip
> Two eyes of poleaxed greenish-blue
>   Everted reddish lip.
>
> A slender convex grooving shows
>   The collar rim is neat
> The base is concave (surely not!
>   The base must mean the Seat)
>
> Straight neck. Grit tempered. What comes next?
>   The height. In cms. plenty
> The waist diam. is most refined
>   It can't be more than twenty.
>
> The Find Spot? Syracuse, N.Y.
>   The Type? J.L. A.1.
> And thereupon I woke to find
>   That pot and I were One!

David Oates, now Professor and associated with the expedition from its fifth until the penultimate season, is a master of mud-brick and has gone on to excavate remains of the middle-Assyrian period at Tell Rimah, ancient Karana in the Jebel Sinjar. There is no better field worker in all Mesopotamia and the main plan of Fort Shalmaneser is largely his achievement. So good a man in the field is wasted in an academic seat, however competent a scholar he may be. Digging is in his bones and one hopes that he may end his days freed from the cares of administration, which is not his métier. No better book of its kind has been written than his *Studies in the History of Northern Iraq*, for he is a geographer as well as a historian. A man of good judgement and generally of good temper, except when reproached for procrastination, when his Cornish hackles come into play, he is kind to a fault and unwilling to give offence; he will leave his mark behind him. At Nimrud we had, at times, so many Davids that he became known as Sheikh Daoud, an appropriate name, for he would have been a happy wanderer with the Arab tribes. Tall and of gentle manners we remember him as an Apollo looking down from an Olympian height on a world which he must often have found distressing and distasteful.

> Sheikh Daoud was indifferent to fury
> Though feeling like Hell
> He swore he was well
> And positively mellow
> But – SUDDENLY – turned *Yellow*!
> The Medical Professor
> Quickly went into session
> With antibiotics
> And lesser narcotics
> With lotion and pill
> To cure or to kill
> With excitements unpleasing
> (And not very easing)
> They plied all their skill
> . . . .
> Now he REALLY feels ill.

The other David was Stronach who served as a fledgling during the bumper season of 1957 and helped to extract the unique collection of chair-backs from Chamber S.W.7 of Fort Shalmaneser. He also worked on the copper fibulae or safety-pins and wrote authoritatively about them. A good mixer, modest, likeable and energetic, not long after leaving Nimrud he was appointed, at an exceptionally early age, to be Director of the newly founded British Institute of Persian Studies in Tehran which has owed much to his endearing personality. His flair for public relations has helped greatly in the launching of that Institute and he has directed with distinction a number of excavations notably at Pasargadae, founded by Cyrus the Great and at the Median site of Nush-i-Jan. It is pleasing to recall the number of archaeologists who have gone on from an initiation at Nimrud to notable careers elsewhere. Two of them, David Stronach and Neville Chittick, have become directors of Oriental Institutes, and five have been awarded University Chairs or Professorships.

More or less contemporary with David Stronach was another Cambridge man, Nicholas Kindersley, not a profound academic but invaluable to the expedition because of his practical ability and skill in looking after transport. He went on to run a successful hotel in Ireland and I wish that he had continued to serve the school. Agatha's ode commemorating his capacity for eating meringues ran:

> Baa baa Michael, what is there to eat?
> Grill chop, plenty, and cream meringues for sweet;
> None for Miss Parker who cannot get them down
> But twelve for Mr Nicholas who's been out in the town.

Another unforgettable character was Marjorie Howard, seconded from the Institute of Archaeology (then in Regent's Park), solemnly engaged in pumping polyvinyl toluene and other chemicals into the ivories. A gifted artist, life was made difficult for her when two colleagues were courting in the pump and Antiquities Room. One of the vaguest women I have ever met, she was passionately devoted to her dog and during her absence from England hired a Jehovah's Witness to care for her father and the dog; she worried solely about the dog. How she reached home we do not know, for she refused to concern herself with such trivialities as Visas. All officials yielded to her in despair.

> Weep tears of Polyvinyl, all
> Ye nymphs of Regent's Park
> But list, there's greater glory seen
> Attend and likewise Hark!

The ruined ziggurat, about 43 metres high, is a landmark visible at many miles' distance from Nimrud. Founded by King Assurnasir-pal II and completed by his son Shalmaneser III (859-824 BC), it was dedicated to Ninurta, god of war and the chase, the patron saint of the city. The original staged tower was approached by staircases, but only the mud brick core now remains, and on the northern side a pilastered facade of burnt brick with ashlar masonry blocks of limestone at its base. The building served as a watch-tower, was doubtless used for the taking of celestial observations, and was closely connected with the Ninurta temple at its foot.

Open-work ivory panel, 8.1 × 6.9 cm, depicting the 'lady at the window'.

Ivory head, height 16 cm, known as the 'Mona Lisa of Nimrud', found encased in sludge, deep under water at the bottom of a well in a room NN of the NW Palace. I was cut from a longitudinal section of an abnormally large elephant's tusk. The dar black tresses of hair are a perfect setting for the face: the crown and stand were originally fitted with ivory studs. The nose has been restored by Sayid Akram Shukri, photograph by Antran. This is th second largest ivory head to have survive from antiquity; it was perhaps made to th order of Sargon II.

Chryselephantine plaque depicting a lioness killing a negro in a meadow of lotus and papyrus plants, which are rendered in carnelian and lapis lazuli and overlaid in gold. Length 10.5 cm, base 9.8 cm tapering at 6 cm at top; thickness at bottom 2.8 cm and at top 1 cm. One of a pair.

Ivory figure in the round, height 13.4 cm. Nubian (?) leading an oryx, carrying a monkey (*cercopithecus*) on left shoulder and leopard skin over right. He wears a patterned, divided skirt tied by a sash and decorated with two full-length *uraei*. Pendant round neck and armlet originally incrusted. Parts of legs restored in wax.

Right: Open-work ivory panel, 14.6 × 8 cm. A browsing oryx.

Above: Open-work ivory plaque, 9.4 × 5 cm.
Cow and calf. Part of a set of furniture veneer.

Below: Open-work ivory panel, 19 × 15 cm, set in a lunette framework 14 mm wide.
Sphinx in quasi-Egyptian style, wearing Pharaonic headcloth and *atef* crown,
pectoral with papyrus design, Phoenician apron with pendant *uraeus* and sun-disc.
Eyes and eyebrows originally incrusted.

Nimrud: Fort Shalmaneser

For Lo! Three Homers and a Half
of famous Marjorie
The Great Sir Mortimer himself
Shall sponsor on TV ! !

High on the list of personalities stands Hamad our watchman, who
served for many years and became so rich that he had to be dismissed.
An enterprising man, he appeared early at Nimrud as an applicant for
the job, dressed in a bandolier stuffed with cartridges, rifle in hand and
was instantly accepted. He was insolent and aggressive and a trial to
everyone, thus perfectly endowed for the office. He had a savage dog
which attacked all and sundry, particularly our epigraphist, C. J. Gadd,
when he sallied forth in the small hours of the morning to the battlements where our open-air closet was situated. When the Minister of
Education Halil Kenna was due to arrive at Nimrud with a large party
of state visitors, we were afraid that Hamad's dog would bite his
Excellency's legs, or have his meat, as the Arabs say, and that would
have done us and him no good. 'As much meat,' I said to Hamad, 'as
your dog removes from the calves of his Excellency's legs, I warn you
that I shall remove from you.' That did the trick.

It was a difficult task to persuade (Professor) C. J. Gadd, author of
The Stones of Assyria, to join us at Nimrud, about which he had written
so learnedly, but eventually he yielded to pressure and, as he was an
open-air man, enjoyed the experience and his period of release from
the cares of Keepership of the Department of Western Asiatic Antiquities in the British Museum. Cyril Gadd fitted happily with the
expedition but suffered acutely from our rather greasy cooking and
longed for an unobtainable old-fashioned bread-and-butter pudding.
I have an ineffaceable memory of him dressed in a second-hand post-
man's uniform which he had used during the war while serving as a
fireman in the British Museum. This outfit he used to don while
attending with the utmost anxiety to the improvised kiln efficiently
built by our architect for baking the cuneiform tablets – an operation
which was entirely successful. In that year, 1952, we found not only
the rich archive filed in the N.W. Palace but also the wonderful hoard
of treasures in its wells. But so pessimistic and undemonstrative was
Gadd by nature, that his colleagues at home were given no inkling that

we had found anything of surpassing interest. Agatha's poem on the subject ran as follows:

The Saga of
THE KEEPER, THE ARCHITECT, AND THE YOUNG EPIGRAPHIST
(Under the auspices of Lewis Carroll)

The Keeper and the Architect
    Were looking at mud brick
They pondered how, and why, and if,
    And how much? And how thick?
And what degrees in Centigrade
    Were best to do the trick

The wind was blowing noisily
    And dustily to boot;
They sighed like anything to see
    Such quantities of soot!!
'The wind is *never* in the North;
    "Prevailing wind" my foot!'

They took the chimney down again
    And built it up anew
And thick and fast the flames at last
    Went roaring up the flue.
'I really think,' the Keeper said
    'That this time it may do.'

'O Tablets!' said the Keeper then,
    'Your time of grace is sped,
Into your pots now, every one,
    The flames are burning red;
In fact one cannot tell them from
    My young assistant's head.'

'What? Burning us?' the Tablets cried,
    Turning a little pink.
'Although we have a hard-baked look
    Our hearts are soft, we think,
And from the fiery furnace we
    Undoubtedly do shrink.'

But fifty Tablets came along
    All ready to be cooked,
And nicely sanded, in their pots,
    Were soon to Hell Fire booked.
(And that seems odd of Mr **Gadd**.
    A kindly man he *looked*.)

'*Away with softness!*' Lenin said
    And I repeat his cry;
'So if you're ready, Tablets dear,
    Shall we prepare to fry?'
But answer came there none because
    Theirs not to reason why.

At dawn the Young Epigraphist
    Obediently did rise,
Broke down the door and sorted out
    Tablets of every size
Holding a pocket-handkerchief
    Before his smoke-grimed eyes.

Whilst Mr Gadd, behelmeted
    Was blasting fast and free.
(His mother would not know her son
    Thus dressed by I.P.C.)
And brave and clear the cuneiform
    Stood out for all to see!

Incidentally, the builder of Gadd's kiln was our friendly and co-operative Scottish architect, John Reid, who has subsequently applied himself to the restoration of ancient Scottish homes. Agatha's ode about John ran as follows:

(N.B. This remarkable dream came to Mr Reid after he had partaken rather freely of a Kouzi. He dreamt that he was being interviewed by the representative of a certain newspaper.)

'I'd like to ask you, Mr Reid,
    What feelings did it rouse
When you were asked by Levenstein
    To build his country house?

What did you feel when first he said
   He'd like a house devised?'
Sucking his pipe, young Mr Reid
   Said: 'Well – I was surprised.'

'When Mr Levenstein explained
   You had *carte blanche* to spend
Expense no object, Mr Reid
   A free hand to extend
What were your feelings, Mr Reid
   Thus nobly patronised?'
Sipping his toddy, Mr Reid
   Said: 'Well, I was surprised.'

'Now Levenstein and Finkelbaum
   Are wealthy men indeed.
Why should they give the job to you,
   I wonder, Mr Reid?
So far you've only built a kiln
   (Though cunningly devised).'
Stroking his thatch of hair, young Reid
   Said: 'Well – I was surprised.'

'When you had struggled gallantly
   With all the devilish kin
Contractors, builders – yes, and forms
   And filled the whole lot in,
When you at last beheld your house
   Just like a dream arise,
What was your feeling, Mr Reid?'
   'INCREDIBLE SURPRISE!'

I must also pay tribute to a succession of Mutesarifs, the Governors of
Mosul who, in spite of their many preoccupations were generous of
time spent on our behalf. Especially kind to us was Sayyid Qazzaz, one
of the most efficient Iraqi administrators, whom I had first met when
he was senior clerk in the British Administration in Mosul under
Major Wilson, who marked him for promotion. He foresaw difficult

times and after he had attained high office as Minister of the Interior, attempted to resign, but Nuri Pasha refused to release him. When Kasim came to power, Nuri's loyal henchman, without any powerful protection, was executed for allegedly having given orders to fire on rioters when he was Governor of Basrah. For any orders given he took full responsibility. Straight as a die, he was a loyal Kurd and a loss to Iraq. Many a time he came out to inspect Nimrud and kept a benevolent eye on us. We lament the loss of an old friend.

The senior members of the Iraq Antiquities Department then serving under Dr Naji el Asil were highly businesslike and co-operative. Taha Bakir, an epigraphist and a most honourable man who later succeeded Naji, was both loved and respected: his colleague Fuad Safar, who later became Inspector General of Antiquities, was a man of unusual all-round ability, clever in linguistics and the renowned excavator of Eridu. These men had the difficult task of adjudicating a fair share of the finds and advised the director with their expertise, sagacity and fairness.

Faraj Basmachi, honest to the bone, was, when we first met him, inclined to be xenophobic, but under gentle persuasion to be xenophile; he was an amiable man who did not mind having his leg pulled, but he was never generous in recommending a good reward for the digger. After our wonderful season in 1952, we sent him off to Baghdad with the ivory Mona Lisa, or Lady at the Well, packed into a hatbox which we draped with a strip of black lining in mourning for her loss.

We also have happy recollections of another Iraqi member of the expedition, Sayyid Izzet Din es Sanduq – Mr Box as he used to call himself, who could produce lightning sketches of any object ever discovered, suitable for the first, but not always for the final record. We all liked this delightful man who was happy because he had near at hand a cousin in Mosul whom he used to visit for long weekends. On one occasion Izzet Din asked me to procure electric light for his cousin's home, very rare and virtually unobtainable. 'You can do it if you try,' he said; so I wrote a letter to the British engineer in Mosul, a well-known misanthropist. 'My friend,' I wrote, 'thinks that I have some influence on the electric light: I have assured him that I have none, but not to write to you would be unfriendly.' Within two weeks, the home of Izzet Din's cousin was fully illuminated. God said let there be light and there was light.

Another good friend, the Iraqi representative of the Antiquities Department, was Tariq el Madhlum who, I suspect, hated all foreigners as exploiters of his country and resented the fact that its development was perforce attempted through them. He had, I believe, bitter memories of conscription in the Iraqi Army. This gifted man and imaginative painter was an asset to our expedition. He loved Agatha for her open-hearted kindliness and she loved him for his strong and sterling character. After completing his term at Nimrud, he came to the University of London and after four or five years of diligent work obtained a doctorate which resulted in an invaluable book on the chronological development of the Assyrian bas-reliefs, illustrated by his own lucid sketches. Subsequently he has directed important excavations at Nineveh, at Sumerian Tell el Wilayah, and elsewhere, and is skilled in maintenance and restoration. Agatha wrote of him:

> In his corner Tariq sits
> Does the catalogue in bits
> All the while his fertile brain
> Urges him to paint again
> 'Compositions' go and come, so he too,
> Pulls out: Female figures, two;
> Ladies at the window? No
> There they hang upon the wall
> Watching Tariq at his toil!

Of our workers I have often spoken – a happy mettlesome crowd, ever ready to quarrel and to be reconciled; they loved a dramatic situation and were prepared to laugh at themselves: to handle them was to understand men and needed fairness, firmness and fire. No one should be a director unless able to make rapid decisions: hesitation is fatal. The cream of our workmen were the skilled Sherqatis from the village opposite Ashur; they were devoted and sensitive craftsmen. Our foremen were Abd el Halaf el Anqud, wise, gentle, tactful, a contrast to the fiery and conscientious but less well-bred Mohd Halaf el Muslah who radiated energy, and was not always of sound judgement. These two kept a watchful eye on the men who turned the soil and tenderly nursed the recalcitrant mud as it yielded to their hands. Some of them were of the third generation in descent from those who had worked for the Germans at Ashur. It will be a sad day when their traditional skills cease to be handed down, for with the growth of industrialization there is danger that this handicraft will become extinct.

I must not omit to mention the services of the Iraqi Police: as a rule a pair of custodians were sent from Mosul to guard our camp – tokens of law and order. They were always inclined to be helpful but were not always wise. On one occasion a Kurdish policeman spotted some criminal, a man wanted on a charge of robbery, happily at work on the dig, and attempted to arrest him. The quarry, however, was too quick for the arm of the law and took to his heels. Our policeman waited for the man to become visible in the plain below the mound as he tried to cover the ground between Nimrud and the village of Naefa. The Kurd, unwilling to forgo his prey, took a long shot with his rifle and winged the man who, with damaged leg began crawling to safety surrounded by an angry posse of defenders from his village. Our policeman, hot in pursuit, had to flee for his life and we had to save him from lynching. He returned to Mosul safely, though not, I fear, chastened.

A more serious view I thought, was taken of robbery than of murder which was by no means uncommon among the tribes. I remember that at the request of the Sheikh of Nimrud I felt obliged to dismiss at the end of one week four men, alleged to have committed murder. I sometimes wondered what our chartered accountants thought when they read against the names in the pay book 'Sacked for murder', and two weeks later 'Reinstated'. The fact is that they had murdered the Sheikh's groom, but the matter was quickly settled by the payment of blood money exacted through the powerful authority of the Sheikh's uncle, Haji Mohd el Najeifi.

Many distinguished visitors came to Nimrud and occasionally lodged with us. Firstly, Ernest and Dora Altounyan from Aleppo whom I have mentioned in the account of our Syrian excavations. Ernest was the devotee of T. E. Lawrence and wrote a notable poem 'Ornament of Honour' which opened with a lovely passage:

You never saw that crooked moon
Behind Aleppo's citadel:
You never saw it shine again
In Dorsetshire.

Ernest's wife, Dora, was an intellectual and, unlike her medical husband, had a profound interest in archaeological writing. She was sister of the philosopher and historian R. G. Collingwood who wrote *inter alia* a book entitled *Speculum Mentis* (Mirror of the Mind) happily mistranslated 'Little Hope for the Mind', a brilliant howler. Dora painted a number of quick sketches of Nimrud which are in my possession, including a happy reminder of the interior of the house and its sagging roof-poles in the dining-room propped up by a heavy wooden pillar. Our roof was by no means watertight and reminded me of Layard's description of the scene in the village of Nimrud when he took shelter under his solitary table while his servant huddled under his cloak in a corner of the room.

Many of us have happy memories of a visit in 1951 of our old friend, Sir Allen and his wife, Lettice, Lane. Allen was the celebrated founder and publisher of Penguin and Pelican books: he had built up his empire from a capital of £100 and although he read little, had a flair for anything capable of arousing the public imagination. Having missed a University education himself he wanted to make good that gap for the ordinary man who had been similarly deprived, by printing readable books of academic quality cheaply. Allen was a man of boundless energy, an opportunist, a born pirate, ready to take on anything. He had been devoted to Agatha since boyhood and admired her both as a person and for her talents. This generous buccaneer who could ride rough-shod over his best friend expected and never resented opportunism. He had a penchant for befriending bad characters whom he helped liberally. I had some business with him in that I advised him to turn his interest to archaeology and after I had done so, for some time he asked me to edit a series of Oriental archaeologies and I supervised some ten Pelican books most of which turned out to be best-sellers. As authors, I chose when I could, young men of high academic capacity whom I believed would make their mark – among them Oliver Gurney for *The Hittites*, Bryan Emery for *Archaic Egypt*, Stuart Piggott for *Prehistoric India*. Eventually I also persuaded W. F. Albright, Leonard Woolley, Seton Lloyd and Roman Ghirshman to contribute books.

Allen backed us in the early years at Nimrud and for this we owe him a debt. Surprisingly, when I offered him a big volume on our discoveries he began to have cold feet, for Penguins were then running into difficulties and I accused him of leading me up the garden path, for he had at the outset encouraged me. His refusal turned out to be my good fortune, for I went on to write a much bigger, illustrated work which broke a record by selling two thousand copies, seventeen hundred at sixteen guineas, the remainder at twenty guineas, bravely sponsored by the firm of Collins for the British School of Archaeology in Iraq and I was duly grateful to my old friend Sir William Collins whose faith was thus justified.

Allen Lane and his charming wife, Lettice, were present at the discovery of the Ashurnasirpal Stela in 1951, but unfortunately had run out of coloured plates when it was exposed. These were the early years in colour photography for the archaeologist and at Nimrud we saw the first of it. Perhaps the warm-hearted Allen will be best remembered by the expedition for his magnificent gift of a whole Stilton cheese, flown over from London on two or three occasions. We were fortunate to benefit from the generosity of this Maecenas.

The dig at Nimrud is inseparable from memories of our mud-brick house perched up on top of the acropolis wall with its view of the ziggurat on one side, and of Fort Shalmaneser and the outer town on the other. The house itself contained, besides the usual offices, a kitchen and a dark room and two long halls, one of them served as a common room and dining-room, the other as the Antiquities Room. Along the walls we had built big mud-brick counters or *mastabas* which provided ample space for spreading out the antiquities and saved the expense of providing wooden shelving. For the expenditure of a little over one thousand pounds we had a palatial but simple abode with ample storage capacity. In it we spent many a happy hour surrounded by our entrancing finds, and towards the end of the season enjoyed the luxury of taking tea on the brick terrace at the back and the magnificent view therefrom. We slept in tents which were usually waterproof, but I have a memory of a terrible windstorm which came up shortly after sunset: the heavens turned to a dull yellow and we believed that the demon Asmodeus had come to remove the roof of the Expedition manor. We were then in danger of removing the entire camp. Loftus had suffered a similar storm in 1854.

In spite of occasional mishaps which were due to extremes of cold, heat, wind and rain in turn, we lived in reasonable comfort and fed off the land on fresh food prepared by a succession of cooks, Persian and Indian; some were the worse for drink, others the worse for sobriety; our domestic needs were catered for by an ample supply of Arab servants who arrived thin and left rotund; our Major Domo was a Nestorian named Michael, who might have stepped out of an El Greco painting. Our healthy open-air lives made for voracious appetites and apart from the occasional stomach casualties, we suffered from no serious ailments. Life on a dig is conducive to *mens sana in corpore sano*.

It is appropriate that I end this account of Nimrud with Agatha, ever generous and radiating harmony. She helped with the repair of the ivories and the cataloguing, in the early days with the photography, later taken over by Barbara Parker.

We built Agatha a little room at the end of the house where for a part of the morning she sat and wrote her novels quickly and straight on to the typewriter. More than half a dozen of them were written in this way, season after season.

Agatha helped me pay the men at a little *guichet* which opened off my office and occasionally a visitor from Mosul was heard to say, 'Come and have a look at the men being paid and Agatha Christie paying them.' Agatha entertained us from time to time with merry odes some of which I have quoted in this chapter; many members of the expedition were commemorated in this way. The odes were allusive and topical, therefore sometimes beyond the comprehension of anyone not familiar with the expedition: I end with a brief composition about myself:

Hark! Hark! the dogs do bark!
Visitors coming today.
Is it the Abbot of Mar Benham
Or could it be Father J?

Sheikh Daoud doesn't like to be rude
But reaches his tent in a bound.
The Director, instead, claps his hat on his head
And hurriedly goes to ground.

I hope that these reflections on our excavations will lead readers to examine a work in which I take some pride, namely *Nimrud and its Remains*. All diggers know that the most exacting part of their activity is the record of it and not all succeed in meeting this obligation.

Nimrud and its Remains comprises over six hundred pages, made more attractive by over two hundred plates, many of them illustrating glorious *objets d'art*. I am conscious of the inevitable defects of the writing of this voluminous work but thankful that I possessed the stamina and the help of devoted colleagues to see it through. I hope, therefore, that this book, no less than the scientific results, justifies the continuous effort of our skilled teams of workers, season after season, during the twelve years from 1949 to 1960.

CHAPTER 19

Academic Institutions and their Inmates

The title that I have chosen for this chapter reminds me of the time when I applied for a vote at Torquay and was preceded by a lunatic: 'Are you,' said the registrar, 'a temporary or a permanent inmate of the local asylum? If temporary you have no entitlement, if permanent you will be granted a vote.'

For many years I was uncertain about my academic status; however, I now come to the last stages of my career when I had earned a name for Nimrud and much to my delight obtained in 1962, a Fellowship at All Souls College, Oxford; and this appointment, which released me from administrative duties, enabled me to finish and publish *Nimrud and its Remains*. It is true that the College elected me in conclave, but I must acknowledge the debt that I owe to Arthur Salter (Lord Salter), who championed me. We came to know each other well in Baghdad, and after the death of Air Chief Marshal Sir Robert Brooke Popham he was an obvious choice for the Presidency of the British School of Archaeology in Iraq.

This little wizard became a dear friend: he was a man who had served his country with the utmost energy and distinction. To his acuteness and drive, in the face of dire opposition from senior officers in the Admiralty, we owe the elimination of the German submarine menace in the First World War. It was his championship of the convoy system that prevented this country from being brought to starvation. His quick and alert mind was allied to a personality that was without a trace of pomposity or flashiness. This great fighter, who turned many a lost cause into a winning one, lived with a constant twinkle in his eye. At the instigation of Nuri Pasha he produced a masterly report on the economy of Iraq, which was promptly pigeonholed. Privately he stigmatized his Iraqi colleagues as 'darned lazy' and, although he recognized Nuri Pasha's achievements, was distressed that he supported in office many who were inefficient. He was devoted to his College, All Souls, which harboured so many distinguished and learned men, but he had little use for academic attainment as such unless it was devoted to public service, an ambition which was often disappointed.

My election to All Souls gave me some elation for at last, at the mature age of 58, I felt that I had through the efforts of my life-work, recovered from the lack of academic distinction in my youth, and I hope that this unexpected achievement, in contradiction to an undistinguished beginning, may encourage other late developers to persist in the effort towards natural fulfilment. When I joined the College and took part in the Meetings of its Governing body I was reminded of the phrase used by that brilliant actress, Vanessa Redgrave, when addressing her class at School: 'You are "the Crème de la Crème".'

At first, therefore, I suffered, as in youth, from a feeling of inferiority and feared to speak in debate. But like Socrates I had a daemon which sometimes came to take charge, and when possessed I was capable of oratory and of exercising sway; though I rarely had the occasion to attempt it in collegiate gatherings, except on one or two occasions, particularly in a diatribe against the erection of an unimaginative and mindless building proposed as a new wing to an otherwise beautiful College.

College Meetings of the Governing body tended to be protracted, and I was often tempted to believe that it was because our Warden, John Sparrow, thought that this kind of torture was appropriate to a body of men who only became corporate on these occasions. Sparrow's performances in the Chair were remarkable, for he had to cope with the most subtle arguments on every kind of topic and was never at a loss for an answer. It was fascinating to watch him as he stood on his feet and asked himself how he might deal with the next chestnut. A brilliant classic, trained as a lawyer, he would have been capable of rising to the topmost flights at the bar or on the bench, but preferred the cloistered life. His influence on the College tended to be negative, and in my opinion he did not properly exploit the rich body of talent at his disposal, neither did he take sufficient interest in the work conducted by the Fellows within the College walls. But he was a civilized man, urbane and charming, and entertained generously and well.

I will not speak in detail of the Fellows, but would mention my admiration for Lord Wilberforce, who inspired confidence in his judgement and great respect for his clear-headed analysis of the most complicated problems. He was a man of sweet temper and charm who would, I believe, have been well contented in teaching the classics in which, as an undergraduate, he had performed with supreme distinction. It was a misfortune for the College that he was never its Warden but instead the law gained a mind of great quality. The College had indeed its quota of distinguished lawyers, one of whom was Lord Hailsham, endowed with courage, probity and ability in equal measure, a devout Christian possessed of qualities often lacking in our lives today, and one wishes that he had attained the office of Prime Minister, one for which his fearlessness and honourable thinking would have made him eminently fitted: perhaps he was too good a man for that unenviable task.

I had a personal affection for Aylmer Macartney, who was a kind mentor to me when I was elected, an organized mind in a rare field, that of Hungarian history. He could be cantankerous and opinionated but, as it always seemed to me, was basically of sound judgement, devoted to his special field of scholarship and contemptuous of what he considered to be bogus in the land of learning.

Ian Richmond, who occupied the Chair of the Archaeology of the Roman Empire, was my only colleague in an allied field: his death at a comparatively early age was tragic, for there is much more that he could have written down for our instruction and entertainment. He was a cordial, warm-hearted friend, as was the eminent historian, Ernest Jacob, who gave body and soul to the College for 40 years. I was proud that before he died he referred to me as his best friend, perhaps because I gave him what little attention I could towards the end of his days. In him was enshrined something of the ancient rural Oxford that had entered into his soul through tramping around the villages and country churches in his youth.

Another sympathetic friend was that renowned historian, A. L. Rowse, for whom everybody that had ever mattered in the Shakespearian scene was still alive. In conversation he could, like a magician, conjure to life these domestic images of the past and bring them into the room.

The College has this year shown its wisdom in electing an eminent lawyer, Patrick Neill, QC, as Warden, a man of charm and good sense, well-fitted to guide it in difficult times, together with a charming and witty wife and ample family to fill the Warden's Lodgings.

The last but not the least of the Fellows in order of mention was that extraordinary Orientalist, Robin Zaehner, Spalding Professor of Eastern Religions and Ethics; and no man was better fitted to sit in a Chair which demanded its occupant to demonstrate the community of thought and inspiration in all religions: a proposition with which he was wholly in disagreement and his honesty in saying so nearly lost him the Chair when it came up for renewal.

Robin Zaehner had an exceptional talent in the mastery of obscure languages, ancient and modern; in Sanskrit and Persian he was deeply versed. He wrote with an entrancing fluency of style innumerable books, mostly on religious subjects, many of them best-sellers translated into many languages; but he tended to write too much and to become repetitive. He was profoundly concerned with the problem of good and evil and prepared to consider the most cranky subjects, and devotees in the pursuit of their objectives. The light could be seen burning through his windows, far into the small hours of the morning, as he browsed endlessly over his task, often aided by the bottle which helped the many quirks of his comic temperament and provided his friends with amusement. One night it was thought that owing to the noise a late robbery was being attempted, and a colleague was about to summon the police when it was discovered that the disturbance was due to Zaehner who, in the dim light, was found to be clinging to the rafters like a bat.

On another occasion when visiting the British Institute of Persian Studies in Tehran he returned in the small hours in a state of intoxication, and as he was therefore unable to fit the key into the lock of the outer door, lay down to sleep in the jube, or open gutter, which ran down the street outside the building. At dawn, a chill wind blew and roused him from his stupor. He was by that time sufficiently recovered to hail the porter and got the key into the outer lock, but could think of no way of winning admittance to the inner door except by putting his fist through the big glass pane which framed it. Again he lay down, this time covered in blood, but no one was the worse for this escapade as he readily made good the damage out of his own pocket.

I have no hesitation in putting down all this for the record, for it is my belief that life is the richer for such experiences. I have no faith in plaster saints. The world is the better for comic and whimsical learned men such as Robin Zaehner; deeply serious down below, he preferred to open his mouth in jest and rarely took part in debate at any assembly. He was a convert to Roman Catholicism, happy and dedicated to his religion. Years spent with an excess of alcohol probably shortened his life, but he died at a good age after achieving the completion of his principal tasks: he was struck down in the High returning to College after Mass – a blissful end; he died in a state of grace.

All Souls attracted a measure of jealousy from other Colleges in the University, partly because it was a privileged body which lodged no undergraduate within its walls, and yet provided more heads of Colleges than any other. It was, in my opinion, unfairly criticized in the Franks Report on various grounds and quite unfairly for evading its teaching obligations. In fact, as much teaching was done within its four walls as in many other Colleges within the University. It was not built to house many bodies and it would have been absurd to attempt to do so: the spaciousness of its architecture was medieval in origin and not designed for that purpose. It is sound in principle that within a University there should be one or more abnormal institutions, and All Souls was indeed a brilliant solecism, as picturesque in the present as it had been in the past. As I sat in my rooms in the Old Quadrangle, which dated back to the founder early in the fifteenth century, I used to wonder if any of the earlier Fellows recorded as elected to the College in 1453 had occupied them; how long it took for the news of the fall of Constantinople to reach the infidel in Oxford, and what impact the event had on it.

Two years before my election to All Souls I began to receive honours which I had attracted from the completed work at Nimrud, honours which should also have been shared by the many devoted helpers who had assisted me in its excavation and publication. First came the CBE in 1960, to be followed by a knighthood in 1968, most welcome because it also conferred a title on my beloved Agatha, who in 1971 was awarded the high honour of being created a Dame after a CBE in 1956. All this was gilt on the gingerbread.

Academic honours also followed, for after my election to the

British Academy in 1955, I became in due course 'plein membre' of the Académie des Inscriptions et Belles Lettres, a rare distinction, and thus was entitled to adopt the title of Membre de l'Institut de France and so to take part in the proceedings which went on in that imposing building facing the Pont des Arts. This honour would have pleased my Parisienne mother more than any other; I wish that she had still been alive at the time. I was also gratified by my election, later, to a corresponding Fellowship of the Royal Danish Academy, an ancient and august institution. I forbear to mention other generous academical awards but must record with special pleasure three medals: one from the USA, the Lucy Wharton Drexel Gold Medal conferred by the University of Pennsylvania; the Lawrence of Arabia Memorial Medal awarded by the Royal Central Asian Society; and in 1976 the first Gertrude Bell Memorial Medal of the British School of Archaeology in Iraq 'for outstanding services to Mesopotamian Archaeology'. I often feel that these awards are in fact a testimonial to the generosity of my archaeological friends, who have exercised forbearance and forgiveness for my often ill-tempered and censorious complaints; but they have known that I have not only felt beholden, but loved and respected them: it is what men have done, not what they have left undone, that moves us. I feel I must also mention here the pleasure it gave me to be elected an Honorary Fellow of my old College, New College, as well as an Emiritus Fellow of All Souls on retirement.

I must now turn briefly to my links with our Oriental Schools and Institutes, for I have at various times, and indeed, on some of them continuously, served on the Councils and taken an active and profound interest in their affairs, to wit, particularly, the Schools and Institutes in Jerusalem, Ankara, Baghdad, Tehran and Kabul, and had a hand in the foundation of the last two through the British Academy. These institutions have for me been the most rewarding aspect of my participation in Oriental archaeology, for not only have they yielded a multitude of friends, but this form of international involvement has conferred mutual prestige on our country and the host country concurrently. We have in this way helped each other to take a pride in the past, particularly in its ancient monuments and remains, and by sharing in excavations have aided in the building up of the great Museums and national collections: in the early days when the Antiquities Laws were less stringent, the UK also benefited from a share of the finds. But it is the consciousness of involvement, of a sharing with our foreign friends in a common task, and of helping with technical training, that has been most rewarding.

One of the happiest outcomes of this effort has been in Tehran where, since the foundation of our British Institute of Persian Studies, more than seven thousand Iranians have passed through our doors, and the lecture hall is usually crammed with an enthusiastic audience. It was to be expected that such involvements sometimes brought with them tensions, especially with changes in the political background – as in Iraq when influence from the USSR began to preponderate. But eventually we must expect such tensions to ease, for with our colleagues from the USSR we have been on the best of terms, and have enjoyed friendly exchanges of visits on the excavations and in this country. Between true craftsmen there is never any real malice, but on the contrary the joy of exchanging a specialized and privileged knowledge. It is through the brotherhood of colleagues that our best hopes lie of averting international conflict.

I can only mention a few of the many who are *en poste* directing our Institutes. They have a difficult diplomatic and technical task which they perform with skill, good humour and good will. The friendly attitude of colleagues in the Antiquities Departments of the host countries is but proof of success in their missions. No director can possess all the qualifications required for this exacting office, which demands diplomacy, ability in administration and, especially, good personal relations with our foreign colleagues. The head of a mission should be respected as a man of learning and as a good digger. At the same time he should, like any diplomat in foreign service, represent the interests of this country, which spends much money on these missions, and show courage in putting forward our domestic case: this duty is sometimes forgotten. Much patience is needed on both sides but there has always been good will in abundance.

In going over the names of some of our Directors, I will mention their special merits. David French in Ankara has found acceptance with the Institute authorities through his natural ability to speak the language, a tremendous asset, but he has been less ready to put across our own aspirations. In Jerusalem, Crystal Bennet, a capable digger, has shown extraordinary capacity to accommodate herself and to override difficulties in the face of Arab-Israeli conflict of interest; the British School has survived remarkably through such tangles. We have yet to open a British Institute in Egypt, a country with which we have had the longest friendly relations, but the Egypt Exploration Society, since the time of W. B. Emery's mission to Saqqara, has taken the place of an Institute and has provided us economically with a permanent base, now exploited by the learned and able Professor H. S. Smith, son of Professor Sidney Smith. Many other rewarding British activities have been conducted elsewhere in Egypt under these auspices.

I have already spoken much of our School in Baghdad; here I would only say that in Nicholas Postgate we have one of our most highly qualified academics, who had already established a reputation in Akkadian and is eventually destined for a Chair in this country. In Iraq he has the exceptional opportunity of combining experience in the field as a digger with expertise in linguistics and ancient history. I have previously mentioned David Stronach, head of our Institute in Tehran, who has had the exacting task of supervising and organizing the erection of our new buildings at Gulhak, a tiring but supremely worthwhile task, the crown of fifteen years' service since the inception of our Institute in Tehran. David has endeared himself to his Iranian colleagues through his modest bearing and natural friendliness. He is a good digger who has achieved signal success in the field, especially at Pasargadae and the Median site of Nush-i-Jan. In the description of his discoveries he is an excellent lecturer, none better, and is all the better for not being weighed down by academic profundities. His publication of the final volume on Pasargadae, founded by Cyrus the Great, will, when it eventually appears, set the seal to the digging of that site where he has wisely benefited from the observations of learned colleagues, particularly Carl Nylander. It is to Stronach's credit that he has always been ready to communicate his discoveries as soon as possible before proceeding to the more exacting task of final or definitive publication.

While on the subject of Iran, I must not omit to refer to David Whitehouse, another archaeologist of exceptional intellectual capacity, who has established a reputation through the excavation with which he was charged by the Institute, at Siraf, a great medieval seaport on the Persian Gulf. This has been the first extensive scientific investigation of a medieval site in Iran in our time and is much to the credit of all concerned. David Whitehouse, like the other David, is an admirable lecturer: clear in exposition, he has the supreme merit of being able to give a written account of results expeditiously, and only a lack of money could delay the final publication. Administration has so far played second fiddle to his archaeological orchestra but this imbalance he will no doubt correct in due course: organized intellectually, human relationships come less easily. None the less, at an exceptionally early age he was appointed to be Director of the British School at Rome because of his technical brilliance, and it is much to be hoped that here he will gradually cement friendships with his Italian colleagues, and with those engaged in the arts. The School at Rome will benefit enormously if he can accommodate himself to it.

Before his appointment in Rome David Whitehouse was, after his work in Iran, the obvious choice for the directorship of the new Afghan Institute in Kabul which I had a hand in founding through the British Academy: he left it after a year, as did Tony McNicoll who returned to Australia, and both men made a most promising start at the important site of Old Kandahar which, associated with the name of Asoka, promises to be a most rewarding site for excavation for a long time to come, and is now in the capable hands of a brilliant draughtsman, Svend Helms.

Finally I must mention the effective, imaginative and argumentative Director of the Institute in East Africa, who has set the seal to his early work on its behalf by the writing of two important volumes on the Islamic trading post of Kilwa, south of Dar es Salaam, directly connected through its medieval ceramics with Siraf. The work which he is at present conducting at Aksum, capital of ancient Ethiopia, bids fair to be an outstanding contribution to African history and archaeology. It is gratifying to remember that Neville Chittick began his Oriental career at Nimrud. Lack of space prevents me from referring to the work of other institutions with which I have been less directly concerned, but it will be seen that the personnel in these distant zones of endeavour have frequently moved from one field to another, greatly to the advantage of archaeological research which, in this way, has recruited for specialist fields men of wide experience.

The doyen of our Institutes is my old friend and learned colleague, Seton Lloyd, with whom I have more than once played Box and Cox, for I followed him in Baghdad when, in 1947, he resigned his post as Technical Adviser to the Department of Antiquities to become Director of the British Institute in Ankara, and thirteen years later, when I was appointed to a Fellowship at All Souls College, Oxford, he succeeded to the Chair of Western Asiatic Archaeology which I had vacated from the Institute in London University. While I have for many years been President of the British School of Archaeology in Iraq, he has held the same office for the Institute at Ankara. Seton, a model of gentleness, has often made me aware of my impatience and roughness, and thus endeared himself to me. By training an architect, he has brilliantly illustrated his own work and, both in Iraq and Iran, has by his excavations at judiciously selected and rewarding sites, reaped rich archaeological and architectural harvests, for he, like David Oates, is a master of mud-brick: his name is a household word in archaeology. On occasion gently caustic, he has enlivened learning through his wit, and his work has been enriched by the warm and loving heart of his wife, Hyde Lloyd who, with her sensitive artistic understanding, has contributed greatly to his endeavours. Hyde has executed a number of pencil sketches for his book *Foundations in the Dust*, one that all Mesopotamian archaeologists should read, and has undertaken much ecclesiastical sculpture in a wide-ranging output that has yielded the wonderful model of a water buffalo in Mosul marble, a massive heavy weight of concentrated nervous power which I rate most highly among my possessions.

Before concluding this brief account of the British archaeological effort in the Middle East, as it is still sometimes called, though it embraces an enormous tract of territory which ranges from Egypt and the eastern shores of the Mediterranean through Palestine, Syria, Anatolia, Mesopotamia, Afghanistan and Iran, I cannot but lament that we have as yet not attempted to establish a British Institute of Archaeology and Linguistics in India, where nothing has replaced that once proud institution, the Survey of India, although Leonard Woolley, and after him, Mortimer Wheeler, did so much to renew and reanimate its traditions. The refoundation of an institution in India on these lines surely deserves the attention of the British Academy and I believe would be warmly welcomed in that sub-continent, where we still have so many friends who remember with respect and affection the long history of combined scholarly endeavours.

When I review my archaeological life I am impelled as a septuagenarian to compare past with present ventures and to draw up some kind of balance sheet for the auditor. I have been fortunate to practise in what the late Sir Frederick Kenyon once described as 'the Elizabethan Age of Archaeology'. In the Orient we had, at least for the first three decades of my career, both the time and the financial resources to dig in the grand manner, on a grand scale. Thirty years ago, when you could hire a man's services for a shilling a day, it was not unusual for big expeditions to work with a labour force which not infrequently numbered two hundred or more with only a small supervisory staff. Ur was the classic example of work conducted on this scale. In the course of twelve years of digging, over periods which sometimes amounted to five months, many hundreds of thousands of tons of soil were shifted, and the evidence recovered was of a high order of magnitude and ranged over a period of some six thousand years. The catalogue register numbered some twenty thousand objects which will be studied and re-examined for as long as Mesopotamian archaeology is deemed worthy of attention – perhaps for eternity – and, with the growth of knowledge, interpretation and reinterpretation will succeed one another generation after generation. But inevitably because of the speed at which operations were conducted, a not inconsiderable volume of evidence was lost, and that in spite of much brilliant field-work which could hold its own by any standards. However, had we worked on excavations by the canons which are accepted today, we should have recovered but one-tenth of the evidence, and the other nine-tenths would probably never have been found. I am, therefore, on balance, an unashamed supporter of the bygone days of digging – the last of the Romantics, as a colleague in Indian archaeology has been good enough to dub me. But given the restrictions of our present economy, no less than the development in scientific methods, we are bound to dig on a relatively modest scale and consequently to put all the evidence through a fine sieve: we therefore miss nothing, and tend to find nothing. Sometimes the evidence recovered is of so light a character that an older generation is inclined to wonder if the effort is worthwhile. Obviously the answer is yes; but there is still no room for complacency, and the application of selective common sense, and a clear and precise vision of one's objective, is more than ever desirable.

To such reflections we must give due weight, but we must now recognize that while the prosecution of archaeology remains an art, it is now predominantly a science – in the methodology of digging, in the classification and compilation of its results, and through the application of scientific ancillary aids for the analysis and determination of every discovery.

The principal ancillary aids are now too well known to require detailed description, but it is worth remembering that two of the most important have only been available since the Second World War, that is, for no more than three decades. The new technology would have been of extraordinary interest and value to the early pioneers who, by means of the incipient stratigraphic method, and through an intensive scientific study of history, were attempting to resolve dating sequences both prehistoric and historic, and to arrive at a precise chronology. Without much prolonged and intensive study, the new scientific methods, both of Carbon 14 and thermoluminescence, would have made but little headway. The application of C. 14 determinations to sufficient remains of organic matter would, have been of untold aid to Leonard Woolley in attempting to date the sequences in the Royal Cemetery of Ur, and would have enabled him to avoid many pitfalls. For a more reliable estimate of the dating sequences in the Early Dynastic period we have had to wait until the 1970s, when material from that time sequence is once more available, particularly at the Early Dynastic sites of Abu Salabikh and Nippur in South Babylonia. These results will furthermore be checked by thermo-luminescence, the method of determining the date at which pottery was originally baked in its kiln by calculating the loss of electrons. None the less, it has also to be remembered that a correction to the inevitable errors which have arisen from the application of those methods depends on a well-calculated chronology. In the case of Mesopotamia, chronology depends both on King lists and Limmu lists, and again on cross-ties with Egyptian chronology which, with varying margins of error, has been mathematically calculated and computed for a century or more. Accurate scientific results depend, therefore, on a combination of modern scientific method with archaeology, with history and with linguistics, which enable us to bring to bear the written evidence where it is available.

There are of course, many other scientific aids in addition to those I have mentioned. It may suffice to mention the analysis of pottery through neutron activation, which enables us to determine both the constituents and the origins of the clay in potsherds, and has been applied with singular success in the region of the Habur. I have already mentioned how gratifying it was to discover that years of scientific research had confirmed the results of ocular examinations of these clays; but this method had gone a step further still in determining the beds from which the clay had been drawn and the extent to which they had been traded. The archaeologist of a bygone age, scientifically less well-equipped than his successor, was equally able by common-sense methods to arrive at the truth; but truth is no longer acceptable unless determined mathematically by computation.

In describing the close of my career I must also make brief reference to a privilege that has been accorded to me as an elder statesman, that is, my appointment to be a Trustee of the British Museum, which since boyhood had been to me an intellectual and spiritual gymnasium: in the first chapter I have explained how much it meant to me in my youth.

For many years I was in the closest touch with the Department of Egyptian and Assyrian Antiquities, later renamed the Department of Western Asiatic Antiquities. My earliest recollection of it is being introduced to the then head of the Department, Dr H. R. Hall, who was rearranging the gallery dressed in a blue suit so old and shiny that one could see one's face in it, and partly covered in plaster. His successors were more orthodox in appearance. First came Dr, later Professor, Sidney Smith whom I have already mentioned. He was a mine of learning and provoked one to thought, if not always to agreement. His stimulating methods were applied to all and sundry, and he had a way of testing the resistance of anyone who came for an interview. Often enough when faced with a newcomer he appeared to say to himself, how can I get under this man's skin? If the victim was unwise enough to fall into the trap he reacted violently, and thus immediately damned himself. But if a man took this form of punishment without blenching, he became a customer worth consideration. How often have

I kept a careful silence at apparently outrageous statements to find that Sidney was prepared to turn round in the face of evidence, for he was possessed of a good measure of common sense as well as of original thought. But for him, to be intellectually wrong was to be morally wrong. This made him a difficult colleague but a most stimulating teacher. His learning was highly respected, however aberrant it might appear at times, and in my opinion his chapter on the Assyrians in the *Cambridge Ancient History* was masterly and made most attractive reading. He had a rare understanding of ancient calendars and his revisions of Mesopotamian chronology, particularly, concerned with the date of the First Dynasty of Babylon and its reduction, have found wide acceptance, and are a product of his imaginative, analytical treatment of complex evidence. This extremely hard-working, and in many ways brilliant, man has left a mark in the annals of his Department at the British Museum. With the humble civil servant he was always generous and considerate. In Baghdad, where he did a spell as Director of Antiquities for about two years, he was well-liked and admired. Mary Smith, his wife, a gifted artist, executed a historic tempera painting of the main street in Baghdad in about 1927 (then called New Street, now Rashid Street), pictured at a time before the motor car had replaced the horse-cab.

The other British Museum colleague with whom I was in close touch for 45 years was C. J. Gadd, who died in 1969, after succeeding Sidney Smith first to the headship of the Department and then to the Professorship in the SOAS. I have written at length his obituary for *The Proceedings of the British Academy*, vol. LVI. Here I must add how much his loss has meant to me, both as a scholar ever ready to be generous with his knowledge and for his whimsical personality, a delightful companion. He was possessed of a ready wit and of what the French would describe as *l'esprit fin*; he had a knowledge of Ancient Western Asia exceeded by none. This man of recondite learning had his blind spots, and little appreciation of the fact that the results of excavation are not attributable to luck but that a good digger will always reap his reward wherever he goes and that a bad one will have little to show for his money. Luck always comes to the man who earns it and is capable of grasping opportunity with both hands. Kindly, also inclined to be waspish, by temperament he was weak but competent in administration and suffered acutely from the necessity of coming to any decision. Inclined to hypochondria, he was instinctively drawn to the extrovert and enjoyed sailing in the hearty company of Campbell Thompson, whom he found as fascinating as the hero Gilgamesh. He was a delight to all his companions during his season at Nimrud, and especially to our caustic young architect, John Reid, who hung on his words in the expectation of a witticism. He made his name at a single stroke of the pen by the publication in 1923, at the age of 30, of a monograph on a cuneiform tablet in the British Museum, entitled 'The Fall of Nineveh', which was celebrated by *Punch* in the following verse:

> They taught us how in six-o-six
> (BC) that godless town fell flat;
> And now the new-found records fix
> A date anterior to that;
> It fell, in fact, in six-one-two,
> So what they taught us wasn't true.

Wonderfully perceptive in grasping the point of any ancient text that he touched, his insensitiveness to some aspects of archaeological discovery was a puzzle. At Nimrud he was oblivious to the fact that we had traced a stone quay-wall at intervals over two miles, and persisted in thinking that this was the wall of a palace, thus misleading his colleagues at home in the face of evidence which had revealed erosion of the quay by water action and the sinking of the blocks into the river bed, a phenomenon finally proved by aerial photography, so that the ancient line of the river between its banks was plain as a pikestaff. I was consoled to find that so brilliant a mind was dark on one side against the flashes of genius on the other. His Department in the British Museum will remember him with pride.

I cannot say much more about the many friendships with colleagues in the British Museum, much as they have enriched my life. Of Richard Barnett, who succeeded Gadd to the Keepership, I have already spoken, for he assisted me in the field at Chagar Bazar and earned universal fame in my wife's book *Come Tell Me How You Live*, because of his specially-designed nightshirt which zipped up a mouse inside it. Richard was another mine of esoteric learning who published too much rather than too little.

With one other Department of the British Museum I have also long been in close touch, namely the Research Laboratories, which were founded by the late Dr Alexander Scott, FRS, in about 1922. Three years later I spent much time there during my appointment at Ur, which provided the laboratories with a rich *corpus* of material to work on, one of its first major tasks in the early days of its experimentation. I used to see the old man stumping about with delight as he recommended different methods of treatment for recalcitrant metals and fragile ancient substances of every kind, ably assisted by Dr H. L. Plenderleith, who gained fame and a fair name in the process. The staff in those days was completed by the presence of an exceedingly lazy old man named Padgham, who had much practical knowledge which he was unwilling to reveal, but as I watched him discreetly from afar, he unconsciously imparted his knowledge to me, in contrast to the young L. H. Bell, then a boy of great dexterity, very clever with his hands. We grew up as Lab. boys together and have remained friends ever since. The objects from Nimrud, with the exception of the great rarities such as the chryselephantine plaques which went for first treatment to Plenderleith, were, however, handled at the Institute of Archaeology and my close contact with the B. M. Laboratories then ceased.

Before taking farewell of the Laboratories I must mention one more episode which might have made an end of them and of me. On a hot summer's day while Woolley was lecturing in the USA I was attempting to prepare the discoveries in the Royal Cemetery of Ur for a special exhibition. At this time I had an alarming experience in the basement, which was covered by a glass roof. On a long trestle table I had arranged the remains of a canopy partly composed of spindle-shaped shell discs and hemispheres, which I had spread out, for safety as I thought, on wet jute sacking, while I was cleaning them with the aid of a bunsen burner in order to melt down the paraffin wax, which in those days we mistakenly used as a protective coating for fragile objects. I left the Laboratories for luncheon at the Museum Tavern and, conscious of the need for haste in the preparation of the multifarious tasks with which I had been charged, returned to my job in less than forty minutes. By that time the sun, shining directly on to the glass roof of the room in which I was working, had set in motion a process of spontaneous combustion which ignited the highly inflammable jute sacking on which the fragments of canopy from the Royal Cemetery of Ur were resting. Low flames were licking the top of the wooden table, which looked like a heath on fire. There is little doubt that had I arrived five minutes later the entire British Museum Laboratories would have gone up in smoke, for at the end of the table, in proximity to the flames, were two Winchesters of benzine: these I seized and removed from the danger zone as I rushed up to Padgham to help me extinguish the flames. I reckon that had I delayed a few minutes longer my archaeological career would have been extinguished likewise.

I have never sat in a more interesting conclave than as a Trustee of the British Museum. The twenty or so men and women who compose it are drawn from a wide variety of experience: diplomatic, administrative, artistic, antiquarian, legal, financial, architectural, educational, scientific and literary. Between them they lay down the framework of policy for the Museum; they stand as a buttress between the Museum and the Government; they have power to raise money and to spend money; and they sanction or disallow all important purchases. This body of distinguished men and women, drawn from many different walks of life, is unpaid and supplies for the Museum an immense expertise; it also approves or disapproves senior appointments. In this and other functions it brings to bear much mature experience and judgement in debate. Before joining I had not realized the wide scope of Trusteeship and its value as a mentor to the professionals engaged in the administration. I have enjoyed the privilege of serving under the Chairmanship of that galvanized wire of energy, Lord Trevelyan, ever ready to apply a vigorous mind to the solution of any problem, no matter how complex; and I have no less appreciated the sensitive artistic bent of its present Director, Sir John Pope Hennessy, who combines in rare measure administrative capacity with aesthetic sensibility in a post which needs a compound of many talents and is mentally exacting. In speech he is a master of the living tongue.

At last I am brought to reflect on my good fortune in having spanned 50 years of activity as an Oriental archaeologist in spite of five years of interruption in the Second World War, which was a no less interesting interlude. It is something to have reached my 72nd year comparatively unscathed, and in writing these memoirs I have, as I reckon, enjoyed the advantage of never having kept a diary in which much trivial matter is for ever stored. What I have written may for all I know enter that category, but it has all been fun and has gone down on to paper because it hâs stuck in my memory; and it has stuck because every day of an archaeologist's life is intellectually thrilling and much of it enjoyable. But I must admit that in memorizing the past I have been able to rely on the main archaeological signposts in my life, signposts which are represented by extensive archaeological writing, both of books and of articles. In this way I have contrived to forget little and all the names came back, after I had jogged my memory, though sometimes it would not be hurried and I had to wait for a month or two. I was also fortunate in that my war experiences were unusual and unforgettable and I hope that they may be remembered as a brief chronicle of those times. The lighter side of archaeological life, or part of it, has, so I have often said, never been more happily recorded than in my dear wife's *Come Tell Me How You Live*, republished by Collins in 1975. I hope that many will read it again.

Epilogue

As I came to the last few pages of these memoirs my beloved Agatha died, peacefully and gently, as I wheeled her out in her chair after luncheon to the drawing-room. She had been failing for some time and death came as a merciful release, though it has left me with a feeling of emptiness after forty-five years of a loving and merry companionship. Few men know what it is to live in harmony beside an imaginative, creative mind which inspires life with zest. To me, the greatest consolation has been the recognition, which has come from many hundreds of letters, that admiration was blended in equal measure with love – a love and happiness which Agatha radiated both in her person and in her books. Requiescat.

Index

Index

Index

Index

Index

Index

Index

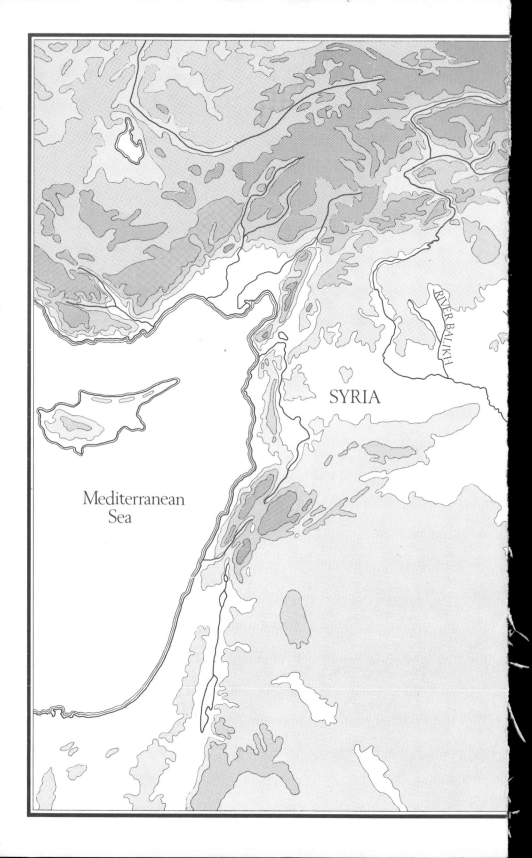